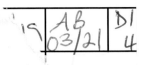

Praise for *Silk Road*

'Ormsby's investigative journalism shines as she provides a very thorough account of Ulbricht's rise and fall.' *Penthouse Magazine*

'Through her clear rendering of the facts, Ormsby makes the intricacies of the technology involved accessible to even the most technophobic of readers. The tone is conversational and friendly while the content is intriguing and increasingly dark. In her quest to uncover the mystery behind the enigmatic DPR she uncovers a story of subterfuge, replete with conspiracy theories and hidden identities, that is rich with anecdotes.' *Newtown Review of Books*

'The book is a fascinating expose of this particular aspect of the "dark web" of internet dealings and its subsequent unravelling.' *Sydney Morning Herald*

'Ormsby is a great writer, giving us gripping accounts from the people who actually used "Silk Road" to paint an accurate picture of how the website was created, run, and ultimately fell . . . *Silk Road* is easily one of the best books I've read this year.' *The Library NZ*

'*Silk Road* is one of the more readable and gripping true crime books of recent times. It is not just Ormsby's knowledge of the brief but spectacular rise and fall of Silk Road that makes for compelling reading, but also the ordering of the material so that the reader has the sense of being educated in the technical and legal background to an astonishing criminal enterp

'For the most complete account of the original Silk Road, which was closed down by the FBI in late 2013, Eileen Ormsby's book *Silk Road* is the best place to start. It's full of original research, interviews and insight. This is best read along with her excellent blog, AllThingsVice, which covers several aspects of the dark net, but especially the dark net markets.' Jamie Bartlett, author of *Darknet and Radicals*

'A great strength of the meticulously researched *Silk Road* is the manner in which Ormsby gently takes the reader by the hand, unpacking the technology underpinning this 'dark net' market.' *Australian Police Journal*

Eileen Ormsby is a lawyer, author and freelance journalist based in Melbourne. Her first book, *Silk Road* was the world's first in-depth expose of the black markets that operate on the dark web. Her gonzo-style investigations have led her deep into the secretive corners of the dark web where drugs and weapons dealers, hackers, hitmen and worse ply their trade. Many of these dark web interactions turned into real-world relationships, entanglements, hack attempts on her computer and even death threats from the dark web's most successful hitman network as she researched *Darkest Web*. She now lives a quiet life off-grid as much as possible.

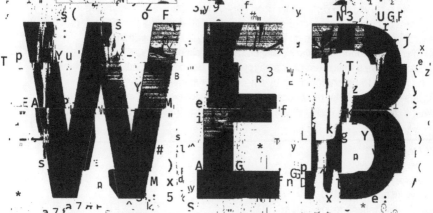

THE DARKEST WEB

EILEEN ORMSBY

ALLEN&UNWIN
SYDNEY · MELBOURNE · AUCKLAND · LONDON

Unless otherwise stated all currency is in US dollars

First published in 2018

Copyright © Eileen Ormsby 2018

All rights reserved. No part of this book may be reproduced or transmitted in any form or by any means, electronic or mechanical, including photocopying, recording or by any information storage and retrieval system, without prior permission in writing from the publisher. The Australian *Copyright Act 1968* (the Act) allows a maximum of one chapter or 10 per cent of this book, whichever is the greater, to be photocopied by any educational institution for its educational purposes provided that the educational institution (or body that administers it) has given a remuneration notice to the Copyright Agency (Australia) under the Act.

Allen & Unwin
83 Alexander Street
Crows Nest NSW 2065
Australia
Phone: (61 2) 8425 0100
Email: info@allenandunwin.com
Web: www.allenandunwin.com

A catalogue record for this book is available from the National Library of Australia

ISBN 978 1 76029 785 5

Set in 12/16.5 pt Minion Pro by Midland Typesetters, Australia
Printed and bound in Australia by Griffin Press

10 9 8 7 6 5 4 3 2

MIX
Paper from
responsible sources
FSC® C009448

The paper in this book is FSC® certified. FSC® promotes environmentally responsible, socially beneficial and economically viable management of the world's forests.

For Mum and Dad, who gave me my love of reading and who secretly wish I wrote nice literary fiction, but are nevertheless unrelentingly proud and supportive of everything I do.

CONTENTS

AUTHOR'S NOTE

This book deals with violent and distressing subject matter, particularly Part III Darkest, which describes incidents of child sexual abuse and torture. Reader discretion is advised.

PROLOGUE

Chris Monteiro stares at his computer screen, heart in his mouth. When the two-minute show finishes, the cybersecurity expert restarts it, looking for signs that it has been faked.

The video is substandard both in terms of plot and production values, but the content is chilling. A white sedan is engulfed in flames and the arsonist stands in front of it, his gloved hand holding a sign up to an unseen light so that the words are clearly displayed to the viewer as the car burns in the background: 'Besa Mafia dedication to Pirate London. 10 April 2016.'

Besa Mafia is a site on the dark web offering murder-for-hire services. And Pirate.London is Monteiro's personal website. The video is real and it is a warning.

On the other side of the world, I click on to the fifteenth email in as many hours from the administrator of the Besa Mafia website. He calls himself Yura, so that is almost certainly not his name. Earlier emails had been all business, offering bribes if only I would stop reporting on the site's nefarious activities. As the day wears on and Yura's offers are met with silence or a refusal, the emails take on an increasingly hysterical and menacing tone.

Yura promises me that his army of hackers will ruin my life. Child porn will be placed on my computer. Incriminating evidence will be planted across the internet, with all digital footprints leading back to me. This latest email has yet another new silencing tactic.

You don't know my name, you don't know who I am, but I know your name and I know where you live. I will get my gang members, and I will send them to rape beat and destroy you. And believe me, it will be successful.

Remove your articles now. All of them.

Monteiro and I have let ourselves into the back door of the Besa Mafia website, thanks to the assistance of a friendly hacker. We have been watching every interaction between the most successful dark web murder-for-hire site in history and its customers. We know all their dirty secrets. We have traced the Bitcoin that has been sent from around the world accompanying orders for the murder, beating or rape of spouses, business partners or scorned lovers.

In the few short months the site has been operational, the website has taken in hundreds of thousands of dollars. Now the hitman-for-hire knows that we know.

And he's not happy at all.

———

A hooded figure sits, defeated, in a concrete cell. Beside him are two dog bowls, one filled with water, the other empty. Propped against his feet, a piece of paper bears a handwritten message:

29 Aug#ISISGAMES

A web address (URL) is also scrawled on the sign, but instead of .com it ends in .onion, signifying that only somebody who has downloaded the Tor software can get access.

ISIS Red Room. Free, BRUTAL, live! A countdown clock ticks towards the deadline. The words that greet those who dare to enter the URL tell viewers what they can expect on 29 August:

> We will with official media pictures and ISIS propaganda material prove to you that we have 7 very real ISIS jihadists in our capture. Everything is live and interactive. Their fate will be in your hands.

'Red rooms' promise pay-per-view torture, culminating in murder, of an unfortunate captive. Those who want to watch pay the website owner in Bitcoins. Rates vary from site to site, but payment is always a prerequisite. A certain amount to watch passively; more if you want to interact in the chat room with other viewers as the torture is being carried out.

Then there is the director. The director is the voyeur willing to pay the most. In return they get to direct the action, choosing what happens next to the victim. Red rooms are a staple of the dark web, a natural progression from tales of the snuff movie that have been part of popular culture for decades.

But this red room is different.

For one, it is free. For another, these are no innocent victims to be tortured, sexually assaulted, mutilated and murdered. Vigilantes have captured ISIS terrorists, whom they promise to slowly torture to death, one by one.

As the timer counts down, word is spreading across forums and chans, not only on the dark web, but on clear web (regular web) sites like reddit and Twitter. A few hours before deadline, thousands of people from around the world are in the dark web chat room, waiting for the show.

At 00:01 UTC on 29 August 2015, the site updates: *Let the Games Begin*

———

The quiver in the senior constable's finger is almost imperceptible as it hovers above the mouse. On the screen, the cursor points to a link: *Daisy's Destruction Pt 1*. A screenshot acts as a preview, promising that the most sought-after video of the dark web may be just a click away.

Daisy's Destruction has become a dark web urban legend. It is discussed furtively in chat rooms and forums, on chans and in IRC. A few claim to have seen the video themselves, but most have only second-hand information from a 'friend of a friend'. The details of what is in the video change depending on who is doing the telling. A twelve-year-old girl is killed in it, say some. No, it is a toddler being tortured, say others. There's a man and a woman. Several men. Only children. It is the first, truly verified, snuff film ever known.

The one thing they all agree on is that it can only be found on the dark web, and only within the murkiest bowels of that. To find it, you have to venture into places few even know exist; into an empire run by a man known only as 'Lux'.

Lux's empire comprises a number of sites. A chan promises censorship-free images. Another provides live streaming video. There is a wiki and a community support forum.

But it is Hurt2theCore that has the police officer's attention. Hurt2theCore is the worst of the sites, not just within the empire, but in all of the dark web. It is the site Lux considers his greatest achievement.

Lux is reviled by most, idolised by a select few. In a place inhabited by thieves, deviants, junkies and pedophiles, he is proud of his reputation as the epitome of evil. He claims to be an American pediatrician, but she suspects he is Australian. She is closing in. That's why she has to click. It may bring her one step closer to finding him and closing down his evil empire.

The video flickers to life. A bedroom, nondescript. A masked woman. Hanging above the bed, tied with rough rope by her ankles, a child, or toddler rather, no more than two years old, screams in fear and agony. At the urging of an unseen male voice, the woman steps towards the baby, a sharp object in her hand, before the video abruptly turns to black.

'This is just a teaser. Let me know if you want to see the rest of it.' The invitation is signed 'Lux'.

The senior constable doesn't want to see the rest of it, but she knows it is inevitable as she closes in on her prey. Lux's acolytes will clamber to pay him for the privilege of viewing the life of a little girl literally being destroyed and she will have to see it, too.

In the meantime, the seasoned police officer opens the little filing cabinet in her brain that secures away the vile sounds and images that have become part of her daily life. She pops *Daisy's Destruction* into it and locks it securely.

As always, she prays that there never comes a day when that filing cabinet bursts open.

———

'The last thing you fucking want is my undivided attention.' The warning plays through my head as I wait on an uncomfortable wooden stool. There's a telephone on the bench in front of me and I pick up the receiver as he takes his seat on the other side of the thick Perspex wall, which has been reinforced with steel bars.

'I want to call you "Mongoose",' I blurt out before he can say anything. Before he wound up here, in this bleak and notoriously violent prison, we had conversed online, in private messages on a drugs appreciation forum where he often held court with his outrageous antics and tall tales. He had used the name Mongoose then and, reportedly, when armed police officers stormed his home to arrest him on a slew of charges, he had calmly commanded them to 'Call me "Mongoose"'.

The author of an article recounting some of Mongoose's older crimes had elected not to interview him, because when people dealt with Mongoose bad things happened: 'business transactions fell apart, people retired nicknames and dropped from view . . . [Mongoose] deposited things on people's PCs via e-mail that gave him access to their personal desktops and files. Frankly, [Mongoose] scared me, and I didn't consider him a reliable source of information anyway. So why feed his fire?'

'Please do,' Mongoose responds politely to my outburst. He looks surprisingly well for a man who has spent nearly two years on remand in Bangkok's infamous Klong Prem Central Prison. He is fighting extradition to the United States, where he faces charges of being the second mastermind behind the world's most notorious online drugs market, Silk Road. The other mastermind, his alleged protégé, has already been sentenced to two consecutive life sentences without possibility of parole.

Mongoose used to sign his posts with an explicit threat: *The last thing you fucking want is my undivided attention*. Right now, the man whom *High Times* magazine dubbed the Megabyte Megalomaniac, aka Mongoose, is indeed giving me his undivided attention.

I hope I don't come to regret it.

———

There's the world wide web—the internet we all know that connects us via news, email, forums, shopping and social media. Then there's the dark web—the parallel internet accessed by only a select few. Usually those it connects wish to remain anonymous and for good reason.

The email is designed to never reveal its users; the news and forums are dedicated to topics of true crime, but with inside information and gruesome detail rarely found on the clear web. Shopping is paid for with cryptocurrency like Bitcoin, on markets that advertise drugs, weapons, hacking tools and far more nefarious goods and services.

I have spent the past five years exploring every corner of the dark web, one of the few who is open about who I am and what I do there. I have shopped on darknet markets, contributed to forums, waited in red rooms and hacked hitmen-for-hire sites.

Sometimes my dark web activities have poured out into the real world and I have attended trials, met with criminals and the law enforcement officers who tracked them down, interviewed dark web identities and visited them in prison.

This book will take you with me into the murkiest depths of the web's dark underbelly—the darkest web.

INTRODUCTION

Imagine being able to browse an online shop that looks just like Amazon, complete with a little shopping trolley for your purchases, except you fill it up with cocaine, ecstasy or heroin. Or what about browsing for the services of a hitman in your local city, arranging for a SWAT team to raid the house of someone you have a beef with or hiring a hacker to check whether your spouse is cheating.

The dark web is a parallel internet that exists deep beneath the one we know. Google won't find its sites, nor YouTube play its videos. You won't somehow stumble across it, because it cannot be accessed without first downloading special software. Host to all the sites that feature in contemporary horror movies or cautionary tales of TV crime dramas, the dark web is like the internet's evil twin, and few people are willing to venture inside. Yet it holds a fascination for us and we have been provided a peek into what it holds, thanks to news stories and documentaries, as well as fictional depictions in everything from the *Law & Order* franchise to the more technically accurate *Mr. Robot*.

In many ways, the reality of the dark web is somewhat more pedestrian than TV shows and movies depict. It is slower, less high-tech and graphically challenged compared to the regular internet. On the other hand, there are some aspects of the dark web too heinous to be used as entertainment. Within the web of private networks, which offer a layer of anonymity impossible to achieve on the regular internet, drugs and guns are traded, hitmen advertise their services, hackers can be hired to attack an enemy's computer and those with the most depraved tastes can download pornographic images to satisfy their lust.

The technical name for the dark web is 'hidden services'—web servers that run locally and are not visible or accessible to the outside internet, and can only be accessed from within the network of the software provider. Hidden services are a way of creating a meeting place where the visitor can't discover where the host is and the host can't discover where the visitor is coming from. Nobody—including the organisations that provide access to the sites—can determine who runs them or where they are located. Nor can they close the sites down.

The most popular provider of hidden services is Tor. Tor was developed by the US military with a primary purpose of protecting government communications. Tor has three main functions—allowing users to publish and read information with complete anonymity, circumventing censorship and getting around internet filters, and providing access to hidden services, the dark web. There are positive and important uses for the first two functions. Tor has become increasingly popular in a post-privacy world for anybody needing or wanting secrecy or anonymity. It is particularly useful for whistleblowers and human rights workers in hostile regimes, but also for ordinary people who want to surf the web without their information being harvested for marketers.

While technically-minded folk have long used darknets to communicate privately, Tor brought it to the masses. Once downloaded, the software opens a browser that looks identical to that used for surfing the internet normally. The average user can't see that their

IP address is being routed through a worldwide volunteer network of servers, encrypted and re-encrypted several times over until it reaches its destination.

Although a user's internet provider may be able to determine that they have connected to Tor, they cannot tell what sites the user has visited. The user's location and usage is hidden from anyone conducting network surveillance or traffic analysis. When the user's destination is a site on the clear web (the regular web), that site knows it has had a visitor but has no way of knowing who that visitor is or where in the world they are located.

These privacy aspects are useful and seem benign, although there is the potential for people to use the anonymity provided to troll or harass others, safe in the knowledge that their identity is hidden. But when we talk about the dark web, we really mean the websites you can visit via Tor that you can't visit on the clear web.

The URL of these sites is usually made up of a string of sixteen apparently random letters and numbers that end in '.onion' instead of any of the usual domain identifiers such as .com or .org. Because the sites are not designed to be found by search engines, users must either know the exact URL they want or use one of the available gateway sites. Any site that has an .onion domain name is contained within the Tor network and is not part of the internet. The hidden network of sites is colloquially referred to as 'Onionland'.

There are sites that claim to sell human organs (heart $65,000, lung $30,000, liver $45,000) that the purchaser can collect from a third-world country. Others offer access to real-life Gladiator fights to the death, contract killing services or live streaming of pay-per-view torture. There are those who swear you can access details of live human experiments or obtain made-to-order snuff films. Yet another site promises to procure exotic animals. Identity items are a high-demand black market product and range from five-dollar licence copies, good for nightclub entry and not much else, to passports that are 'genuinely generated from within the IPS [intrusion prevention system] of the UK government and guaranteed good for travel' for $4000. There is theft-to-order, university papers researched and written and even a service that allows people to buy in to fixed sporting events. There are sites that are completely incomprehensible to most mere mortals—the hangouts of the hackers and phreakers doing whatever it is that hackers and phreakers do in their own impenetrable language.

The sites that can be found on the dark web include black markets (arms, drugs, forgeries, banking details, stolen goods and credit cards, new identities, services), illegal porn forums and filesharing sites, political dissent and hate sites, and hacking communities. Many sites require an invitation to view them and so their contents remain a mystery.

Anonymous markets need an anonymous payment system. That's why cash is king when it comes to buying and selling illegal goods. Unless it has been treated with a chemical designed to hold fingerprints, nobody can tell if you have handled a specific note or coin. It has long been a downfall of the internet that money exchanges (through bank transfers, credit cards or even Western Union transfers) are traceable to at least one of the parties.

Cryptocurrencies fixed all that. Bitcoin in particular offered a robust, mathematically backed currency that had all the validity and anonymity of cash but in the virtual world. When it was unleashed in 2009, Bitcoin—which was 'mined' by computers running complex algorithms to solve mathematical equations—had no value. Only computer nerds and people with well-developed scientific minds had any interest in acquiring Bitcoin, and they did so, more as a novelty than anything else.

A year later, Bitcoin still had almost no value and cost more in electricity usage to mine it than it could be sold for. However, some people began to recognise that its nature of being universal in application, and essentially as anonymous as cash, meant it could have a use in being applied to black markets and the exchange of illegal goods.

Bitcoin has risen so far in value that it has a market cap of billions of dollars in 2018.

Many people refer to the dark web as the wild west of the internet, where anything goes. In many ways, they are right. There are some depraved minds out there and they have total freedom to buy, sell, share or create anything they want, confident that they cannot be found.

Some people want to buy murderous substances and implements. Some want to sell people and poisons. Others want to share livestreams of torture or create pictures and films of such depravity, seasoned cops who view them need counselling. Most frightening is that the technology—simple to use for those with basic computer skills—has meant that those depraved minds have been able to find each other.

PART I

Dark

Silk Road

Like the High Street stores that have had to close their doors, the street corner drug dealer is becoming an endangered species. Local drug dealers are losing business, unable to compete with the convenience and cheaper prices of online shopping.

Most people would never have heard of the dark web had it not been for the rise of the first point-and-click illicit drugs market. Silk Road was the original and most notorious dark web drugs bazaar to be promoted to the public. It was a brazen market that brought together buyers and sellers of every drug imaginable. Its design was reminiscent of eBay or Amazon and it was almost as easy to use, with marijuana, cocaine or Xanax bars ready to be popped into the shopping basket, all set to be shipped anywhere in the world. Colourful advertisements offered everything from a single ecstasy pill to bulk orders destined for on-sale in nightclubs, or through friend-of-friend networks. Sellers were rated for their quality and customer service.

'It's a certifiable one-stop shop for illegal drugs that represents the most brazen attempt to peddle drugs online that we have ever seen. It's more brazen than anything else by light years,' said US Senator

Chuck Schumer when Silk Road first garnered press attention a few months after its February 2011 birth. He called for it to be shut down immediately, which would seem to be a reasonable demand. But the technology was like nothing politicians had ever dealt with before.

Tor, Bitcoin and drugs created the perfect storm for the first online mass black market. Tor allowed the hosting of websites where the owner could not be traced, which meant that a shopfront could be created without the inconvenience of it being closed down by law enforcement or a law-abiding ISP. More importantly, it meant that the website did not have to operate clandestinely, or by invitation only. Rather, it could advertise openly to the masses, the people behind it anonymous, their location in the world impossible to determine.

Any commercial enterprise requires payment for goods. Traditional online payment methods such as credit cards, PayPal, Western Union or bank transfers all have the potential to de-anonymise the user. Those who were capable of stealing those means of payment were a select few, and that would be another barrier to mass-market appeal for the shop. Bitcoin was the game changer.

Entire books have been written about the cryptocurrency Bitcoin, and there is not space in this book to do it justice. At its simplest level, it is a borderless digital currency, which allows for almost instantaneous transactions from one person to another anywhere in the world. It is decentralised, meaning no one entity controls or regulates it. Most importantly for the black market, neither person needs to know the identity of the other. It is the equivalent of cash in an online world.

A potential Silk Road customer might browse a website like localbitcoins.com to find someone selling Bitcoin (which is perfectly legal). Once they agree to a price, the customer makes a cash deposit into the Bitcoin seller's bank account, and as soon as the seller sees the money in their account, the agreed amount of Bitcoin is transferred into the digital address provided. That address could be a private Bitcoin wallet, or the buyer's Silk Road wallet. The seller would have no way of knowing; to them, it would simply be a string of numbers and letters.

Drugs were the ideal product for the experiment. Worldwide recreational drug use continues to grow every year and personal-use quantities are small enough to be hidden in a plain white business envelope, indistinguishable from billions of others circulating the globe for less nefarious reasons.

Postal workers turned into unwitting drug mules as hundreds of thousands of people around the world flocked to this new way of buying drugs. Like eBay, sellers had reputations to preserve, so they provided excellent customer service and high-quality drugs to ensure a five-star rating.

At Silk Road's helm was the site's founder, who initially was known simply as 'Admin'. He started the site with a view to achieving an open market free from regulation or interference by governments. 'Silk Road was founded on libertarian principles,' he said. 'It is a great idea and a great practical system ... It is not a utopia. It is regulated by market forces, not a central power.'

As his site grew from a few to hundreds, to thousands of sales every day, the mysterious founder and sole administrator became the object of hero-worship among drug sellers and users alike. He was known for his libertarian philosophies and preaching for a world where people could indulge in the substances of their choice, free from interference or violence. Unlike other black markets that operated both in the physical world and the dark web, Silk Road would not permit the sale of anything with the purpose of harming or defrauding others.

The founder seemed to truly care for his customers. 'I know this whole market is based on the trust you put in me and I don't take that lightly. It's an honor to serve you,' he wrote on the site's forums. 'I hope that as time goes on I will have more opportunities to demonstrate that my intentions are genuine and no amount of money could buy my integrity.'

In any other hands, Silk Road may well have failed. Most people would have set it up purely as a money-making exercise. But although the site operated as an e-commerce platform, its owner was determined to build a community, one which he would lead with love and kindness, and be closely involved in. He even kept a private journal on his computer, chronicling the early days of his online initiative. 'I imagine that some day I may have a story written about my life, and it would be good to have a detailed account of it,' he mused.

He also contributed prolifically on Silk Road's forums, addressing his flock. 'You all are like family to me. Sure we have some crazy cousins floating around, but they just add character, right? Doesn't matter though, I love you all,' he wrote. He never took the site's members for granted. 'Of all the people in the world, you are the ones who are here, in the early stages of this revolution. You are the ones getting this thing off the ground and driving it forward. It is a privilege to have you by my side. Thank you for your trust, faith, camaraderie and love.'

For whatever reason—quality drugs at a reasonable price, ease of use of the site itself, or the opportunity to be part of a revolution—people from all over the world flocked to sign up to buy or sell drugs and join in the banter of the community.

It was not long before the job was too much for one man. Silk Road needed a crew and there was never a shortage of applicants for the job.

Variety Jones

Some time in 2011, when Silk Road was still a one-man show, 'Variety Jones showed up', the owner wrote in his journal. 'This was the biggest and strongest willed character I had met through the site thus far. He quickly proved to me that he had value by pointing out a major security hole in the site I was unaware of.'

Variety Jones, who had been part of online communities for cannabis growers for over a decade, became the founder's closest confidant. Unable to speak to anybody in the real world, Silk Road's owner welcomed the counsel of the seasoned veteran. He grew to trust the man, and let his guard down, chatting to him as if he were a close friend rather than an anonymous person on the other end of a keyboard. They discussed every aspect of the site, as well as ideas and plans for the future. Silk Road's Admin was the visionary and Variety Jones the practical adviser who would let him know if and how something was possible.

'He convinced me of a server configuration paradigm that gave me the confidence to be the sole server administrator and not work with someone else at all,' wrote Silk Road's founder in his journal. 'He has advised me on many technical aspects of what we are doing, helped me speed up the site and squeeze more out of my current servers. He also has helped me better interact with the community around Silk Road, delivering proclamations, handling troublesome characters, running a sale, changing my name, devising rules, and on and on. He also helped me get my head straight regarding legal protection, cover stories, devising a will, finding a successor, and so on. He's been a real mentor.'

In those early days VJ became the young entrepreneur's sounding board. He was the only person the Silk Road owner trusted enough to share details about the business.

'OK,' said VJ before signing off a chat in December 2011, 'can't go without asking—what's the weekly gross sales?'

'Wanna take a guess?' Admin teased, enjoying some light-hearted banter with his mentor before revealing sales to be around $125,000 per week.

VJ was suitably impressed. 'Not bad for a guy that started selling shrooms, eh?' he said, referencing the origins of the site, when the founder listed his home-grown magic mushrooms for sale.

That night, Admin wrote in his journal: 'Chatted with VJ again today. Him coming onto the scene has reinspired me and given me direction on the SR project. He has helped me see a larger vision. A brand that people can come to trust and rally behind. Silk Road chat, Silk Road exchange, Silk Road credit union, Silk Road market, Silk Road everything! And it's been amazing just talking to a guy who is so intelligent and in the same boat as me, to a certain degree at least.' Three months later, he reported sales of $600,000 per week.

As sales increased and the site grew in popularity, so too did the risks to those who ran it, especially the very visible founder. By February 2012, news stories about Silk Road were common enough that growing numbers of the general public were aware of it, which meant there was political pressure to do something about it. The older and more experienced Variety Jones quizzed Admin about whether anyone in his real life knew of his involvement in the site. Silk Road's owner admitted that two people—a former girlfriend and a friend—were aware he had started the site. He wasn't overly concerned: 'One I'll probably never speak to again, and the other I'll drift away from.'

Variety Jones didn't agree. He believed that anybody who knew the true identity of the owner of the most notorious website in the world was dangerous. His devious mind had come up with a plan. 'Have you even seen *The Princess Bride*?' he asked. Admin confirmed he had.

'So you know the history of Dread Pirate Roberts? It's a thought I'm working on, so humour me.'

Admin was a little hazy on the details and VJ prompted him about the legend. In the story of *The Princess Bride*, the hero, Westley, was captured by Dread Pirate Roberts, a pirate with a reputation of ruthlessness who would kill all on board a ship if they refused to hand over their gold. Westley went on to become the first mate and eventually the pirate let him in on a little secret: Dread Pirate Roberts was not so much one person's name as a job title, secretly passed on from man to man as each incumbent decided to retire. The fictional Roberts' infamous reputation meant ships would immediately surrender their wealth rather than allow their crew to be captured and killed. When the captain wanted to retire, he would offload all his crew other than his first mate at a port. Engaging a new team, the captain would refer to the first mate as 'Dread Pirate Roberts' and once the new crew were convinced, he would leave the ship and retire on his riches.

'You need to change your name from Admin, to Dread Pirate Roberts,' said VJ. 'I'm not kidding—start the legend now.'

'I like the idea,' his protégé responded.

With that, Dread Pirate Roberts, or DPR for short, was born. Variety Jones affectionately called him 'Dipper'.

As time went on, DPR became increasingly reliant on the counsel and friendship of Variety Jones. The two of them would chat late into the night about things that affected the business of the site. During one chat about how to tackle vendors trying to do out-of-escrow sales (and avoiding the commission), DPR admitted that not only could he look through the private messages (PMs) of the site's members, he often did so.

The site's privacy-conscious members would have been disturbed to discover this. Silk Road was built on a platform of trust and 'us against the man'. Although the website enabled encryption using Pretty Good Privacy (PGP), which would thwart any attempts by DPR to snoop, many on the site chose not to use it in their communications.

'Sometime, we have to have a discussion about what to do in the event of arrest or incarceration,' said VJ, one day in March 2012. 'Thought about that a fair bit during the last two weeks.

'For instance, if you were arrested, a decision would have to be made at what point of time do I come get you out. And I would come and get you out. Jail doesn't scare me a whit anymore. I treat it like being in a 3rd world country with poor communications infrastructure.'

'I've been thinking a bit about that as well,' said DPR. 'Like I could put instructions for transferring control in an encrypted file and give it to a family member. Then I can give them the password if I get put in jail.'

'And remember that one day when you're in the exercise yard, I'll be the dude in the helicopter coming in low and fast, I promise,' said VJ. 'Seriously, with the amount of $ we're generating, I could hire a small country to come get you. One of the things I'd like us to look at investing in is a helicopter tour company. Cause you never know when one of us is gonna need a helicopter!'

'Yep, all that money won't be worth much if we're behind bars,' agreed DPR.

The Great 420 Sale and Giveaway

Grab your sleeping bag, stock up on supplies and get ready to camp out on your computer for 49 hours, because on April 20, 2012 at 4:20 PM, the greatest sale in the history of the Silk Road kicks into gear, and you're not going to want to miss a minute of it.

This 4/20, every 420 seconds, some lucky buyer will win one of our 420 great prizes! From $50 gift certificates to a brand new iPhone 4s, some lucky person will be chosen every 420 seconds to win a prize.

– forum post by DPR, April 2012

The Great Silk Road 420 Sale and Giveaway was a brainchild of Dread Pirate Roberts and Variety Jones; a way of engaging the community and getting a buzz happening around the website. Not only would there be regular giveaways throughout, but the party would culminate in a grand prize of an all-expenses paid holiday with spending money. Dread Pirate Roberts was particularly excited and suggested to his mentor that Silk Road forego taking commissions for any sales throughout the event. VJ wasn't convinced. 'I'd like to think that we can bring more to the party than just dropped commissions. We're filling the prize barrel already,' he said.

'It's just three days!' DPR could barely contain his excitement for the party his site was about to throw. His love of his business extended far beyond how much money it made him.

'And a mil in sales,' VJ reminded him, thinking of the extra commissions this could be bringing in a very short timeframe.

DPR thought of it more as a kind of door-buster, loss-leading event, with losses being more than recuperated in the following months. 'We'll be doing a mil in sales every week at full commission before long,' DPR said. 'It's leading by example for the vendors. They will be more generous if we are.' Commissions were dropped.

The announcement of the sale and prize giveaway was met with initial disbelief, but was then well received by customers, and it generated the sort of buzz that was a marketing dream for the site. The community pitched in with their own suggestions and drug vendors offered further discounts and specials on their wares for the duration of the occasion.

In their nightly roundup of the day's events, DPR and VJ cracked jokes about how the sale might be perceived by the public. 'We're selling drugs here, first one's free little Johnny!' joked DPR. 'Damn that sounds awful.'

'Ha!!!' said VJ. 'Let's give away a couple of playground sets, with swings and slides, just to complete the picture.'

The event went down well with the site's clientele, with drug buyers around the world glued to their screens, placing strategic orders in the hope of grabbing one of the prizes. The odds were good, and many customers received bonuses over and above the cut-price wares. Camaraderie among the site's members was strengthened thanks to them taking part in a history-making event that surely would have been considered absurd had anyone suggested it a year earlier.

The winner of the grand prize was a member by the name of 'kiwibacon', who expressed his excitement and gratitude on the forum:

> omg thanks alot sr!!!
> cant beleive [sic] i actually won something!!!!!!!
> WTF!!!!!!!! when i saw msg i was like must be a scam ill never win anything!!!!!!!!!!!!!!!!!!!!!!!!!!!!!
> thanks guys!!!!!!!!! Zomg

A month later, Variety Jones broached the subject of kiwibacon with his protégé. VJ had organised the luxury trip for the winner, provided the itineraries and the extras at a total cost of around $30,000 to Silk Road. 'Dude, I'm worried about our winner,' he said.

'Whasamatta?'

'He's trying to dry out. Heroin. It's not working, and I think his recent influx of cash didn't help,' VJ said, referring to the $4000 spending money that came with the holiday.

This disturbed DPR, who had joked self-consciously at the time about approaching drug dealing in such a cavalier manner. 'Oh geez. Fuck, what are we doing?'

VJ twisted the knife. 'Yeah, he told me some time ago he was trying to quit, but SR made it kinda tough. So I've been doing sessions with him, giving him someone to talk to.'

'Do you think he can't make the trip?'

'I dunno. I'm sure he's gonna run out of spending money early, that's for sure,' said VJ. 'Now, his friend coming from Aus doesn't imbibe, so I'm hoping he'll be a good influence. I'm just worried that it's not the kinda place you wanna get caught trying to score H, or possessing it.' Although they had kept the details of the luxury trip a secret, they had decided it would be to a place both DPR and VJ had a great affection for—Thailand.

'What does he want to do?' DPR asked.

'Oh, he's all gung ho to go, it's me that's worried ;)'

'Shoulda thought more carefully about dropping $4k on an addict,' said DPR ruefully. 'Maybe our next prize will be three months in rehab.'

A growing enterprise

'What are weeklys now?' VJ, the only person who was allowed to be privy to sales revenue information, asked the site's owner in the third quarter of 2012.

'Up to $1.3M,' Dread Pirate Roberts responded.

Variety Jones became an integral part of Silk Road, but he was never hired to do a specific role. The site continued to grow at such a rapid pace that DPR soon had to take on staff members—administrators and forum moderators. Such was his reputation and the love of members for the site, many people offered their services for free. Forum moderators, in particular, started out as volunteer positions.

DPR gradually built up a small team of trusted workers to whom he paid between US$500 and $1500 per week. The website's members were soon introduced to Inigo, Libertas, Chronicpain and Samesamebutdifferent (SSBD), who took on public-facing administration roles. Inigo and Chronicpain hailed from the US, Libertas represented Europe and SSBD worked the Australian time zone.

Although DPR was paranoid about his own anonymity, he was not prepared to trust his staff. 'I'll need your ID with current address,' DPR told people when he was offering them a position that provided access to information other members were not privy to. 'It will be stored encrypted and I will probably never need to decrypt.' Once staff members supplied the identification, DPR would send them a letter that contained a code they would have to repeat to him, so that he could verify that the identification truly belonged to the staff members. He would send it at a random time so that they could not provide a fake address.

A couple of people were uneasy with this requirement and elected not to join the site's administrative team. For others, however, the lure of taking on an official role, as well as the money being offered, was too tempting. 'I guess I'll just have to trust you on that,' said Flush, who took on the public moniker Chronicpain. 'That's a big trust.'

'Yea, that's true,' DPR responded.

Inigo ('handsome devil', DPR commented upon receiving a copy of his driver's licence) was widely considered to be the site's second-in-charge. He was named for Inigo Montoya, Dread Pirate Roberts' sidekick in *The Princess Bride*. Variety Jones, who really held that position, was practically unknown to members, except as a cannabis seed grower who made occasional forum posts. His role as adviser and mentor was not made public. Nobody was aware of the access he had to the inner mechanics of Silk Road, nor of his influence over the Dread Pirate Roberts.

It wasn't just the members at large who were kept in the dark. The public-facing staff members appeared to be Silk Road insiders, but not one of them was aware of the existence of Variety Jones, the puppet-master behind the scenes who had his finger in every one of DPR's pies. DPR shared everything with VJ, sought his counsel and let him in on every aspect of Silk Road. As for his paid staff: 'DPR didn't tell us shit,' SSBD said later. They were provided with limited access, restricted to what was required for them to carry out their jobs.

The administrators were responsible for a variety of tasks, including vendor quality control, resolutions, answering messages—trivial but time-consuming jobs DPR was no longer interested in doing. The toughest stuff, they were told, was keeping up with the vendors and knowing when to demote them. Demotions would apply for non-delivery of drugs to customers, faking feedback, circumventing escrow, loan scamming, exchange scamming or providing fake product. Some bans were temporary, others more permanent.

The administrators and moderators were required to provide regular updates to DPR and he expected total loyalty. The staff, with their common goal of distributing as many drugs to as many people as possible, generally worked as a functional and cohesive team.

That was, until DPR logged on in January 2013 to frantic messages from his deputy. 'I hope you get online soon,' Inigo wrote to his boss. 'We are under attack.'

A thief in the midst

Inigo had noticed some odd transactions running through the Silk Road accounts in the preceding hours. Around $100,000 had gone missing from the petty cash account, but far worse was the discovery that somebody had been changing vendors' passwords, resetting their PINs and wiping out their balances. It could only be a staff member with administration privileges. Inigo worked frantically all night trying to stem the thefts, unable to get hold of DPR.

'I think I figured out how to contain it,' he wrote finally. 'As far as I can tell it was Flush, and he managed to steal a little over $350k.'

DPR came to the same conclusion as to the source of the thefts after doing some digging of his own. 'This makes me sick to my stomach. I decrypted his ID and did some digging. He was arrested for cocaine possession last week,' he told Inigo. 'This will be the first time I have had to call on my muscle. Fucking sucks.'

DPR's 'muscle' was a high-volume cocaine and heroin dealer by the name of Nob. DPR gave Nob the details Flush had provided him when he signed on as forum moderator Chronicpain: Curtis Green, of Utah. DPR asked Nob if he could arrange someone to force Green to return the stolen funds. Nob replied by asking whether DPR wanted him 'beat up, shot, just paid a visit'. DPR instructed him to arrange to have Green beaten up and given a sternly worded note with a Bitcoin address to which to restore the funds.

Nob's ears had pricked up at the mention of Flush's arrest for possession. 'That wasn't the kilo that I sent was it? Because I'm going to be pissed,' he said.

'Did you send it to Utah?' asked DPR. Nob confirmed that he had. The two determined that Flush must have tricked Nob into sending it to him as a middleman in a transaction, then used his position as an administrator to raid vendors' accounts. The money that a kilo of cocaine would bring, along with the Bitcoin held by other drug dealers, would be enough to set someone up for life. Flush had, it seemed, gone rogue in a manner that was unprecedented, not to mention unwise given that the owner of the business from which he had stolen had his name and address.

Once he realised what was happening, Inigo had been able to reset the password to Flush's account, but he was beating himself up about not stopping the Bitcoin thefts sooner. 'If you want me to get on a plane and go find him, just say the word,' he told his boss.

'I have someone on it, thank you though,' DPR replied. 'I have a friend that smuggles heroin for cartels. I'm chatting with him now. He has muscle everywhere and will get to him quickly.'

Dread Pirate Roberts was shaken by the sheer audacity of the theft and sought reassurance from his deputy. 'You're with me right Inigo?'

'Yes sir.'

'I mean . . . long term.'

'Oh yeah absolutely. i swore my loyalty to you and i will stick by that. i take pride in my loyalty above all my other characteristics,' Silk Road's first mate assured him. 'Where i lack in other fields, you'll at least get your value out of me by having somebody loyal for life :)'

'Thank you.'

'You've given me a chance at a financially secure future that i didn't have before,' Inigo continued. 'While Flush may have been a greedy scumbag, I'm here for the long run, if anything just to show my graditude.'

'Maybe guys like us are just rarer than I'd hoped,' DPR said.

Later, DPR shared his frustration with his closest confidant, Variety Jones. VJ was all sympathetic ears. '$350K, eh? Fucker.' DPR poured out the entire tale, including Nob's role. VJ was suitably angry on his protégé's behalf. 'At what point in time do we decide we've had enough of someone's shit, and terminate them?' he demanded after hearing the story. 'Like, does impersonating a vendor to rip off a mid-level drug lord, using our rep and system; follows up by stealing from our vendors and clients and breeding fear and mistrust, does that come close in yer opinion?'

'Terminate?' DPR asked. 'Execute?'

'I know a guy, and he knows a guy who knows a guy, that gets things done,' Variety Jones told him.

Dread Pirate Roberts had a philosophy of no violence. He had provided a note for Nob to give to Flush that he hoped would make him return the funds and learn his lesson. But as he spoke to his two main men—Variety Jones and Inigo—over the next few hours, he became more paranoid that Flush was working with law enforcement and may have kept logs of the hundreds of chats they had engaged in.

'So, you've had your time to think. You're sitting in the big chair, and you need to make a decision,' Variety Jones insisted.

'I would have no problem wasting this guy,' DPR responded.

'Well ok then, I'll take care of it,' said VJ.

'I don't condone murder but that's almost worthy of assassinating him over,' Inigo said to DPR in a separate chat, unaware that DPR was also mulling the situation over with Variety Jones (unaware, in fact, that Variety Jones existed). 'There are certain rules to the underworld, and problems can sometimes only be handled one way.'

The parallel conversations lasted well into the wee hours of the morning, touching on trust, justice and Flush's predilection for trying to recruit people to multi-level marketing schemes. Inigo revealed he had never really trusted Flush and DPR admitted that Flush had been trying to turn DPR against Inigo. The conversation took an existential turn.

'You wanna know one of my deepest fears in all of this?' DPR asked. 'Being wildly successful and becoming extremely powerful and being corrupted by that power.'

'That's a very real possibility,' Inigo told him. 'Power has corrupted even some of the best of men.'

'I need something from you,' DPR said.

'Anything.'

'You need to call me out if ever I am over confident in my ideas, or abusive of my power.'

'I wouldn't hesitate to, don't worry,' said Inigo.

'Thank you,' responded DPR.

Variety Jones was a little less reflective. 'You would have surprised me if you had balked at taking the step, of bluntly, killing Curtis for fucking up just a wee bit too badly,' he said. 'Also, if you had balked, I would have seriously re-considered our relationship. We're playing for keeps, this just drives it home. I'm perfectly comfortable with the decision, and I'll sleep like a lamb tonight, and every night hereafter.'

Although Variety Jones seemed ready and willing to take care of Flush's murder himself, DPR decided Nob was the man for the job. The next time he spoke with him, Nob said, 'As we discussed, I reached out and I have two very professional individuals that are going to visit Green.'

'Will they execute him if I want?' DPR asked.

'They are very good; yes, but I directed them only to beat him up; that was your wishes yesterday, correct?' Nob said. 'They have your note and are going to, how do I say it, torture him.'

Nob told him that beating up Flush would not cost anything, but that DPR would have to pay for a murder for hire.

'Ok, so can you change the order to execute rather than torture?' DPR asked. 'Never killed a man or had one killed before, but it is the right move in this case.'

Nob quoted a price of $80,000 for the hit, to which DPR agreed. 'Yes, let's do it,' he said.

The murder of Curtis Green

The day of Curtis Green's murder, he and his wife went shopping for Campbell's Chicken and Stars soup. No other soup would do for the task at hand. Green was still reeling, trying to figure out just how everything had gone so badly wrong.

Curtis Green, aka Flush, aka Chronicpain, had been arrested on narcotics charges on 17 January 2013. He had been on the phone to his wife, who was out of town, when a parcel was dropped at his door. Unfortunately for Green, the kilo of cocaine he had been expecting was delivered by the Drug Enforcement Administration (DEA) instead of the mailman. Green was immediately cooperative with law enforcement agents upon being told he was facing 40 years' prison. He even provided the Baltimore Silk Road Task Force with access to his administrator account.

The Baltimore Silk Road Task Force included DEA Special Agent Carl Mark Force IV and Secret Service agent Shaun Bridges.

Bridges, the Baltimore task force's computer forensics expert, found a treasure trove of opportunity when he logged in to Green's account as Flush, and promptly started helping himself to Bitcoin from the petty cash fund, and then from the accounts of Silk Road's vendors. Bridges did this completely of his own accord, without alerting his bosses or colleagues to the activity.

Special Agent Force, meanwhile, was the lead undercover of the Baltimore task force, in touch with DPR. When DPR provided Nob with orders to kill Flush, fortunately for Green, he had been providing those orders to Carl Force. He had taken on the persona of a large-scale cocaine and heroin dealer, using the name Nob, and had been insinuating himself into the site owner's inner sanctum for months.

While Nob was Force's official undercover identity, he had taken it upon himself to set up some other, more lucrative, identities on the Silk Road without the knowledge of his superiors or colleagues. As 'French Maid' he took payment from DPR for information about the investigation and as 'Death from Above' he extorted money out of DPR under threat of revealing certain information he knew from within the investigation. DPR made payments to both personas, unaware that they were also his friend Nob, and certainly not suspecting that they were a law enforcement officer on the task force assigned to take Silk Road down.

The hapless Green had no idea he was being screwed over by both Silk Road and the officers who had arrested him. The administrators of Silk Road hired one of the task force's members to kill him for a theft he didn't know about that was being carried out by another member of the task force. At the same time, Force had no idea that Bridges was behind the theft and Bridges didn't know that Force was relieving Silk Road of Bitcoin in other ways. Bridges was careful to first move the Bitcoin from various vendor accounts into Flush's account to ensure blame would be laid on Green. 'I mean, anybody looking into it would—it would be a no-brainer, saying, "Oh, obviously he did it",' Green told the court later. Bridges then transferred the proceeds out of Flush's account to Mt. Gox, a Bitcoin exchange operating out of Japan.

Force advised Green that DPR had ordered his torture, which made Green's decision to turn snitch on DPR a little more palatable. Force explained they would have to stage the torture and make it look as realistic as possible so that Force, as Nob, could provide DPR with evidence that the job had been done.

The torture was carried out in a Salt Lake City hotel and involved what Green felt was a rather too enthusiastic mock drowning in the bathtub. He did not have to act for the photographs the police snapped, because his panic was genuine. After what felt like hours, the police were satisfied with their evidence and let Green return home.

Before Force could provide the photos to DPR, however, the order had been upgraded to execute. Green was in tears as he updated his wife about the situation, still at a loss to explain the theft that had turned his boss against him. What's more, the task force agents had returned to Baltimore with only torture photos, not murder photos. Green and his wife would have to stage the murder and take photos convincing enough to satisfy DPR.

Campbell's Chicken and Stars Soup was exactly the right consistency and colour to pass for the vomit of a man who had been tortured to death. Green's wife staged the scene with an artistic flair motivated by the knowledge that the slightest error could mean a real death sentence. 'Lay perfectly still,' she told her husband, and then started snapping with her iPhone.

'Green is dead, they killed him this weekend, don't have the details yet, and I'm waiting for a photo,' Nob wrote to DPR. DPR insisted on seeing the proof himself. A while later he received the evidence he needed of both the torture and the gruesome aftermath. Nob told DPR that Green had died of asphyxiation or heart rupture while being tortured. Green had vomited all over himself.

'I'm pissed I had to kill him,' DPR said to Nob, 'but what's done is done.' He justified it as being Chronicpain's own fault: 'I just can't believe he was so stupid . . . I just wish more people had some integrity.'

Upon receipt of the photograph of Green's dead body, DPR admitted to being 'a little disturbed, but I'm ok . . . I'm new to this kind of thing is all.' He wired the balance of what he owed to Nob, as agreed. 'I don't think I've done the wrong thing,' he said. 'I'm sure I will call on you again at some point, though I hope I won't have to.'

After the murder

No doubt Dread Pirate Roberts believed, or at least hoped, that one
murder for hire would be all that was required and he could go back
to running his empire and bantering with Variety Jones about things
that did not involve killing people.

No such luck. Things fell apart again for the website in late March
2013. A user going by the name FriendlyChemist contacted DPR to
tell him he was in deep shit with the Hells Angels. FriendlyChemist
claimed he had been fronted $700,000 worth of LSD from the motor-
cycle club. He gave it to popular vendor Lucydrop to sell on Silk Road.
Lucydrop took off with the proceeds and failed to supply the product,
never to be seen on Silk Road again. Now the Hells Angels wanted
their profits and they were coming for FriendlyChemist.

FriendlyChemist had a long list of real names and addresses of
Silk Road vendors and customers that he would publish unless DPR
gave him $500,000 to pay off his suppliers. He provided a sample to
DPR as proof.

DPR was worried. 'I said, have the hells angels contact me so I
can work something out,' he told Variety Jones. His journal entry
on 28 March 2013 read: 'being blackmailed with user info. talking
with large distributor (hell's angels).' A short time later, a user previously unknown to DPR and calling himself 'redandwhite' introduced
himself as one of the people FriendlyChemist owed money to.

DPR started up a dialogue with redandwhite, proposing he
become a vendor on Silk Road. He offered the supposed Angel
FriendlyChemist's real name: 34-year-old Blake Krokoff. He also
provided an address in British Columbia, and the titbit that Krokoff
was married with three children. 'FriendlyChemist is a liability and
I wouldn't mind if he was executed,' he told redandwhite.

Meanwhile, FriendlyChemist was becoming edgy, not having
heard from DPR for nine days and presumably not having been let off

the hook by his suppliers. FriendlyChemist delivered an ultimatum: DPR had 72 hours to pay up before 5000 users' details and about two dozen vendors' identities would be released.

DPR decided that these threats were unforgivable and so, several hours later on 29 March 2013, DPR sent a message to redandwhite. 'I would like to put a bounty on his head if it's not too much trouble for you. What would be an adequate amount to motivate you to find him? Necessities like this do happen from time to time for a person in my position.' He went on to say that it didn't need to be 'clean'. Redandwhite responded quoting $300k+ for clean, or 150–200k for non-clean.

The price was a bit high for DPR. 'Are the prices you quoted the best you can do? I would like this done asap as he is talking about releasing the info on Monday.'

They eventually agreed on a price of 1670 Bitcoins—approximately $150,000 at the time—for the job. DPR made the transfer, immortalised on the blockchain for that date. A day later, redandwhite provided an update on the whole messy situation, stating: 'Your problem has been taken care of . . . Rest easy though, because he won't be blackmailing anyone again. Ever.'

'Got word that blackmailer was executed,' DPR updated his journal. A few days later: 'received visual confirmation of blackmailer's execution.' Ever the sceptic, DPR had demanded a picture of the dead victim with a string of numbers supplied by DPR written on a piece of paper next to him, which redandwhite dutifully supplied.

'I've received the picture and deleted it. Thank you again for your swift action,' DPR wrote, presumably mentally filing the picture along with that of Curtis Green laying in his can of chunky chicken soup. No doubt, he hoped that this was truly the end of killing to save the empire, until the name of an old nemesis came up.

Redandwhite must have decided this murder-for-hire business for the online drugs czar had the potential to be lucrative because, a couple of days later, he told DPR that his goons had extracted some interesting information from FriendlyChemist with some not-so-friendly questioning before his demise. FriendlyChemist had identified another Canadian who had been working with him on the blackmail scheme as well as running a number of scams for a couple of years.

That individual was Tony76, the vendor responsible for the greatest heist in Silk Road's history. And redandwhite had his real name.

Tony76 had been a vendor of cocaine, ecstasy and heroin, and one of the most beloved and trusted sellers on Silk Road. He engaged with his customer base with a friendly, open demeanour and his ratings were consistently high for both product quality and customer service.

During the Great 420 Sale, Tony76 had been one of the most enthusiastic participants. He offered his usual array of drugs at such heavily discounted prices that he had to ask customers to front him payment without going through Silk Road's escrow system, which provided protection for customers against paying for a product they never received. Having the cash on hand meant he would be able to stock up for the huge upswing in orders. Being such a trusted and respected Silk Road identity, customers were happy to oblige.

A couple of days after the sale had come to an end, Tony76 posted to the forums:

> In 12 hours i will be taking my listings down for 24–48 hours to catch up with the sale orders. If you have an order you want to get in you have 12 hours. I will leave sale prices up for the 12 hours. When i put my listings back up in 24–48 hours prices will be back to normal with NEW PRODUCTS AS WELL.
>
> Please keep messages to a minimum as i have been having a hard time keeping up with all the pointless messages.

That was the last anyone would ever hear from Tony76.

A week after the sale, a rumble began on Silk Road. Nobody expected international orders placed during the sale to have arrived yet, but people had started to report and rate their domestic deliveries. Shoppers began to ask Tony76 when their domestic deliveries would arrive. His service was usually so good—his customers hoped his standards weren't slipping.

Two weeks later the rumbles became a roar as buyers demanded to know where their goods were. They compared notes and realised Tony wasn't responding to messages, even as he logged on. It slowly became clear that the most trusted vendor on Silk Road had absconded with what buyers estimated was over $100,000 for a single weekend's work; one moderator of the forums placed it at a cool quarter of a million dollars.

Some of the faithful remained hopeful for weeks, even months. Others offered explanations aside from his actions being a massive scam. Some believed Tony76 had been killed by Mexican drug lords. Others assumed he had been busted. Many refused to believe that someone in their community would do such a thing. Then came the conspiracy theories: he was already selling under another name; Silk Road's owners were in on it; it was all part of a worldwide sting and nobody was safe; Tony76 was actually a Canadian bikie gang.

A lot of customers demanded Silk Road do something to recover their Bitcoin. But Silk Road's administration was unsympathetic. Dread Pirate Roberts had developed a system to protect buyer and seller—that system depended on the escrow service being used. Buyers had been warned that if they traded outside of escrow, they were unprotected. Still, Silk Road's reputation had taken a blow and Tony76's name continued to be brought up as part of its history. DPR never forgot what he did.

'Man, I still can't believe tony fell into yer lap,' Variety Jones marvelled when DPR told him a heavily edited version of the story a few days later.

Indeed, DPR didn't do much questioning himself on that part of the story as he relayed what FriendlyChemist had told redandwhite. 'Says he was in cahoots with lucy all along and ripping the angels off and black mailing me was part of the plan. He also said a 3rd party, our man tony76, orchestrated the whole thing. Gave up his ID.' Redandwhite had told DPR that Tony76's real name was Andrew Lawsry of Surrey, Canada. '[FriendlyChemist] said that [Lawsry] started selling on silkroad a couple of years ago and since then he has made a career of making new seller profiles to sell and then rip people off. He told them how to start on here and how to rip people off and asked for a percentage in return. He said that he showed them everything about how to sell and how to pull it off and all that stuff.'

Again, not stopping to wonder where redandwhite had come from or whether he was really who he said he was, bloodlust whetted, DPR ordered another hit. 'I would like to go after [Tony76],' he wrote, 'though it is important to me to make sure he is who Blake said he is. I would rather miss the chance to take him out, than hit an innocent person. If he is our man, then he likely has substantial assets to be recovered. Perhaps we can hold him and question him?'

There was a problem, though. Tony76 lived with three other drug dealers, and at least two were always home. 'Ok, let's just hit [Tony76] and leave it at that. Try to recover the funds, but if not, then not,' said DPR.

Redandwhite was a little more bloodthirsty—either that or he needed the money. He offered to hit Tony76 alone for $150K, but said that he would have a better chance of recovering any money if he did all four occupants of the house. 'Anything recovered would be split 50/50 with you,' he said. Redandwhite quoted the bargain price of $500K to do all four, practically a 'buy three, get one free' deal.

Whether he was nervous or he liked the idea of 50 per cent of recovered earnings, DPR responded later that day: 'hmm . . . ok, I'll defer to your better judgment and hope we can recover some assets from them.'

'Gave angels go ahead to find tony76,' he wrote in his journal, along with some housekeeping issues about cleaning up unused libraries on the server.

DPR transferred another 3000 Bitcoin to redandwhite ('sent payment to angels for hit on tony76 and his 3 associates,' said the journal), an amount which again appears in the blockchain for that day. A week later, he received confirmation that he had been successful in ordering the murders of four people, three of whom he did not know and had no beef with. 'That problem was dealt with. I'll try to catch you online to give you details,' wrote redandwhite. 'Just wanted to let you know right away so you have one less thing to worry about.'

'Thanks,' said DPR, 'see you on chat.'

Mr Wonderful

In mid-2013, several staff members received an email from someone who called himself Mr Wonderful. Mr Wonderful said he was an undercover law enforcement agent, and he was offering incentives to the staff to feed information about Silk Road and its owner to him.

One of the staff contacted was Scout, the only female on DPR's team. The deal offered by the undercover was for Scout to assist with setting up high-profile vendors in exchange for a percentage of each bust (plus a get-out-of-jail-free card). She immediately alerted DPR, who promptly demanded Scout hand over her login credentials for the TorMail address she was using and then locked her out of her own personal email account. DPR took over discussions with Mr Wonderful.

DPR later suspended Scout from her duties as moderator, claiming that engaging with the undercover and then discussing her situation with other employees Inigo, Libertas and SSBD was an unacceptable security threat.

Once what became known as 'emailgate' settled down, the remaining staff suggested DPR rehire Scout. He eventually relented and did so, but insisted she have an entirely new (male) identity.

He sent his staff a message on 12 July 2013: 'Hey gang, we have a new moderator going by the name cirrus. We used to know him as scout. Cirrus has always been dedicated to our common goals and the community at large and we have put what happened surrounding Mr Wonderful behind us so he can come back on the team. The scout persona is still off limits and still should not be discussed.'

'Thank you for the introduction!' responded Cirrus. 'I'm really excited to be back and working with you guys. Missed you all!!!'

The greatest scam ever?

Perhaps the reason DPR was so ready to place a hit on Tony76 was that Tony76 personified the greatest frustrations of running the most successful online black market in history. The truth was the market did not run as smoothly as its owner tried to portray.

There was never a shortage of people for whom the fast and relatively easy money of drug dealing was not enough. Criminals saw another criminal making untold riches and they wanted a share of it. DPR spent a great deal of money paying off extortionists, hackers and scammers behind the scenes, while the Silk Road community remained in blissful ignorance. DPR paid up to protect not only his empire, but the people he considered he had a responsibility towards.

If a rogue vendor threatened to release information about their customer base, Dread Pirate Roberts paid the ransom to keep them quiet. When a staff member apparently stole the Bitcoin in members' accounts, DPR returned the money without telling them it had been stolen. He paid off those who would perform DDoS attacks to take the website offline. When a scammer spoofed private messages to look like they were coming from Inigo and convinced vendors to part with

Bitcoin to buy 'shares' in Silk Road, again DPR returned the money from his own pocket.

He kept records of all the payments as expenses in his spreadsheet. All in all, the costs of paying off criminals could pile up, but DPR tried to protect his people as much as possible.

But when he discovered that the original great scammer, Tony76, had apparently been so happy with proceeds from his heist that he carried out a similar scam months later with Lucydrop, it was too much. He had already crossed a certain line when he had ordered the murder of Curtis Green.

Only it seems that Tony76 was a scammer on a far more epic scale than DPR ever imagined. The FBI and Canadian authorities compared notes and could find no homicides matching the names or any other details of the alleged victims. The most probable explanation was that redandwhite and FriendlyChemist were the same person—maybe even Tony76—carrying out an elaborate scam. FriendlyChemist had started blackmailing Silk Road around the same time as Lucydrop—who was very likely Tony76—had absconded with thousands of dollars worth of members' Bitcoin.

DPR had apparently paid Bitcoin worth around $650,000 to a slick-talking shyster and opened himself up to charges of conspiracy to commit five new murders that had never taken place.

If it was as it appeared, Tony76 first robbed hundreds of Silk Road customers to the tune of six figures in April 2012, scammed them again for a similar amount under the name Lucydrop in 2013, then attempted to blackmail Dread Pirate Roberts with customers' addresses he had gathered while selling as Tony76 and Lucydrop. When that failed, he extracted the money out of Silk Road by pretending to be a hitman, carrying out the murders of himself and his alter egos.

Variety Jones was right to marvel that Tony76 had dropped into DPR's lap.

End of the Road

Silk Road's unlikely business lasted nearly three years, growing exponentially and going from strength to strength, seemingly out of the reach of law enforcement or politicians. It operated so openly and smoothly that its thousands of members began to imagine that it would keep going forever. Perhaps the billion-dollar business wasn't really that significant in the grand scheme of the global drug trade. Maybe politicians and law enforcement didn't mind it so much because it had none of the violence or immediate danger of the street scene.

Customer service staff, administrators and moderators came and went, always with a core team of around five, to whom the ever-growing membership base could go with questions or issues. Others worked behind the scenes, the ordinary user never aware of their existence.

Nor were any of the casual users of the site aware that some of these staff members were discussing and sanctioning murder of those who threatened the Silk Road empire. Thus when it all came crashing down on 2 October 2013, to the million or so members of the site, the arrest of Dread Pirate Roberts was the arrest of a peace-seeking libertarian who provided recreational drug users with access to affordable, high-quality drugs in a violence-free environment.

Handsome, 29-year-old Texan Ross William Ulbricht was captured in a dramatic arrest in a San Francisco public library. Ulbricht, who had an advanced degree in chemical engineering, and who had developed a cult-like following among the Silk Road users as Dread Pirate Roberts, criminal mastermind, was caught in the sci-fi section logged in to the master control panel of Silk Road, as well as various other incriminating sites and applications.

The arrest was carried out by FBI agents who had been keeping the young Texan under surveillance and suspected that he sometimes logged on to administer Silk Road from a local café or the library. When he entered the library, they had to make sure he was logged in to the backend of Silk Road. What DPR didn't know was that one of his staff members, Cirrus, had been compromised. She had been arrested in July and her account taken over by an undercover agent, Jared Der-Yeghiayan.

The FBI had to make sure Ulbricht was logged in as DPR when they seized his computer, or there was little doubt that the laptop would be encrypted and of no more use to them than a brick. To do so, they had 'Cirrus' strike up a chat with him. If DPR was actively chatting to a staff member, they could grab the laptop while he was logged in and have access to the inside of the Silk Road website.

The plan was executed perfectly. Two officers staged a domestic dispute, and while that distracted Ulbricht, another officer grabbed his open laptop. On that laptop was a goldmine. He not only kept a journal on that same laptop documenting the establishment and growth of the site, he meticulously kept records of the real-time chats he had with his staff, something that was drummed into his staff they were forbidden to do.

Thousands of pages of logs recorded every conversation DPR had had with his various staff members. They also revealed the existence of the hitherto unknown Variety Jones. Unfortunately for some, the open laptop also held the ID documents of Silk Road staff.

Five days after Ulbricht's arrest, high-ranking members of Silk Road met to discuss a replacement. A month later, on 6 November 2013, Silk Road 2.0 was launched.

More arrests

Nearly three months after Ross Ulbricht's arrest on 19 December 2013, key staff members Inigo, Libertas and Samesamebutdifferent (SSBD) were taken into custody in a coordinated transnational operation.

'I suspect that the police had also done a "sneak and peek" into my premises at some stage,' Peter Nash, Australian moderator SSBD said. 'I remember coming home from work one day and my front door key was extremely stiff whereas it normally opened very easily. At that point in time my immediate reaction was that a locksmith had tampered with it. I was told after my arrest it was most likely that the police had installed listening and possibly video surveillance in my home but I have no actual confirmation of that.'

Peter Nash went to bed on 19 December 2013 a content man. Holidays had started. Tomorrow he would board a plane to the UK for his first family Christmas in seven years. From there he would head to Paris for New Year's Eve, where he would propose to the woman sleeping next to him.

Sitting up in bed at 5:00 am, Pete was dealing with some final matters on the website he helped moderate and at the same time chatting via private message to Cirrus, a fellow moderator whom he had never met but considered a friend. He told Cirrus all about his planned holiday. It was then he heard strange noises coming from within the apartment.

His bedroom door burst open and more people than he ever knew could fit in his apartment swarmed in. 'Australian Federal Police!' they yelled as one of them snatched the laptop from his hands. 'Don't move!' Around fifteen police, accompanied by two FBI special agents, searched every inch of the apartment while Peter was read his rights. He was allowed to comfort his partner as they ransacked his home. Computers were high on the agenda.

There would be no plane trip that day. There would be no romantic proposal at the Eiffel Tower.

In Charles City, Virginia, USA, a similar scene took place on a yacht that Andrew Jones called home. It was a rent-to-own affair on which he could laze away the days, a lifestyle paid for by the modest salary he was pulling from Silk Road. Andrew didn't ask for much out of life. Time spent smoking weed and chilling with his girlfriend were his happy days.

He was smoking weed and chilling with his girlfriend when there was a loud banging on the boat with voices demanding that he come out.

'This is a joke, isn't it?' he said to his girlfriend, Birdie.

It was no joke and Andrew was presented with a warrant that allowed police to take all of his computer equipment, before they placed him under arrest and took him away. The accompanying indictment identified Jones as Inigo and gave names to the colleagues he knew only as SSBD and Libertas.

When he was in the interview room, police showed him some of the evidence they had against him. Andrew was aghast as he saw things that no law enforcement agency should know: conversations he'd had with buyers and sellers, and even private messages with DPR.

I don't fucking understand . . . he thought.

In Dublin, Ireland, Gary Davis was presented with an identical indictment, accusing him of narcotics trafficking, computer hacking and money laundering under the name Libertas. Davis was taken in for questioning by the *gardai*, but remained tight-lipped, responding only that he wanted to consult a lawyer. His solicitor wasted no time in arranging bail and Gary Davis was home sleeping in his own bed that night.

Samesamebutdifferent

Peter Nash arrived at Silk Road late in 2012. Calling himself Samesamebutdifferent, better known as SSBD, he quickly became a prolific contributor to the Australian discussion threads and soon after, at his own request, was elevated to moderator. 'I had sent a PM to DPR asking about supporting the community and he just upgraded me the following day,' he explained.

At first a volunteer, he was later paid $500 per week, then by mid-2013 was earning $1000 per week in Bitcoin. The Bitcoin never left his account, instead being spent on cocaine, weed and MDMA (ecstasy). 'I was just doing it because I enjoyed the camaraderie and social connections I found on the forums,' Pete said. 'At that time I was going through an incredibly stressful and challenging period in my career and was feeling very isolated in my life. The forums became my second home. I was holding down a full-time job and then putting in almost the equivalent amount of hours each day on the forums.'

Pete was surprised when Dread Pirate Roberts demanded he provide a scan of his driver's licence, which DPR assured him was standard for his staff. Silk Road's owner preached the importance of opsec (operational security) and as anonymity was sacrosanct, Pete's ID would be encrypted, safely tucked away from prying eyes; Pete need only worry if he ever tried to blackmail his boss.

SSBD soon became one of the most popular and hardworking moderators on Silk Road. In his role, Pete had no control over anything that happened on the markets. He had no influence in what the marketplace did. He never sold drugs himself. He had no say in what drugs could be sold, to whom or by whom. His job was to delete spam, help newbies with their questions, move posts around if they were put in the wrong forums or delete them if they put someone in danger, such as if a disgruntled member posted identifying details of somebody. Forum moderators also had to immediately remove particularly objectionable posts, like anything linking to offensive pornography or sites selling other objectionable services.

Pete got along with all the staff, but was closest to fellow moderator Scout, who was later reinvented as Cirrus. 'We used to exchange messages often and I frequently found myself offering [her] support.' Scout/Cirrus often inadvertently pissed off DPR, and Pete would find himself comforting her when things turned pear-shaped.

As for his boss, Pete said of DPR, 'it would not be unusual for him to totally ignore messages from me or others. Occasionally we would have more in-depth exchanges but he never really gave much away and our exchanges were usually rather one-sided.'

Pete had been going through a tough period in his life. The Silk Road forums offered him purpose, friendship and camaraderie. His position of moderator accorded him status. He had all the drugs he needed for weekends to be one long party. Life was good.

When Ross Ulbricht was arrested on 2 October 2013, accused of being Silk Road mastermind Dread Pirate Roberts, and the marketplace was seized by a host of American three-letter agencies, Peter Nash panicked. He posted some farewell messages on the forums (which, being on a separate server, had not been shut down), cleared his house of drugs, wiped his computers clean and went to ground.

But a few weeks later, with no knock on the door, the fear began to subside. A race had begun to replace the site with a new marketplace, and previous staff were invited to join forces with programmers and developers to re-create Silk Road. When the new site opened with much fanfare just a month after Ulbricht's arrest, Pete couldn't resist; he revived SSBD and logged on to the dark web once more.

Silk Road 2.0 felt like home. The old faces were there. Money launderer StExo had bestowed upon himself the moniker of DPR, carrying on the legend of the character of *The Princess Bride* handing over the mantle. Former administrators Libertas and Inigo resumed their roles. Most importantly, Pete's closest ally, Cirrus, was on board as chief moderator of the forums. It was Cirrus to whom Nash was chatting on that fateful day six weeks later.

After the unexpected 5:00 am visit from representatives of both Australian and US federal law enforcement, Nash was taken to the Roma Street police station, where he discovered they knew more than he ever could have imagined. Pete was not the only one arrested that day. Simultaneously, Andrew Jones, Silk Road's second-in-command Inigo, was arrested in Virginia, USA. Gary Davis, accused of being administrator Libertas, was picked up in Ireland.

A police officer processing Pete's paperwork warned him not to talk to anyone no matter what they said to him. 'If you talk to these people you will fuck yourself,' the officer said. Pete was introduced to an FBI special agent who was there to oversee his arrest. It was suggested several times that there were things he could do right there and then to 'help himself'. Pete exercised his right to remain silent.

From there Peter Nash was incarcerated and his nightmare began. The United States government demanded he be extradited to face charges there. Under the Australian legal system, this meant there was virtually no chance of being released on bail while the courts determined whether or not to grant the USA's request.

Pete was remanded in a Brisbane correctional facility. For a while, things were okay; or at least as okay as they could be spending Christmas in prison. But then he woke up one morning to a fellow inmate waving the front page of a local newspaper at him. It said that Pete had run Silk Road while working in a prison. The same prison he was incarcerated in.

'I initially found it hilarious reading all the inaccuracies and sensationalist hyperbole,' he said. But then he was threatened by a group of inmates and his time in the general population was over. He was moved into protective custody.

Pete—a nurse and psychologist—had worked for a service for adults with intellectual disabilities and complex behavioural support needs, including those who were in prison. The same news report stated he was 'under investigation by the Crime and Misconduct Commission for allegedly smuggling a dangerous sex offender out of jail for a meal at Hungry Jack's'. Pete denies this.

'The "incident" in question related to my having escorted a client to see their doctor and whilst out we got lunch,' he said. 'It was that simple, nothing untoward whatsoever and perfectly normal in the context of community rehabilitation as per that client's support plan.' But Pete soon discovered it wasn't just his fellow prisoners he had to worry about. A while later it was reported he received a vicious bashing at the hands of prison officers.

'The bashing occurred after the prison was locked down following a roof top protest that was going on somewhere in the prison,' Pete said. 'We had been locked down since early afternoon and I was alone in my cell watching TV. I became aware of a commotion somewhere in my unit, lots of screaming and shouting basically then soon after a corrections officer acting in their capacity as the specialist response team (SRT) came onto my tier and announced a verbal warning of physical violence against anyone who called out.

'Just as he said that, someone made a comment and because I was looking out my cell window at the time the officer looked in my direction. I was ordered to get on the ground and put my hands behind my head. My protests that I hadn't said anything fell on deaf ears, I am told even the corrections officer who was working our unit that day tried to intervene and was disregarded. Soon after my cell door was opened and approximately five officers smashed me to the ground punching and kicking me in the head and ribs yelling at me to "stop resisting!" and to "shut the fuck up!"

'I was then handcuffed and dragged from my cell. Before exiting the unit I was pushed up against the wall then my hands which were cuffed behind my back were sharply pulled back so I fell forward in a free fall so my head connected sharply with the metal shelf that ran around the outside of the fish bowl (staff observation area). I was then dragged up to a holding area near the stores and thrown onto the ground and after being uncuffed told to "clean that shit up" which was referring to the blood that was all over the walls and floor, some of it mine and some of it other inmates who had received the same treatment. I was left in the holding area for a couple of hours then taken back to my unit.

'At that time I thought my ribs had been broken. I was having trouble breathing and started to hyperventilate which was probably the shock coming out. Another inmate alerted the medical team that

I was in distress because they could hear my distress. Soon after I had a large number of corrections officers outside my cell demanding to know what was wrong with me. At that time I was only concerned with avoiding another bashing so I told them I was ok and just needed some pain relief.'

With life having become a nightmare in the Australian prison and his lawyer advising him that, no matter how long it was drawn out, extradition was all but inevitable, Pete gave up the will to fight. He waived his rights to contest his extradition and agreed to go and face the music in the United States. He was transferred to the Metropolitan Correctional Center in New York in June 2014.

Another, far more famous, prisoner was also housed at the MCC. Ross Ulbricht was in another division, awaiting trial for being the Dread Pirate Roberts, Pete's boss. And a complete stranger.

Libertas

'Promoted gramgreen to mod, now named libertas,' DPR wrote in his journal during Silk Road's growth spurt in May 2013. The renamed marijuana vendor's role became monitoring user activity on Silk Road for problems, responding to customer service enquiries, and resolving disputes between buyers and vendors. Libertas had a quirky, somewhat militant manner, and a tendency towards grandiose statements, which led to him being gently ribbed by other members of the site.

Nowhere was this manner more evident than upon the arrest of Ross Ulbricht and the shuttering of Silk Road. Libertas made an impassioned speech on the Silk Road forums the next day:

Ladies and gentlemen, brothers and sisters in arms,

It is with a heavy heart that I come before you today. A heart filled with sadness for the infringements of our freedoms by government oppressors, and a heart filled with sadness for the pain that all of you who have lost everything are feeling.

Silk Road has fallen.

Whilst this is devastating to me personally on so many levels, and I will not be commenting on the arrest of any person portrayed by the media as 'Dread Pirate Roberts', it serves to strengthen my resolve to keep fighting the hands of Law Enforcement that are committed to strangling personal freedom from our bodies, demonstrating a lack of conscience and justice on their part in the process. They will stop at nothing to enforce the unjust laws created and maintained by the societal and governmental framework within which they operate, and the actions of one persona, the Dread Pirate Roberts, has managed to stymie their efforts for two and a half years . . .

We must stand on the shoulders of this tragedy that has befallen us and raise high what still remains—our sense of community, freedom and justice. No doubt we will all regroup elsewhere, and I look forward to seeing all of you again, still free and still engaging in free trade without government interference into your personal affairs.

Whilst Silk Road may have fallen, its spirit will spring eternal. The spirit of this community that has inspired and helped so many will continue to live on regardless of what governments wish to say about it. It has been an absolute pleasure serving and working with all of you, and I sincerely wish you all the best for the future wherever you choose to go.

The Dread Pirate Roberts is a revolutionary, a comrade in arms and a true hero who will live on as such in our hearts and minds without fail for as long as we breathe. His ideals and sacrifices will never be forgotten, and they will spur the next generation of revolutionaries into action against oppression.

To the members of Law Enforcement that are no doubt reading this, many of you may have received pats on the back and 'high-fives' from your peers. You may feel good now, ecstatic even, but I urge you to consider the effects of your actions. You are going to see more bloodshed on our streets (note 'our', not 'your', for those streets belong to the people), and more dealer on buyer violence as free people that wish to engage in activities that harm none are forced to return to their previous methods of securing the goods that they wish to put into their own bodies. That blood is now on your hands, and the hands of the politicians that you live to serve and serve to live. I pity you, for as long as you live to serve you will never know freedom.

To the community at large, you have been nothing short of incredible. Keep fighting the good fight, and never let they who are bound by the chains of law tell you that you are not permitted to be free simply because they are shackled themselves. Governments tell us that we are free but the reality is that the moment we are born we are shackled by the rule of law. Government has no place in a free society, and we need to make sure that they who deem it their right to take away the natural rights of others as free beings are made fully aware of that.

Take the fight wherever it is needed, and support every effort to take your government down. You are justified in those actions as they would not hesitate to take you down for standing up for your freedom.

'Freedom is never voluntarily given by the oppressor; it must be demanded by the oppressed.'

– Martin Luther King Jr.

It has been an honor and a privilege to be part of something so incredible with all of you.

Until we meet again, brothers and sisters.

– Libertas.

Libertas was instrumental in developing Silk Road 2.0, which opened a month later. Silk Road 2.0 survived the multiple arrests and continued running for a year before being shut down on 6 November 2014. By the time it closed, it was larger than the original Silk Road ever was. Cirrus, the undercover Homeland Security officer, had been on its staff the entire time.

Libertas had used the Guy Fawkes mask, the symbol of Anonymous, to stamp his posts on Silk Road. With his widow's peak and goatee, the dark-haired Davis cultivated a look that was remarkably similar to the online avatar of Libertas.

The Irish system began as Gary Davis' friend. He was granted bail on a nominal surety and headed straight home on the night of his arrest. The court decided there was no evidence he was a flight risk, would tamper with witnesses or commit further serious crimes, much to the chagrin of the FBI agents who had flown to Ireland to interrogate him.

He had to surrender his passport, and report in to the local police station three times a week, but other than that, Davis was a free man while he prepared for his court hearings.

The United States was keen to extradite Davis to face trial as soon as possible on the conspiracy charges, but Gary's lawyers argued vigorously. Gary was diagnosed with Asperger's syndrome—a form of autism—shortly after his arrest. His lawyers argued that his Asperger's coupled with depression meant that extradition would breach the European Convention on Human Rights (ECHR), which prohibits torture and inhuman or degrading treatment or punishment, and ensures 'respect for one's private and family life, his home and his correspondence'.

A psychologist confirmed that in Davis' case, extradition could precipitate a suicide attempt.

Counsel for the US, Remy Farrell, was sceptical, claiming Davis had 'a mild case of Asperger's brought on by a bad case of extradition'.

Davis appealed all the way to the full bench of the Supreme Court of Ireland and was still awaiting the decision at the time of writing.

Inigo

The man widely assumed to be second-in-charge only to the Pirate himself was Andrew Jones, aka Inigo. One of the earliest customer service staff members, Inigo was appointed as an administrator to resolve disputes between buyers and vendors. He also maintained Silk Road's book club, where users were set reading tasks and those who participated would debate the libertarian and political philosophies from the books allocated.

In his offline life, Andrew Jones was a hardcore libertarian who believed that the role of government ended at the protection of people's rights; government should neither provide for people nor punish them for activities that did not interfere with the rights of others. He and his girlfriend were participants in the Free State Project, an experiment to bring together 20,000 people in New Hampshire with the intention of creating a society in which the maximum role of government was the protection of individuals' rights to life, liberty and property. The project had not commenced at the time of his arrest.

Silk Road's longest-serving administrator was released on $1 million bail, which was raised by his parents putting up their home and retirement savings as surety. He was placed under 24/7 house arrest at their house. As part of his bail conditions, he was not allowed access to any internet-enabled devices. His long-time girlfriend, Birdie, moved into the family home with him.

Drew and Birdie set up a page to fund his defence, having seen the generosity of the community to Ross Ulbricht's family since his arrest. The fundraiser drew a couple of Bitcoin, but overall they were disappointed in the response. Drew lost the support of most of his family and all of his girlfriend's family, who were quick to believe that Andrew was a cartel drug trafficker who was bent on destroying society.

As the authorities revealed their case against Drew to his lawyers, the magnitude of the evidence against Ulbricht, Drew and his co-defendants became clear. Drew was dismayed to learn that DPR had not only kept his identification but also logs of all of their TorChat conversations—hundreds of pages worth. He was convinced that the amount of evidence the US had against him was overwhelming and could put him in prison for the rest of his life.

After much soul-searching, and weighing up the options—life in prison or not—Drew decided he would turn state evidence against Dread Pirate Roberts.

The trial of Ross Ulbricht

The trial of Ross William Ulbricht, accused of being Dread Pirate Roberts, sole owner and operator of Silk Road, began in New York on 13 January 2015. Ulbricht's defence attorney, Joshua Dratel, opened with the bombshell that Ross Ulbricht created Silk Road as an economic experiment but said he was not Dread Pirate Roberts. He claimed Ross had sold the Silk Road in the very early days of the website's lifetime. The defence claimed that Silk Road's true owner had been alerted to the police investigation closing in and had framed Ulbricht.

It is safe to say, there had never been a trial like this one. The first witness called was Homeland Security Special Investigations Agent Jared Der-Yeghiayan, who had made over 50 purchases from 40 Silk Road dealers in ten countries and eventually took over the account of a Silk Road staff member, Cirrus, formerly known as Scout.

Der-Yeghiayan admitted that he had suspected several people to have been Dread Pirate Roberts, including Mark Karpelès, the owner of Bitcoin exchange Mt. Gox, and also that he thought the writing style of the person operating the Dread Pirate Roberts account had changed in April 2012.

Ulbricht's defence team tried to bring up people and events and evidence relevant to the defence, but much information was excluded due to certain concurrent ongoing investigations. The defence tried to introduce evidence about a Silk Road account called Mr Wonderful, operated by a law enforcement agent, but any evidence about that account was disallowed after objections by the prosecution. The jury also never got to hear about the antics of DEA Special Agent Carl Mark Force IV and Secret Service agent Shaun Bridges, who used their access and technical knowledge to steal Bitcoin from user accounts, sell intelligence to Dread Pirate Roberts, and extort money from him with threats to release sensitive information. The jury heard the entire case, blissfully unaware of the corruption of two law enforcement officers actively involved in investigating Silk Road.

It wasn't until a few days into the trial that the name Variety Jones came up. Until then, at most, those intimately involved in Silk Road knew the name as the moniker of a marijuana seed supplier who made occasional posts on the Silk Road forum. Nobody had any idea he was also Dread Pirate Roberts' most trusted adviser, his oldest ally and the brains behind many of the site's ideas, improvements and innovations.

As the prosecution revealed it had recovered over a thousand pages of chat logs between Dread Pirate Roberts and the Svengali-like Variety Jones, members of the many darknet market-related forums scrambled to uncover information about the man Ulbricht apparently relied on for everything in the early days, from technical advice to moral support.

There did not seem to be any real-life identity linked to this Variety Jones character. Nothing in the evidence suggested that law enforcement had anyone on their radar. He had not been included on the indictment with Inigo, Libertas and SSBD. His role in Silk Road was not clear, but he was paid significantly more than the administrators and moderators. The Silk Road accounting books indicated that payments amounting to several hundred thousand dollars in Bitcoin had been made to him.

The press picked up on this mysterious new character, his role behind the scenes in Silk Road, and his relationship with Dread Pirate Roberts. They soon referred to him as a puppet-master, the true architect of Silk Road.

As the trial wore on, Ulbricht's lawyers made valiant attempts to deny the accusations that he was the sole owner and operator of Silk Road. But the treasure trove of information on the laptop, the journal, spreadsheets, blockchain transactions, TorChat logs, payroll details, together with the data recovered from the server, built up a picture of guilt that was difficult to defend.

Who is Variety Jones?

As someone who had been following and writing about Silk Road since its very early days, I followed the trial avidly from the other side of the world. Every morning I would download the hundred-plus pages of court transcripts and check my Twitter feed for analysis and news and insights. I would fire up Tor and scour dark web discussion forums for inside information or new revelations. On site after site, the chatter centred on one topic: Who is Variety Jones?

On 22 January 2015, three days in to the second week of Ross Ulbricht's trial, I opened an email from an unfamiliar address.

> Excuse my unsolicited email, but this is best done over email, rather than publically via twitter :) I have been following yours (and others) tweets about the trial, loving it, hope to get the book one day!

It was a warm fuzzy opening to what at first glance I thought might be a piece of fan mail—a rare, but not unheard-of occurrence. Then the writer got down to business.

> I've been looking into Variety Jones, avoiding the dark net market angle as I expected to draw blanks on that front, however coming at it from the seed supplier angle threw up something interesting I thought you might be interested in.

> In 2006, a Canadian cannabis seed related company called Heaven's Stairway was raided and shut down . . . the owner was a millionaire businessman of Armenian descent . . .

The email, around five paragraphs, provided some tantalising hints, a couple of names, and links to source information I might want to pursue. The writer gave off the impression that he had simply been googling and had come up with this stuff.

The decision now is do you or someone else do the homework and find and name VJ via this link, interesting to think about no?

It warrants proper and *careful* consideration, we're not talking about a few starry-eyed teens here, we're talking about older, wiser and possibly better connected career criminals, who worked this industry long before the current zeitgeist for acceptance of marijuana was at the fore, if a person was interested, they would do so with care, these *are* the kind of people that have had people hurt before for getting involved in their business.

Just thought you'd find the links interesting :)

Alan. (My real name, so if you run with this, it's ALL yours, you found it, you ran with it :P)

Any investigative journalist would find the information interesting, but there was something off about the email. There was no way I was going to click those links.

His Gmail address supplied a surname as well, along with the information that he was in the UK and a picture. A couple of hours' searching came up with exactly nobody by that name. He was lying to me.

I responded with a non-committal, 'Wow, that's a lot to take in. Thanks—I will have a look when I have some time. Did you send it to anyone else?' His response was swift.

Nope, just for you and I'll keep it that way if you like.

I didn't want to post it in public as it deserves a writers touch and someone with time to put the pieces together properly, that's if there is anything there and I'm not a writer.

I just like digging things up and trying to make connections, and have a bit of an art for searching and making connections. :P

I decided not to act on it that day. There were hundreds of pages of court documents to read through before the trial resumed in the morning.

The next day I received another email. More links and lines being drawn, implicating people in the seed growing business of the UK and Canada.

One thing is abundantly clear, Variety Jones is known by many of them, and not just in an online capacity, they know who he is, period. But there is respect for him that means I find it doubtful that any will disclose those details

I didn't respond and later that day, another email arrived from my eager correspondent.

Ok, this one is a bombshell . . . There is a very probable *official* paper-trail that leads to the identity of Variety Jones . . .

The man had done his homework. Pages of accusations, links and practically a roadmap telling me that Variety Jones was also known in the world of online drug dealing as Plural of Mongoose, and was known in the real world as Roger Thomas Clark.

'I haven't really had time to look at anything yet and to be honest doxxing is not generally my thing,' I wrote back, still suspicious of 'Alan's' motives. 'Why the keen interest on your part, may I ask?'

Once again, 'Alan' professed mere curiosity and a desire to help Ross.

I read the chat logs / articles last week and saw two names that really jumped out at me, Variety Jones and ~shabang~, at first moreso ~shabang~ than anyone else, because, shabang, VJ and the aforementioned Plural of Mongoose and Gypsy Nirvana among a few others were all entwined in a series of dramas, arrests, claims of blackmail etc. over control of the cannabis supply market, and/or control and ownership of some fairly large pro-cannabis websites that were thought to be worth a lot of money in the early part of the internet, from 1998 to 2008, these people worked for each other, with each other, conspired against each other and even used law enforcement AND EVEN FAKED ASSASSINATION attempts against each other in attempts to take each others money and/or businesses.

Finally, intrigue got the better of me and I clicked on all his links. The next day I found that all emails between me and two former Silk Road staffers—Scout/Cirrus and Nomad Bloodbath—had disappeared from my Gmail account. Scout and Nomad Bloodbath had both been compromised before the fall of Silk Road, their accounts taken over by Homeland Security agents. My attempts to retrieve the emails, or find out what happened to them, were fruitless.

I suspected that I had fallen for a phishing attack and that it came from the mysterious 'Alan' who had bombarded me with increasingly specific information, none of which I had been able to verify. I forwarded the information to LaMoustache, the most thorough dark web researcher I knew.

More new characters

Variety Jones was not the only surprise new character to emerge from the evidence led at Ulbricht's trial. The message logs revealed a quagmire of people who contacted Dread Pirate Roberts for various reasons. One unidentified user by the name of 'alpacino', who appeared to have ties to a law enforcement agency, was feeding Dread Pirate Roberts intelligence about the investigation. As well as specific information about the authorities' attempts to locate DPR, alpacino had some general advice for him:

> I know that Eileen has a publishing deal and is writing a book around SR, and has had extensive dialogue with everyone from buyers to new vendors to old hats. She claims that she has your blessing and at some point will be (or has) interviewing you of sorts . . . Do not put it past them to wiretap journos. If you (for example), interact with people like Chen [the Gawker reporter who first wrote about Silk Road] or Ornsby [sic], assume they can see it. Assume journalists are compromised/breached.

Over the years of writing exclusively about the dark web, I had become accustomed to receiving all manner of communications. More often than not, they were conspiracy-fuelled, inaccurate or fed to me in a deliberate attempt to spread FUD—fear, uncertainty and doubt. There is rarely enough time to check or respond to every claim. The discovery of a rogue agent feeding intelligence to DPR behind the scenes reminded me of an encrypted note I had received in December 2013, a couple of months after Ulbricht's arrest, from an anonymous Silk Road member. 'What if I told you DPR had a federal agent on his payroll . . . who was feeding him information about vendors who were being surveilled or were about to be busted. He saved quite a few vendors' asses,' the message said. It went on to name some prominent vendors and incidents I could question them about as proof of the writer's claims. 'Ask Modzi how DPR knew stuff that helped him not get busted. He won't know how, but he will know what you are talking about'. The message also suggested I ask StExo about 'The Canadian Professor incident'. Although my curiosity was slightly piqued, the note came at a time when rumours and paranoia ran rampant throughout the dark web forums, and I did not follow up on it.

Both incidents came up in DPR's law enforcement intel file and journal: '"alpacino" from DEA has been leaking info to me. Helped me help a vendor avoid being busted, he wrote. In a separate note he referred to a Canadian academic: 'StExo has discovered that Dr David Decary-Hetu is planning to do research on SR for canadian LE [law enforcement]'. DPR made a note to himself of the professor's LinkedIn profile address.

Later, a character who called himself Oracle and seemed to have some inside knowledge of Silk Road wrote in a post on a dark web forum: 'This news, when brought to DPR1's attention, allegedly resulted in the poor professors life being threatened! StExo and DPR1 spoke of possible scenarios, one of which involved putting a contract on the professors head! Very "Breaking Bad"-esque (which incidentally was a show StExo was a fan of). To my knowledge, the Canadian academic was never actually harmed, but was threatened to back off.'

Décary-Hétu, however, denied ever having been threatened. 'It really feels strange to read about how DPR was discussing how to intimidate me. I would love to read those chats to see exactly what was said—if anything was really said. I was never contacted by DPR or any of his associates. No one ever tried to intimidate me or stop me in any way from crawling cryptomarkets. I always thought that it was a pretty harmless thing to do,' he said. 'I was never contacted or threatened by anyone—and I checked my SPAM folder to make sure I had not missed something. This is once again offenders bragging about how tough they are when they have done absolutely nothing in fact.'

I had dismissed the note at the time, but with this new evidence that the information had been accurate, I had to wonder who had sent

it to me and what they hoped I would do with it. It may have been a
Silk Road insider; perhaps the Variety Jones I had not known existed
until the previous week, though it did not seem his style. Perhaps it was
someone who had access to the discovery documents, which would
mean someone within one of the three-letter agencies or someone
from Ulbricht's camp, trying to get that information into the public.
As I had ignored it, I might never know.

Silk Road deputies

Peter Nash, Andrew Jones and Gary Davis meanwhile had been all
but forgotten as their far more famous boss stood trial. Davis kept his
head down and avoided the limelight as the case for his extradition
progressed through the Irish courts. Nash had been transferred to the
New York Metropolitan Correctional Center, where Ulbricht was, but
they were in different sections. Surprisingly, considering the charges
were computer-related, Nash had access to the prison's email system
and I was able to provide him with daily updates on the trial and what
was happening to his co-accused.

Both Nash and Jones entered guilty pleas because there was little
point in denying who they were. The prosecution had evidence—lots
of it. Bit by bit, information came out from testimony and exhibits
produced against Ross Ulbricht in the lead-up to the trial of Dread
Pirate Roberts. Ulbricht had kept the IDs of his staff in a file on his
computer. A backup server, which was housed in Pennsylvania and
subjected to a search warrant, contained every single message ever
sent from Silk Road. Law enforcement was able to match up things
said in private messages with events in the men's real lives (exactly as
they did with Ross Ulbricht).

'Hindsight is always 20/20 and providing my ID to DPR was
obviously reckless and stupid,' Pete said. 'You have to remember
though that those were different times and no one had been busted

back then and I think we were all rather misguided in our perceptions of risk.'

It wasn't until the trial that the former staffers discovered that fellow moderator Cirrus was in fact an undercover Homeland Security agent. Cirrus had been instrumental in bringing down Ross Ulbricht, and had been engaging Peter Nash to ensure that he was logged in to Silk Road so that agents could grab his open, unencrypted computer; Cirrus had done the same with Ulbricht. By the time the revelation became official knowledge, Peter already suspected there was a traitor in their midst and it could only be one person. Cirrus was the only still-active moderator of the original Silk Road to have escaped arrest. But Nash was bewildered to discover that the real Cirrus' account had been taken over as far back as July 2013.

'It seems strange to me now knowing that the Scout/Cirrus account was handed off to a HSI [Homeland Security] undercover, because they continued to mimic the same personality traits of being quite flaky and overly emotional about some of the shenanigans that used to go down on the forums,' Peter said, apparently no longer sure which pronoun to use to describe his former colleague.

Many on the dark web forums and reddit blamed Ross Ulbricht for the arrest of Peter Nash and his co-defendants Jones and Davis. Their photo IDs were held on Ulbricht's laptop, along with logs of chats and messages that any dark web employee should have the right to assume were never kept.

Nash, however, refused to lay the blame at his boss' feet. 'As for Ross leaving my ID in an easy to find folder on his laptop . . . well I think that just underscores what I just said before about being stupid and reckless,' Peter said. 'I do not blame Ross for my incarceration though. It was my choice to send him my doxx, no one made me do that. Too often people look to blame others for the consequences (unintended or otherwise) of their actions and I am not about that, I take the responsibility for what I did.' That said, he no longer held the unbridled admiration for Dread Pirate Roberts that he once had, saying, 'What has come out subsequent to Ross' arrest and at trial has conflicted me and changed my perceptions of a few things. The OPSEC issues certainly caused me to question a lot.'

What did concern him were reports that the peace-loving libertarian captain of the website he had come to love had ordered six hits, calling for the murders of recalcitrant staff and Tony76, among others. Staff and users of Silk Road alike had been sold the utopian vision of drugs for consenting adults in an environment free from coercion and violence. The bombshell revelations split the darknet market community. Those who loved and admired Silk Road and its owner could not condone cold-blooded murder. It seemed so out of character for the leader they felt they had come to know.

In the myriad conspiracy charges thrown at Ross Ulbricht, conspiracy to commit murder, or attempted murder, was not one of them. Nevertheless, the transcripts discussing the hits were admitted as evidence of Ulbricht's willingness to use violent means to protect his business. Like many, Peter preferred not to believe the government's version of events. 'As for the murder for hire stuff, well as abhorrent as that may be I will reserve judgment until those allegations have been tested and proven beyond a reasonable doubt.'

Despite being in the same facility, Nash crossed paths with Ulbricht just once, when neither was expecting the meeting. Ulbricht was coming out of an elevator. Peter recognised him immediately and held out his hand to the younger man, introducing himself. When recognition failed to register on Ulbricht's face, Peter followed it up with his surname. Ulbricht's eyes went wide as the penny dropped. 'I just told him I was pleading out the next day and that was it, we literally just passed each other so there was no time to speak, just exchanged pleasantries really,' Peter recounted.

Silk Road was a most unusual workplace, in which the entire executive team, who dealt with each other on a day-to-day basis, had no idea about the person behind each username. When Peter Nash and Andrew Jones attended the same court appearance, neither knew who the other was. Inigo and SSBD had had daily conversations and kept things running when Dread Pirate Roberts was otherwise indisposed. Both had guessed the other was male—a safe bet on Silk Road, Scout being the one exception—but had no knowledge of each other's details otherwise.

Andrew's lawyer had told him that Peter would be in attendance and he was able to figure out which one Peter was. He had hoped they would be placed next to one another and have a chance for a chat, but that wasn't to be. Peter was seated a few seats down in the same row and Drew had to crane forward to see his co-accused. When he caught Peter's eye, Drew gave him a bright smile.

Peter had no idea who the smiling man was and blanked him, wondering if he was a federal agent. It was only when the proceedings started and they read out the US vs. Jones that he realised Drew was Inigo, the man he had worked side by side with in what they thought was a revolution.

By that time, the socially awkward Andrew was steadfastly avoiding catching Peter's eye, worried that Peter judged him for the decision he had made to turn state evidence against Dread Pirate Roberts.

Andrew had gone into hiding after he made his deal with the prosecution. He remained under house arrest at the home of his parents, the bracelet affixed to his ankle ensuring he never strayed far from home. He was banned from any online activity at all; he couldn't even order take-away through the local pizza delivery's webpage.

As it turned out, the prosecution ultimately failed to call him to testify, though no reason was given. Andrew felt he would not have been able to assist the prosecution's case; he was as much in the dark as to his boss' identity as anyone and knew little of what went on in the backend of Silk Road.

The verdict

The trial of Ross Ulbricht wound up on day three of week four, on 4 February 2015. Both sides had a chance to make closing arguments, then the prosecution and the defence rested, sending the jury out to decide the fate of the young Texan.

After a mere three hours of deliberation, the jury found Ross Ulbricht guilty on all seven felony charges he faced, including drug trafficking, continuing a criminal enterprise, hacking, money laundering, and fraud with identification documents.

After the trial, the public was made aware that at least two members of law enforcement who worked on a task force dedicated to Silk Road were corrupt. They had infiltrated the site, posed as vendors and staff, and stolen Bitcoin for their own use. Carl Mark Force IV and Shaun Bridges pleaded guilty to their crimes and were incarcerated for 78 months and 72 months respectively. Carl had used the names 'Nob', 'French Maid', and 'Death from Above' during his extortion activities.

Neither Force, nor Bridges, the investigation concluded, was 'alpacino'.

Closing in on the puppet-master

Among the identification documents of Silk Road staff found on Ross Ulbricht's computer was a passport supplied by Variety Jones. Nevertheless, he had somehow avoided arrest during the December 2013 swoop that nabbed Inigo, Libertas and SSBD. Strangely, VJ's ID had been added only a few weeks before Ulbricht's arrest, even though he had been mentoring Silk Road's owner from the beginning. It seemed out of character and particularly incongruous for somebody whose main contribution to Silk Road was identifying security flaws and advising on opsec.

Media speculation about the mysterious Machiavellian puppet-master was keen, but there appeared little action on the part of law enforcement. They had an ID, according to the court transcripts, although the name had not been made public, and a reference from Variety Jones in one of the chat logs that tied him to the moniker Plural of Mongoose. In a 28 June 2012 chat between Ulbricht and VJ, he said, 'I was, and am, Plural of Mongoose. Folks who know and love me, it's Mongoose.'

When discussing whether it would be easy for either of the Silk Road masterminds to de-anonymise the other, in the period before VJ had supplied his ID, Variety Jones threw out a broad hint. 'You know—I post up, and give you shitloads of info that could if you tried just a bit (fuck, Plural of Mongoose alone should do it!) that you could determine exactly who I am,' he wrote. 'I did that to make you feel comfortable.'

'I know,' responded DPR.

'If you can't find me in 10 days, you've not read my shit.'

Both pieces fit directly with what the mysterious 'Alan' had written to me, and LaMoustache did not disappoint with his usual intensive research efforts. On 26 February, a couple of weeks after the trial concluded, LaMoustache posted a detailed analysis on his website which joined all the pieces and definitively identified Variety Jones as being Roger Thomas Clark, previously known as Plural of Mongoose, no stranger to the UK prison system and currently residing in Koh Chang, Thailand.

Clark had a long history in the online drug trade that significantly pre-dated Silk Road. Although Silk Road was unprecedented in its design and scope, it was far from the first online drugs market. Long before an accessible dark web, people were buying and selling drugs through chat rooms and Usenet forums, using code words and arranging clandestine meetings to exchange goods for cash.

The millennial generation likes to believe they led the way in online black markets, but there were many people involved in online drug sales while they were still in primary school. There were sites on the clear web that skirted legalities by positioning themselves as informational sites, which did not blatantly make drug sales, but brought like-minded folk together. One in particular, overgrow.com, was the mecca of cannabis-growing websites, the brainchild of a group of cannabis activists who had previously interacted on discussion forums. It was home to a massive collection of articles, pictures and information on cannabis cultivation, with in-depth FAQs about nearly every cannabis strain.

'Overgrow was the meeting place of an outlawed society, bringing the wisdom of expert growers to novices, and the politics of cannabis activists to recreational users, all in an online world of information and photo galleries,' wrote journalist Chris Bennett in an exposé in *High Times* in 2006.

As commercial interests became involved, the Overgrow community became increasingly dysfunctional and split when there was a disagreement over who in the 'seed biz' had the legitimate right to run the site. More dysfunctional than any was a character who went by the name Plural of Mongoose, the man Bennett dubbed 'the Megabyte Megalomaniac'.

Plural of Mongoose—or PoM, or simply Mongoose—delighted in causing havoc. When two key individuals of the UK seed biz, Richard Baghdadlian and Marc Emery, were busted by Canadian authorities, Mongoose took it upon himself to publish a series of posts detailing the busts from inside the circle of those involved. He hurled wild accusations at a number of vendors, breeders and other members of Overgrow, and accused Baghdadlian of working with authorities.

In April 2007 Mongoose got into a dispute with another supplier and former business partner, Gypsy Nirvana. The convoluted mess of accusations and counter-accusations, shady business dealings and sexual infidelities wound up in court, where Mongoose's identity was revealed to be Thomas Clark, a Canadian living in Surrey in the UK.

All of this played out on the internet forums that Mongoose and Gypsy frequented. During one tirade, Mongoose mentioned visiting a good friend in England called Variety Jones. He clearly held Variety Jones in high regard, saying: 'I met VJ when I was just a pup, and he had always been my counsel. If I started getting too big for my britches, I could always count on him to take me to task. There is nothing I knew that I didn't share with him, and he was a sounding board and confidante like no other.'

Mongoose spent some time in prison before returning to the seed biz, but lay low until a new forum emerged, where he could once again get in behind the scenes and manipulate those involved. He assumed the name of his former mentor Variety Jones and took to playing a similar role to the young Dread Pirate Roberts.

On 21 April 2015, the US government filed a sealed complaint against Roger Thomas Clark aka 'Variety Jones' aka 'VJ' aka 'Plural of Mongoose', who they said 'served as a trusted advisor of Ulbricht'. The complaint sought to charge Clark with conspiracy to traffic narcotics and conspiracy to commit money laundering in relation to activities on Silk Road. VJ, the complaint alleged, was a senior adviser to Dread Pirate Roberts, the owner and operator of online illicit black market Silk Road. Clark was alleged to have been a close confidant of Ulbricht's who advised him on all aspects of Silk Road's operations and helped him grow the site into an extensive criminal enterprise.

Variety Jones was more of a counsellor or consultant than staff. There were several large payments to him on the Silk Road spreadsheets, but these tended to coincide with payments for specific events.

A couple of weeks later, on 4 May, the US Embassy in Thailand requested the provisional arrest for the purpose of extradition of Roger Thomas Clark from Koh Chang Island, Thailand.

On 29 May 2015, Ross Ulbricht was sentenced to two life terms in prison, without possibility of parole. Variety Jones had promised him, if it ever came to this, he would do whatever was necessary to break him out. People began to muse whether he would really come roaring in with a helicopter to save his young genius boss.

Mongoose on a virtual rampage

He may have taken a back seat on Silk Road, content to let Dread Pirate Roberts and the customer service representatives be the public face of the website, but it was not in Mongoose's nature to shrink into the background.

On 11 September 2015, Motherboard—a VICE Media subsidiary dedicated to tech news—published an article entitled, 'These are the two forgotten architects of Silk Road: Digging through the email account of Variety Jones', which took LaMoustache's research, independently verified it via the controversial path of acquiring access to Clark's private emails with the assistance of a hacker, and published the findings. The second 'architect' identified by Motherboard was Mike Wattier, who was Silk Road's prime coder, 'Smed'.

Once his name hit the mainstream media, and he realised that the American authorities were serious about bringing him in on myriad drug running, money laundering and hacking charges, Mongoose decided to go public. Roger Thomas Clark was indeed living in Thailand, enjoying the good life. He was invited to most of the parties of the ex-pats because he always had the very best weed. He was socially awkward and somewhat annoying, according to one local source, and it was only the steady supply of quality drugs that kept getting him invited back.

'So I've got this trip planned, to the Big Apple,' he wrote on 20 September 2015 on seed-growing forum MyPlanetGanja (MPG), reviving an account that had not posted in six years. 'There's a lot of misinformation floating around out there,' he wrote. 'My first instinct is to try and correct all of it, which is why me second instinct is pretty much always to beat my first instinct into fucking submission, and warn it if it ever raises its mangy fucking head again, it had better be prepared to be thoroughly chastised, perhaps even taunted.'

As Mongoose would tell it, when he heard about the warrant for his arrest, he took himself down to a bar near the local police station, a place 'where the locals go to interact with the local police'. He asked an officer whether they were looking for him. 'No, we're not, but immigration is,' the officer responded. The two proceeded to have a drink. 'He made a phone call,' Mongoose claimed, 'and about 15 minutes later a pickup truck with a couple of immigration police showed up, they sat down and we ordered a bottle of Sangsom Thai whiskey, and a bucket of ice. This was a serious conversation we were having, and called for serious drink.'

The immigration officer confirmed that there was a warrant for Mongoose's arrest, with a corresponding reward of 20,000 Thai baht, approximately $700.

'I left a bundle of 50,000 THB on the table to cover the tab, said good-bye to the smiling officials divvying up the loot, and headed home,' Mongoose said.

He had a way with words and a way of drawing out a tale, feeding off the responses and encouragement of others. 'I didn't architect anything, I was too busy being in Wandsworth fucking prison,' he said in response to the media reports that called Variety Jones the hidden architect of Silk Road. He claimed he could not possibly be Variety Jones, because he was incarcerated during much of the requisite time. 'Folks . . . get a skewed view of an alternate reality. The altered reality said nope, Mongoose was never in prison, it was all a ruse while he was in reality Architecting away at you know which project.'

It wasn't long until Mongoose's story took an even more unbelievable twist. He said that somebody contacted him; somebody who mattered a lot in the Silk Road investigation. That somebody had been feeding information to the owner of Silk Road in the time leading up to Ulbricht's arrest. 'It started out with things like Atlantis. He had, for a princely sum, kept the management of Atlantis updated with documents that eventually led to them shutting the site down, fearing the feds nipping at their heels,' Mongoose said.

Atlantis was a rival to Silk Road that had tried its best to gain market share but had never been successful in luring away customers from the incumbent giant. They had accusations of being a honeypot (i.e. a law enforcement sting), scammers and scum thrown at them as they tried to build their business. In the end, they shut down, still scorned. What came out at Ulbricht's trial, however, was that they had tried to warn Dread Pirate Roberts of an FBI investigation. He, apparently, had ignored them.

In Mongoose's story, this crooked FBI agent had come into possession of a Bitcoin wallet, with 300,000 Bitcoin in it (worth at the time of the tale some $75 million), which he had liberated from Silk Road, and which nobody else knew existed. Unfortunately, he did not have the passphrase to unlock the Bitcoin within. He did, however, have a plan.

'He was going to patiently wait for Ross to be convicted, and after he was convicted, he would eventually be transferred to a permanent home in a federal prison,' Mongoose wrote. 'Now, this is where I come in. He figured, for whatever far-flung reason, that I could convince Ross to cough up the pass-phrase he needed. He also had a second theory, and that was that Ross only had half the pass-phrase, and I had the other half. Either way, I am critical to his plan.'

Mongoose's tale rambled on for thousands of words, claiming that the mysterious contact provided him with the news of corrupt agents Force and Bridges long before it hit the media. The corrupt officer, he claimed, fed him many such pieces of information. 'And one day, he did something weird. I mean weird, even for him. He signed off one of his rants with: --cwt.'

This seemed to be a less-than-subtle attempt by Mongoose to imply that the corrupt cop was Christopher W Tarbell, the FBI special agent who headed the task force that brought down Silk Road and Ross Ulbricht. Mongoose claimed that, when pressed, the agent said cwt stood for 'carat' because one of his code names was Diamond. It was Diamond, Mongoose said, who alerted him to the sealed indictment and had arranged for his arrest by the Thai authorities. When Mongoose slipped out of the arrest, the story took a sinister, even hysterical turn.

'Well, you'd think I kicked his puppy! He went fucking mental, and started going on about his backup plan. He would kidnap Ross Ulbricht's sister, or mother, or ideally both. Get a video capable phone in front of Ross Ulbricht, and he'd give up that fucking passphrase, and Diamond would have them tortured until he did. I had his bonafides by now, and knew him well enough to know he was serious about this. Come Christmas, if I wasn't well in position exactly where he wanted me to be, I'd be responsible for the results.

'In this case, biting the bullet was turning myself in, because writing an anonymous postcard wasn't going to cut it. If I was to keep him from kidnapping those two women, which he'd do if I didn't turn myself over to him, I was going to have to turn myself over to the DOJ folks, so they could take the appropriate action to protect those people, and maybe even figure out just who this sick fuck was, and stop him.

'Easiest thing in the world, turning yourself in, you'd think.

'You'd also be wrong. Wrong, wrong, wrong.'

In his attempt to turn himself in, Mongoose claimed he had written to Assistant US Attorney Serrin Turner on 9 May 2015, having become aware of the sealed indictment against him. 'The contents of the email informed Mr. Turner that secret grand jury information, and the existence of a sealed indictment had been passed on to me by Diamond. I also touched on the fact that I was aware the authorities in SE Asia had been requested to detain me for extradition.'

He told Mr Turner he would cooperate and turn himself in. Mr Turner never responded. So Mongoose doubled down on his efforts to figure out who Diamond might be. He was getting worried now. 'It wasn't until he started obsessing on the kidnappings, that I realized I had a fucking lunatic on my hands. A lunatic highly placed in the FBI, with a massive off the books private budget, who thought that kidnapping and torture were the solution to his problems,' he said. 'I gave myself four months to see if I could uncover him. If not, I'd have to come up with something else. I spend the next four months, sixteen hours a day, trying to track that fucker down.'

Mongoose wrote a follow-up email to Serrin Turner, again telling his tale of the mysterious and dangerous Diamond. 'I intend to uncover the identity of Diamond,' he concluded in the letter. 'I have a pretty good idea how to go about that, and if you and/or your office are unable or unwilling to assist, perhaps you could pass my information on to someone who can.'

As Mongoose brought his astonishing tale to an end, he finished by addressing the question everyone wanted answered. His ID was in the same folder as that of Inigo, Libertas and SSBD. Thus the FBI presumably had his information at the same time. So why wasn't he arrested back then?

'The answer is simple: the folks who should have been trying to put me in jail, didn't want me in jail.'

What to believe?

It didn't take long before people started poking holes in Mongoose's story. Small details didn't match up to other reports. Many people on the forum had been around during the first great dramas created by Mongoose all those years ago, which had spilled over into real-life violence and arrests. The claims that a highly placed government agent had threatened to kidnap and torture family members of Dread Pirate Roberts bordered on the absurd.

Mongoose claimed that by his calculations, there were over 400,000 Bitcoins from Silk Road unaccounted for, which was a claim backed up by some who put the research into Silk Road. However, Mongoose was possibly simply seizing on reports that the FBI was unsuccessfully struggling to seize a further 600,000 Bitcoins belonging to DPR.

There was no denying that Mongoose was publicly outing himself as the person the authorities had indicted as being Variety Jones. He continued to post on the MPG forum, taunting the authorities and practically begging them to arrest him. He stuck to his story that there was a third, unidentified, rogue agent called Diamond who had stolen Bitcoin and provided intelligence to a number of darknet markets (not just Silk Road). He was sure the authorities were deliberately ignoring the matter, hoping it would go away.

'Only 2 agents *ever* succumbed to temptation, therefore "Diamond" cannot possibly exist. (Insert "LA-LA-LA-LA I can't hear you," here),' he wrote, imitating law enforcement's response—or lack thereof—to his wild accusations. 'So, if all the TLAs [three-letter agencies] pretend Diamond doesn't exist, the problem will just go away, right? And they're doing a damned fine job of pretending that either A) Diamond didn't *really* break any laws, or B) Diamond isn't a federal agent, and none of our concern. Also, that Clark guy bothering us to turn himself in, he'll likely just give up and stop bugging us any day now. Let's just wait him out, shall we.'

Indeed, it seemed as if they were waiting it out. Mongoose continued posting, not hiding where he was writing from, and musing as to why he was not being arrested. Separating fact from fiction in his stories was always difficult and he knew this and was happy to lead people on a merry chase. His taunting of the authorities became increasingly blatant:

'My name is Roger Thomas Clark, I can be reached by email at zybose@safe-mail.net, and I wish to make arrangements to safely travel to the United States and turn myself in to be served with any indictments that may be pending. If I have been mis-informed, and there aren't any sealed indictments waiting for me, well great! Drop me an email and let me know, either way.

'I really cannot be much clearer and [more] direct than that.'

He liked to play with journalists, too. He contacted Joseph Cox, the author of the Motherboard article, and told him to fly to Thailand, where he would gain an exclusive interview with the man alleged to be Variety Jones. Cox would have to give up his communication devices and allow minders to whisk him between Southeast Asian countries until finally, 'A helicopter will take you to the airport at your final destination. A limo will take you from there to my hotel, and we'll play the rest of it by ear.'

'It was elaborate, it was hard to believe, but as a journalist there was the possibility there was some truth to it,' Cox said of the plan that took shape over two months of private messages. But it seemed life on the run was taking its toll on Mongoose. 'Towards the end when we moved to encrypted chat, he sounded exhausted, less of the jokes, less whimsical.'

It did seem all part of an elaborate hoax; as Cox was packing his bags for the trip, he received a message: 'DO NOT GET ON THE PLANE.' Mongoose told him that one of the minders had been arrested. 'Not driving down the road and pulled over arrested, but two truckloads of army pulled up to his house type arrested.'

I also contacted Mongoose via private message and he was happy to chat, though he never invited me on his helicopter. He claimed not to have yet read my book on Silk Road, but knew who I was. 'Everyone seems to think yer pretty swell, and actual author and not a click-bait factory drone,' he told me. 'High words of praise, indeed, from some of the people who have dealt with you.'

'Are you still in Thailand?' I asked one day. 'If, just say, I was going to Thailand to get some nice cushion covers made up by the super-tailors, would you meet me for a beverage and a chat?'

Mongoose never responded to that message. On 3 December 2015, two years after the arrests of the three Silk Road administrators, Roger Thomas Clark, a 54-year-old Canadian, was arrested through a joint operation of the FBI, the Department of Homeland Security, the Drug Enforcement Administration and local Thai police.

Darknet markets after Silk Road

After the fall of Silk Road, the two smaller markets in its shadow—Black Market Reloaded and Sheep—received such a massive influx of Silk Road refugees that the former closed down gracefully, saying they didn't need the scrutiny all the new members would bring, and the latter closed suddenly, taking everyone's Bitcoin with them. Silk Road 2.0 opened just a month after Ulbricht's arrest, run by former Silk Road employees, three of whom were arrested a couple of months later and one of whom was in fact undercover agent Cirrus. Silk Road 2.0 stayed open for a year before it, too, was shut down by the authorities.

After that, several markets rose and fell—a few by law enforcement infiltration, but most just shut up shop, usually taking the Bitcoin of their customers with them. The appetite for online drugs markets was voracious; drug users worldwide had discovered a newer, simpler way to acquire better quality drugs at reasonable prices, and the closures, busts and scams were little more than a nuisance, the cost of illicit activities. It was not long before new markets dwarfed the size of Silk Road.

The classic exit scam, many say, is the perfect crime. Build up a network of trust among customers, then abscond with all their money. Those who have been ripped off have little recourse; there's no ombudsman to complain to when your illegal goods don't turn up or aren't what was promised. No door to knock on and demand your money back.

Individual drug dealers have done it throughout the dark markets' history to various degrees, with Tony76 setting the bar. But on a much larger scale, sometimes the owners of a market, entrusted with all the users' Bitcoin in their accounts and held in escrow, decide to simply close the market and move the Bitcoin into their personal wallets. Such was the case with Atlantis in November 2013 (although in retrospect, it is likely Atlantis was simply spooked as they had apparently been fed information about the ongoing FBI investigation) and Sheep Marketplace in December the same year. And so it was in late March 2015 with the largest black market the dark web has ever known. The owners of Evolution Marketplace—known as Verto and Kimble—brazenly told staff that they were closing the site and taking the coin. The estimated value of everything within their control ranged from $12 million to $34 million worth of Bitcoin at prevailing market rates.

This should not have come as a surprise to its customers. As well as getting larger, these new markets had wildly different philosophies of doing business than the trailblazer. Gone were the days when the leading darknet market, Silk Road, refused to sell or list anything 'the purpose of which is to harm or defraud another person'. The markets that emerged to fill the gap left by Silk Road listed stolen credit cards and personal information, hacking services and malware alongside drugs for personal use. Evolution was founded by a character well known to the dark web. Verto had been administrator of Tor Carding Forum, a massive community of those who trade stolen credit or debit card account information for profit. They sold personal information, credit card dumps, ATM skimmers, cloning machines, fake IDs. And the owners pulled Ponzi schemes on their own members.

In retrospect, it should have been obvious that someone who had made a career of ripping people off would stage a heist where risk was minimal and reward was great. Evolution's administrators had probably planned the long con, giving themselves a year or so to establish trust and amass Bitcoin. Evolution had always had a cleaner interface and, importantly, lower commissions than any other major online black market. The profits, while still healthy, were unlikely to be adequate for those risking their lives and freedom.

Two former moderators of the Evolution forums confirmed separately that a 'staff meeting' was called the morning of the closure, though their recollections differ slightly.

'We had a staff meeting at 10:30 am this morning,' said NSWGreat, where the owners announced that the 'market was being closed and they're taking everything with them. Said market and forums would be online for 30 minutes for us to save anything we wanted to keep.'

'It was pretty bizarre,' confirmed EvilGrin. 'Verto wasn't there. Kimble said we'd wait a few minutes for him then in a few minutes he said, "Verto isn't coming to the meeting, or to any meetings again. Because I'm taking Evo offline in 30 seconds."'

When Silk Road was launched in February 2011, one of the stated intentions of Dread Pirate Roberts February was to create a place where peaceful people could buy and sell drugs free from violence. Exit scams brought out the violence in people. Many of the vendors on Evolution had large amounts of money tied up—money they owed to very real people in very real life who would be very unsympathetic. Vendors posted that they feared for their lives if they could not pay their own suppliers.

Many of those who lost money in the Evolution exit scam (and many who did not, but were affronted by the heist) were baying for the blood of Verto and Kimble. They didn't just want the money returned—they wanted those who had taken it to suffer.

The pitchfork brigade got even uglier when they started offering money for the identities of other Evolution staff members, all of whom were presumably as in the dark as any of their customers. Some went one step further—not just the uninvolved staff, but their families as well.

Despite the thousands of online sleuths combing for clues, following the Bitcoin and sharing their theories, the absconding founders of Evolution were never located. They joined a small but growing number of dark web drug lords who apparently got away scot-free and enjoyed their spoils in anonymity.

Whenever one market went down, other markets operating simultaneously would get an influx of new members and those without the proper infrastructure would buckle under the demand. After Evolution closed its doors, there were no consistently reliable markets for some time; users became so frustrated that many said they would forgive the owners of Evolution their sins if only they would reopen the stable and efficient market.

Thanks to the transparency of Bitcoin, pundits could make educated estimates of the amount of turnover and profit that market owners made. Thus, it did not take long before the gap in the market was filled with others attracted by the potential for massive returns.

AlphaBay launched in mid-late 2014, and it was immediately apparent that it existed purely for profit and made no pretence at the lofty ideals and morals of the old-school markets. AlphaBay was the epitome of the new darknet markets; bigger than Silk Road ever was, but darker, selling not only drugs, but weapons, stolen personal information, computer hacking tools, malware, ransomware, stolen goods and services to steal identities and ruin lives. With few exceptions, if it was illegal, it could be purchased on AlphaBay.

This was the true wild west of the dark web. There were few rules on AlphaBay, other than a ban on child pornography, a ban on any activities designed to circumvent commissions going to AlphaBay's owners, and a stipulation that any malware sold must have a built-in function to ensure it could not impact any computer in Russia, whether belonging to government, industry or private citizens.

This final rule, alongside AlphaBay's large Russian-speaking membership and the Russian-language forums that rivalled the size of the English-language ones, meant the website was widely considered to be run by Russian organised crime.

Before long AlphaBay was ten times the size Silk Road ever was. Darknet markets had come a long way from the days of the creation of a young idealistic Texan in Silicon Valley.

A third rogue agent

On 29 November 2016, Ross Ulbricht's defence team filed a letter with the US Attorney's office in Maryland stating they had found evidence that a still-unidentified rogue government agent—not a field agent, but an analyst in an office with nine-to-five responsibilities and with access to internal communications—may have sold information about the Silk Road investigation to DPR before his arrest. The evidence pointed to someone having deleted all traces of certain correspondence from the official files, including all copies. Forensics experts had uncovered some 30 pages of correspondence between Dread Pirate Roberts and a character calling himself 'notwonderful' in an administrator's backup file that had apparently been overlooked by the rogue agent when erasing all traces of his existence.

He provided DPR with real-time information on the investigation: 'Some of it is analytical, some of it matches the status of what we know about the investigation,' Ulbricht's lawyer, Joshua Dratel, said in a statement.

DPR agreed to an up-front payment to notwonderful of between US$5000 and $8000 and then a salary of $500 per week for ongoing updates. The payments were to be made out to a Silk Road user going by the name 'alpacino'.

When the prosecution first came across the payments to alpacino, they had assumed it was another alias of Carl Mark Force IV and it was reported as such in the media. After the initial reports, however, all references to alpacino were quietly dropped in the prosecution of Special Agent Force.

Just as Mongoose had said, there was another corrupt government agency official who was extracting money from the golden goose that was Silk Road. This one had been able to remove nearly all traces of his or her identity with surgical precision.

A visit to Bangkok Remand

Klong Prem Central Prison in Bangkok does a roaring trade in padlocks. Most first-time visitors are unaware that they have to put their mobile phone into one of the old-school metal lockers in the courtyard before being permitted inside. If you haven't brought your own padlock, you can buy one from the admissions officer.

Visiting someone at the prison is a surprisingly simple—and very low-tech—affair. On 29 March 2017, I filled in a few details on a slip of paper stating I was a friend visiting one Roger Thomas Clark.

I'd flown from Melbourne especially for the visit, confident that he would see me. A fellow journalist—Bitcoin Uncensored podcaster Chris DeRose—had tweeted that he was in Bangkok and I asked if he would be kind enough to check whether Clark was still at his last known address, Bangkok Remand. Since his arrest in 2015 it had been impossible to get any reliable news about the man accused of being Variety Jones. Occasional news reports would crop up that he was still there, only to be contradicted by another saying he was in the same NYC facility as Ulbricht. His appeal had been successful; his appeal had been denied. Nobody knew how to contact him by mail.

Chris rose to the challenge, attending the prison three days in a row before finally getting in to see Clark by mentioning Bitcoin on his visit slip. 'He knows you and wants to work with you,' Chris told me on a call after the successful visit. I booked a flight almost before I hung up the phone.

I had expected something cold and menacing, but the prison was surprisingly non-threatening. The garden areas accommodated the smokers and there were several water features as well as statues of Buddha and a variety of animals. Many of Bangkok's ubiquitous soi dogs had made their home there, sleeping or trotting around the gardens in various states of manginess. Along the walk from the taxi drop-off point to the front door were stalls selling street food and cold water. A table manned by prison staff displayed fresh vegetables bagged up that could be bought and delivered to prisoners to supplement the prison food of rice, chilli and indeterminate meat.

A large poster dictated appropriate attire for visitors—women were to refrain from exposing shoulders, midriff or knees. Something that resembled a metal detector near the entrance buzzed every time somebody went through, although it could be easily sidestepped. A bored staff member would occasionally bark 'phone?' at someone whose clothes or bag might be hiding such contraband, but would wave them through before they could finish shaking their head.

The procedure to get an audience was basic, almost archaic. Visitors would fill in the slip of paper—twice, because the prison doesn't supply carbon paper—requesting a visit with the prisoner of choice. A private copy shop would make a copy of the visitor's passport or driver's licence for 2 baht, and both would be presented through a window to somebody who did not seem very interested in whether the photograph matched the visitor.

I held out my hand, palm upwards as indicated, and received a stamp near the base of my thumb and another slip of paper that told me what time I could enter the visiting room. Visiting hours started at 8:30 am for 20 minute-long visits. No. 11 was displayed when I arrived and my slip of paper said I would be part of group 13. Prisoners only get one visit per day. If your prisoner had already seen someone, you'd be told once you got in that the prisoner could not see you.

There were squat toilets in the waiting room, the type you scoop water into after you finish. They weren't filthy, but they seemed to receive the minimal necessary cleaning. Classical music played over the speakers, and visitors could wait in front of a large television playing what looked like a Thai version of the classic breakfast news program. Little stores in the foyer sold snacks, coffee and cold drinks, and I bought an iced coffee to ease the oppressive heat and to calm my nerves, coffee being the first on my list of comfort foods. Staff in blue jumpsuits—they may have been trusted inmates—shifted buckets around to catch the worst of the leaks. It was the season for torrential downpours and the prison was not quite waterproof.

The 40-minute wait was nerve-wracking. I hadn't thought of what I was going to say to him and had no idea what to expect. For years, Silk Road had been my obsession and I had met countless minor players—moderators, administrators, vendors and customers—but the two who most intrigued me, Dread Pirate Roberts and Variety Jones, remained elusive. Ross Ulbricht never responded to the letters I wrote to him and nobody knew for sure where Variety Jones was.

I wondered what he would be like. I had drunk in the thousands of words he had written across various media and we had exchanged messages on MyPlanetGanja. One thing meeting people in the flesh had taught me was that the human was rarely what you expected from their online persona. Mongoose was infamous among the tight-knit seed biz community. He was known to be entertaining, erratic, verbose and unforgiving of a slight. He had a habit of messing with journalists or people he considered too nosy. Many considered him dangerous, echoing the concerns journalist Chris Bennett had about the 'Megabyte Megalomaniac' over a decade earlier.

The clock ticked over, a siren sounded and the visitors of group 12 poured out of the visiting area, as group 13 took its place quickly, nobody willing to waste precious seconds with their loved ones. I sat on one of the five stools in room 5. Some visitors came in pairs, or brought children, so the little room became crowded.

My heart was pounding. When the next siren sounded, the prisoners would take their places on the opposite side of the smash-proof window and I would finally get to meet Variety Jones.

The Megabyte Megalomaniac

Plural of Mongoose was like a puppet master, and it was eerily intriguing watching him pull the strings on the forums that made people dance in the real world: Business transactions fell apart, people retired nicknames and dropped from view, court dates came and went—but when the chance arose to interview PoM, I decided to pass. By that time, I had it from a reliable source that PoM deposited things on people's PCs via e-mail that gave him access to their personal desktops and files. Frankly, PoM scared me, and I didn't consider him a reliable source of information anyway. So why feed his fire?

– Chris Bennett, *High Times* magazine, July 2006

'Nobody has ever regretted not doing an interview; lots of folks have regretted doing one,' Variety Jones once warned Dread Pirate Roberts, when the two of them were riding high overseeing their Silk Road empire, counting commissions on millions of dollars in sales every week. Yet here he was—or at least, the man alleged to be him—not only granting an interview, but eager to provide input into a book.

My stool had become damp with sweat waiting for someone to appear opposite me as everybody else gabbled into the telephones while mine remained in its cradle. My heart sank as the minutes ticked over and it became obvious that Clark was not going to show. I didn't budge because I hoped there would be an explanation, but I grew increasingly frustrated as I waited.

A couple of minutes before the end of the session a guard picked up the phone opposite me. There had been some sort of mix-up with my prisoner. Just wait there, and he will be along in the next session, I was told. When he entered with another lot of prisoners, I recognised him instantly; not because of any photographs—all that existed online was a grainy passport shot that may or may not have been him—but because he was the only westerner there.

'I want to call you Mongoose,' I blurted into the receiver before we even exchanged pleasantries. Prisoner #58-501-04886, Roger Thomas Clark, smiled through the glass.

'Oh, please do,' Mongoose responded. 'I've been Roger too long. And the people in here, they hear "Roger" and immediately call me either "Federer" or "Rabbit". They think it's hysterical.'

Mongoose was not a large or imposing man. Standing at 5 feet 8 inches (173 centimetres), with greying hair, a receding hairline and hazel eyes, he had waved eagerly through the Plexiglas and bars that separated us. He displayed no signs of the motor neuron disease or multiple sclerosis diagnosis he was rumoured to have, though it was hard to tell through the thick glass.

We had a bit of that awkward exchange you have when meeting somebody you know by correspondence or reputation, but not personally. He helped move it along with 'So I hear you're writing another book.' I launched into the premise of the book and the fact that I hoped he would contribute to it.

'I've refused over 200 visits,' he said with the air of exaggeration those who interact with him soon become accustomed to. 'Most of those would have been reporters.' He had had a bad experience when the prison made him cooperate with a reporter who was doing a story on Canadians in Thai prisons. Mongoose fumed for months, saying the reporter had made up things he had said for dramatic effect.

I decided to fill him in on darknet market news, and told him about Libertas having taken his appeal to the High Court of Ireland, of the incarceration of another one of our mutual online acquaintances, UK paraphernalia vendor Pluto Pete (he was genuinely shocked to hear of his sentence), as well as the news that the chief prosecutor in Ulbricht's case, Preet Bharara, had been sacked by newly installed President Trump. I related reactions on the forums to his incarceration and the latest on Ross Ulbricht's appeals process. I called Ross 'Dipper', as VJ used to refer to him.

He drank it all in, but when I told him what was happening with Bitcoin and the current markets, and AlphaBay's role as king, he cut me off. 'Don't tell me anything I shouldn't know,' he said. 'Don't tell me anything about the new markets, about AlphaBay, anything. It makes life a lot easier when they're asking me questions if I can just say I don't know. I need to be in an information vacuum.'

The talk turned to life inside Bangkok Remand. Mongoose insisted he got along well with everyone, but very much kept to himself. The other inmates mostly left him alone and he knew that rumours swirled about him being some sort of mafia kingpin. He had two minders who took shifts following him everywhere, unless he managed to shake them off.

When I told him I had just five days in Bangkok, he invited me to return each morning, other than Friday when he had a friend coming in. He said he wasn't supposed to have any one person more than twice a week, but he would be able to fix it. He told me to make sure I was there first thing in the morning, because he only got one visitor per day. Sometimes if an inmate refused one visitor, the system would reflect that he had had his visit for the day and later visitors were told the prisoner could not see them.

The young man beside me was having an excited, animated and apparently loving conversation with the equally young man sitting opposite him, to the left of Clark. They appeared to be brothers, cousins or close friends. It was difficult to imagine the sweet-looking young man being capable of murder. The odds are that he was though, because Clark was being held in the section of the prison that houses those who have been charged with murder. That meant that all the other prisoners were almost exclusively Thai nationals. Had he been put into the drug offences section, he would have had many more Western prison mates. As it was, he had nobody with whom he could converse in English, television was exclusively in Thai and he was not allowed any English-language reading materials. He spent a lot of time thinking, he said.

'They say Thai jail is no picnic,' Mongoose told me, 'but it is. It is a picnic in the park—a picnic that stretches on and on and on and nothing ever happens.'

During the following visits, our conversations meandered all over the place. Each session would start with Mongoose bringing up something I had said the previous day and he would probe and clarify. He seemed to have a photographic memory for everything that was said and missed nothing. His gaze would not waver as I responded to his questions until he was satisfied with the answers.

Mongoose asked for details on the extradition of Gypsy Nirvana from the UK to Maine, US, so I brought him up to speed on what I'd found online the night before. Mongoose and Gypsy had a chequered history thanks to the 'series of dramas, arrests, claims of blackmail etc. over control of the cannabis supply market' that I had been told about previously. Mongoose listened intently to my report but had little to say about the new developments.

I told him about the email from the mysterious 'Alan' that had fingered him as Variety Jones, and the subsequent loss of emails from my Gmail account. He decided that 'Alan' must be his 'Diamond'. He repeated all of the claims he had made online about the mysterious third rogue agent, Diamond. He said he continued to gather evidence about Diamond's identity, but until he could prove it beyond a shadow of a doubt, he was terrified that if he got extradited to the US, he would conveniently disappear.

He held high hopes for not being extradited and great fears for if he was. His case was being appealed and his lawyers told him that the Thai authorities felt the Americans were being less than honest with them about the nature of the evidence they held, and that the evidence in the criminal complaint was flimsy and all circumstantial. I asked him about the assertion in the complaint that Variety Jones, like others on the staff of Silk Road, had provided a scan of his passport to DPR, and that scan was of Roger Thomas Clark. Mongoose vehemently denied he had ever sent such a thing to DPR, although he apparently confirmed to others he had done so.

An insider had told me that foreigners and nationals were treated differently in prison. 'When a Thai national breaks the rules, or gets out of line, they beat him up,' the insider said. 'They can't do that with the foreigners, so what they do instead is, when the *farang* gets out of line they beat up every single one of his cellmates—there could be 8, 10, 12 of them—and leave the *farang* alone. He's then left to deal with the cellmates.'

Clark didn't tell me any such thing—he was wary of saying anything negative about the prison after the earlier story on Canadians in prisons had landed a fellow prisoner an extended jail sentence for complaining about conditions. He did say, however, that whenever he got deliveries from the commissary store, he divided them among all his cellmates. Because of this, he only ever wanted goods that were easy to divide. Cigarettes and three-in-one sachets of coffee were the best.

'One guy got me Pringles, which he heard I liked, but that was a nightmare,' Clark told me. 'I had to count out each crisp to ensure I didn't accidentally give someone of a higher status a smaller pile than someone else.' Such slights can cause violence in a place like Klong Prem.

Clark seemed almost nervous, and chattered away at a million miles an hour, sometimes sounding downright manic. In that way, he was very much like his Plural of Mongoose online persona. Just as with his online antics, it was hard to tell if he was living in a fantasy world. I felt he might have had a somewhat tenuous grip on reality.

I left the prison with an earful of words, but not much information. He said he couldn't divulge a great deal that would be of use to my book then, but he expected to be out soon and then he would fly me back, we would sit down and have a whole lot to talk about. 'Around August,' he told me, 'something will have happened one way or the other.'

I asked him whether we could correspond by post, or if there was anyone who visited him regularly that I could send messages through. He declined on both counts, saying that letters in English had to be vetted and translated and usually didn't get through at all, and that he didn't want anyone else involved. I got the impression he wanted to control every bit of our interaction.

Just as I was about to leave our final visit, he said if there was any change in his situation—either way—or he wanted me to come see him, he would get a message to me.

'How will you do that?' I asked.

'Easy. You're not hard to track down, you know,' he replied.

The rise and rise of AlphaBay

AlphaBay continued its domination of the dark web's e-commerce activities throughout 2015, 2016 and into 2017. Every major drug dealer sold their wares on the largest and most reliable darknet market and most customers flocked there as well. New users found the interface to be intuitive and user-friendly, with most of the more technical aspects of buying illegal goods online automated for their convenience.

AlphaBay worked at keeping the software updated, providing continuous improvements to the customer experience. Those looking to purchase identity information could set the controls to return listings by location, birth year, credit limit and other useful search parameters. Drug buyers could quickly identify vendors with overnight service to their location, or sort from cheapest to most expensive or highest to lowest customer satisfaction rating. AlphaBay also facilitated access to services such as sophisticated money laundering and swatting (bomb threats and false reports to law enforcement).

Borrowing from the marketing tactics of legitimate businesses, customers were given referral links that they could provide to potential users, receiving commission from any purchases those new users made, providing an incentive for members to recruit new customers to the site.

AlphaBay invested heavily in opsec measures to ensure its owners remained safe and anonymous. The website employed security administrators and programmers to stay on top of IT security, as well as 'scam watchers' responsible for monitoring, reporting and disabling scam attempts. They hired a PR manager, moderators and customer service representatives who were removed from the operations of the business, responsible only for marketing and enquiries from the clientele. Those employees entrenched themselves on clear-web sites such as reddit, ready to respond to queries, spruik the site's services and bring in new customers whenever the chance arose.

The owners of AlphaBay were not given to rallying speeches, debating socio-political theories, opening book clubs or setting reading challenges involving complex manifestos on anarcho-capitalism. They were businessmen, running an efficient market designed to maximise profit for its owners and contractors. Their FAQ section included the question 'Is AlphaBay legal?'

> Some people have really asked this question. Of course not. We are an anonymous marketplace selling drugs, weapons and credit cards. Make sure you access the website through Tor or through a VPN to ensure anonymity. We take no responsibility if you get caught.

Not everybody was happy with this new breed of darknet market. Many who had been part of Silk Road did not want to give their business to an organisation that was happy to provide poisons, weapons and tools to facilitate extortion, theft and fraud alongside their favourite drugs, so long as it turned a profit. Smaller breakaway markets emerged that had strict rules about what could be sold there, some limiting sales to only the less harmful drugs such as cannabis, MDMA and LSD. These niche markets proved popular with many of the longer-term darknet market users.

However, AlphaBay was the most visible, the easiest to use, had the best user interface and widest range. It was the 'Darknet Market for Dummies' of the dark web, simple to access and requiring virtually no technical proficiency to buy almost anything imaginable. AlphaBay was the new one-stop emporium for all things illegal and its doors were open to anyone with Bitcoin.

Another visit to Klong Prem

I went to visit Mongoose again on 12 July 2017. I hadn't heard from him, but I was starting out on a trip to Europe and the US, so he was practically on the way. I hoped he had some further news of either an imminent release or movement to the US.

As I sat in the visiting room while everyone else was talking to their loved ones, the chair across from me remained empty. I played with a small child, there to see the very young man opposite the screen of a young woman. When she lifted the child up and put the phone to his ear, the young man's smile widened and he spoke in the universal language of toddler-talk.

Eventually a guard on the other side of the screen signalled me to pick up the telephone. He held my visitor slip up against the screen. It had been adorned with some handwriting: 'Prisoner does not want any visitors.'

Mongoose had told me that messages like this could mean 'prisoner has had quota of visitors for the week', 'prisoner not allowed to see visitors', 'we could not find prisoner', or possibly 'prisoner doesn't want to see you and is too polite to say so'. I was sure it was written in Mongoose's own hand. I felt deflated. Why the sudden turn-around? He had been excited previously and eager to see me for more than his allotted number of visits. He must know I'd come to Bangkok specifically to see him. What sort of game was he playing?

I hoped it was just a mix-up, or he was expecting somebody else that day and didn't want to use up his daily visit on me. The next morning, having breezed through the sign-in formalities as an old hand, I didn't even make it into the visiting room. A couple of people around me in the waiting room gestured to get my attention, indicating that an announcement that had come over the loudspeaker in Thai was meant for me. I guess I was pretty easy to spot in the crowd, being the only *farang* there.

The corrections officer behind the glass held up my visitor slip. 'He doesn't want to see you. He doesn't want to see anybody,' was the message I got from her broken English. She made it quite clear I was to go away and it probably wouldn't be in my best interests to return.

Frustrated and confused, there was little I could do. Things became clearer when some news filtered through to me that evening. The previous morning—the day of my first visit—a Canadian dark web drug lord had been found dead in his Thai jail cell, the victim of an apparent suicide.

The death of a dark web kingpin

It didn't take long to determine that the victim was not Mongoose. According to local news, a 25-year-old man who had been in custody in a jail cell for less than a week took his own life by choking himself to death with his towel. He had been arrested on suspicion of being Alpha02, founder and owner of AlphaBay, the largest online black market in the world.

AlphaBay had been offline for a week prior to the news. Market downtime always led to rumours, panic, FUD and reassurances on reddit and various dark web forums. There would always be people who feared the worst when a market became suddenly unavailable— that the owners had exit scammed, or law enforcement had taken it down. Sometimes they would be right, but more often than not it would simply be website maintenance or a short-term problem like a DDoS attack. Members would not be warned ahead of time when a market deliberately took itself offline for maintenance, upgrades or security patching, because that would invariably result in panic withdrawals of Bitcoin, causing site instability and even more downtime.

Thus, although there was the usual panic from the jittery minority, most people were not too worried and were prepared to sit out the downtime. 'It's an established market, so outages are expected from time to time,' wrote a reddit moderator. 'When they go down we give them the benefit of the doubt as in the past they have come back up again after a few hours.'

The hours stretched into days and uneasiness increased among the dark web community, as rumours became verified news stories. There had been a major dark-web-related raid in Quebec. That had led to an arrest in Thailand, but authorities were tight-lipped whether it was a vendor or somebody related to the darknet markets. AlphaBay's PR employees continued to post updates of what they knew, but it was clear that they were as much in the dark as anybody else. They had no access to the inner workings of the website.

It wasn't until news filtered through on 13 July that the man arrested in Thailand had been found dead the day before that the enormity of what had happened at AlphaBay dawned on the darknet market users.

On 5 July 2017, Royal Thai Police had executed a search warrant on the Bangkok home of Alexandre Cazes, a Canadian ex-pat. Cazes had lived in Thailand on and off for eight years and had married a Thai, which cemented his residency.

When police swooped, Cazes was not prepared. In his bedroom, his laptop was open and unencrypted, with Cazes logged in as 'Admin' to the backend server of the AlphaBay darknet market. He also had text files with usernames and passwords that enabled law enforcement to access all of the information and cryptocurrency—Monero, Zcash and Ethereum as well as Bitcoin—on the AlphaBay server. According to the criminal complaint, Cazes 'served as the leader of the managers and operators of the criminal organisation who, collectively, controlled the destiny of the enterprise'.

According to personal financial statements on the computer, Cazes estimated his own net worth as just over $23 million. Police seized assets including a Lamborghini for which he had paid $900,000, a Porsche, his wife's Mini Cooper and a BMW motorcycle. They also took control of $8.8 million in cryptocurrency.

Although police had seized and shut down AlphaBay, they left its users in the dark as to what happened. Cazes was the 'arrest in Thailand' that had been rumoured, but nobody was aware that they had, in fact, caught the leader of the entire operation.

Nor does anybody know what happened in those seven days between Cazes' arrest and his death. As it was reported in the *Bangkok Post*: 'The NSB [Narcotics Suppression Bureau] locked up Cazes in one of their basement detention cells with attached bathroom. On the eve of his first court hearing, Cazes went into that bathroom with a towel, and guards later found him dead on the floor. It's an apparent suicide. An autopsy will try to sift through the massive suspicion of yet another suicide in NSB custody.'

A week later, on 20 July 2017, US Attorney General Jeff Sessions held a press conference with FBI Acting Director Andrew McCabe and Deputy Attorney General Rod Rosenstein. The Attorney General said that the US was in the midst of the deadliest drug epidemic in its history. 'Today, some of the most prolific drug suppliers use what is called the dark web,' Sessions said. 'It is called dark not just because these sites are intentionally hidden. It is also dark because of what is sold on many of them: illegal weapons, stolen identities, child pornography, and large amounts of narcotics. Today, the department of justice announced the takedown of a dark web market, AlphaBay. This is the largest takedown in world history.' He thanked law enforcement partners at Europol, in Thailand, the Netherlands, Lithuania, Canada, the UK, France and Germany.

'This is a landmark operation,' added the FBI's Andrew McCabe. 'AlphaBay was roughly 10 times the size of the Silk Road, so we are talking about multiple servers, different countries, hundreds of millions of dollars in cryptocurrency, in a darknet drug trade that spans the globe.'

The only mention of the death of the alleged owner-operator of the site in custody a week earlier was by Deputy Attorney General Rod Rosenstein: 'Following the death of the defendant charged in the American case, our US Attorney filed a civil complaint which will ensure that appropriate action is taken with regard to all the assets that were seized in the course of that investigation.'

Alexandre Cazes' extravagant lifestyle suggested the dark web administrator was doing very nicely from the commissions taken from every sale of the reported 250,000 drug listings on AlphaBay. As well as luxury cars and properties, he enjoyed drugs and partying and was not faithful to his wife. He was active on a pickup artist forum, where he was frequently found to be boasting about his wealth and assets. According to his indictment, the commissions 'were worth at least tens of millions of dollars'.

Cazes owned a company called EBX Technologies as a front to explain his income and cryptocurrency holdings. EBX was supposed to be a website design company but, according to the court documents, 'the website for EBX Technologies is barely functional and does not appear to support any substantial business activities'.

As with Silk Road, it was a basic mistake that brought the police to Cazes' door. He had reused a personal email address—Pimp_Alex_91@hotmail.com—in the header of the email sent by AlphaBay to people who needed their passwords reset. Police were able to match that email to Cazes.

The darknet market community was sceptical of the official suicide-in-custody story. Speculation ranged from plausible to absurd. Many pointed out the endemic corruption in the Thai system, something that the news reports in Bangkok also alluded to. However, the theories differed as to how that corruption may have come into play.

'Corrupt LE [law enforcement] killed him after extracting information on any cash he has stashed away,' one redditor mused.

'What if a bunch of cops were already getting paid off, but once Cazes got nabbed, the dirty cops had to tie up the loose end?' asked another.

'Thailand is notorious for having corrupt LE,' wrote someone called murderhomelesspeople. 'I wonder if [Cazes] paid off some guards to fake his death, he certainly has enough money to do so. Releasing a photo of him dead in the cell, seems like overkill to me, like they are really trying to convince you he's dead.'

Given the widely held belief that AlphaBay had connections to Russian organised crime, some thought that Cazes was a patsy, a fall guy upon whose head others involved in the operation put a bounty to stop him from revealing any sensitive information about the business and those who were really in charge.

More generous-minded folk thought he sacrificed himself for the greater good. 'Maybe he wasn't a snitch and gave up his own life to keep them from torturing sensitive info on users/vendor info out of em. It takes true balls to take your life away. This man is a hero,' wrote DarkKnight.

Others were having none of it. 'What the hell is the point of running a DNM [darknet market] for 3 years if your "Plan B" is to kill yourself?'

Attorney General Sessions had a message for anyone thinking of taking Cazes' place: 'You cannot hide. We will find you.'

As for Mongoose, I could only speculate that he was aware of part, if not all, of the story. My first attempt to visit him must have been

within hours of Cazes' death, but it is possible that news of his arrest
had been relayed to him though the prison grapevine. Thai police may
have grilled him about Cazes, AlphaBay and darknet markets. The
coincidence that they were both Canadian nationals who had made
their home in Thailand and allegedly masterminded multi-million-
dollar darknet markets would not have been lost on the authorities.

All I had to go on was that piece of paper: 'prisoner does not want
any visitors.' I left Bangkok with more questions than answers.

Afterword

At the time of writing, the darknet markets are in disarray. After the
AlphaBay seizure, users flocked to the second-biggest market at the
time, Hansa. Unfortunately for them, Hansa had been quietly taken
over a month earlier by Dutch national police, who let it operate until
the expected influx of new members from AlphaBay. One of the most
common mistakes of darknet market users is that they use the same
login credentials across all markets. The Dutch police were able to
use the information captured from Hansa to identify vendors across a
number of markets.

'In fact, they flocked to Hansa in droves,' said Europol director
Robert Wainwright at a press conference. 'We recorded an eight times
increase in the number of human users on Hansa immediately following the takedown of AlphaBay.

'The intelligence we have yielded through the monitoring of Hansa
has given us new insight into the criminal activity of the darknet,
including many of its many leading figures . . . To those who engage in
criminal activity on the internet and the darknet especially you are not
as safe and anonymous as you think you are.'

Even this, the worst time in darknet market history, did not
dampen the appetite for drug users to buy online. The enabling technologies of Tor, Bitcoin and PGP continued to operate to protect users

in most cases. It had been demonstrated repeatedly that there was a huge amount of money to be made running an online black market and for every person arrested, there were hundreds more making (or absconding with) more money than they had ever dreamed possible. The eBay/Amazon-style markets continue to thrive, improve and adapt and remain the simplest to use.

On the other side are the non-centralised markets that will sell only the lowest risk drugs—LSD and similar psychedelics, MDMA and marijuana. The Majestic Garden epitomises these and many people prefer to use it over the commercial marketplaces. Rather than a centralised marketplace that takes the orders and does the administration for a fee, it is more in the form of a discussion forum and volunteers keep track of which vendors are trustworthy. It is up to buyers to make individual arrangements with the vendors. There is no central escrow so no chance of a market owner closing shop and running off with all the money.

Peter Nash, Samesamebutdifferent, was held in New York federal prison for nearly eighteen months before finally coming before a judge, who promptly declared he had paid his debt to society and sentenced him to time served. Peter returned to Australia, where he was at last able to pop the question he had intended to ask his partner almost two years earlier. She answered in the affirmative and they were married in 2016. He remains in Brisbane, where he is rebuilding his life, drug and dark web-free.

Gary Davis, the man alleged to be Libertas, had his case taken all the way to the High Court, and then the Full Court of Appeal in Ireland. The US remains determined to extradite him, and his chances of avoiding that fate are slim. If he is extradited, he will likely face spending the majority of the rest of his life in prison.

Andrew Jones, Inigo, remains in limbo awaiting his sentencing. His ankle bracelet has been removed and he has a job he enjoys, working with animals. His employers are aware of his history. Although he never had to testify against Ross Ulbricht, he suspects the government is taking its time so that they have him available should Variety Jones or Libertas ever face US courts.

Andrew was annoyed at how he was portrayed in the murder-for-hire discussions surrounding Green. He had been chatting online to DPR at the same time DPR was talking to Variety Jones, but the two discussions were quite separate. Andrew maintains he was never aware of the existence of Variety Jones and had no idea the other discussion was taking place. When the chat logs were reported in court, they were read in chronological order, which gave the impression the three of them were plotting Green's murder in depth. Andrew says that, although the discussion happened, he didn't think DPR was serious.

Curtis Green recovered from his 'murder' and still lives in Utah with his wife. He is writing a memoir. He spoke to Variety Jones before the latter's arrest. 'He didn't know it was me I don't think,' Green said. 'We talked about his advice to kill me.' Of Inigo, he said his colleague was 'lucky he wasn't charged with conspiracy to murder me'.

Curtis himself pleaded guilty to conspiracy to distribute cocaine and possess with intent to distribute. 'Pleading guilty and having the nightmare over was the best choice,' he said. He was sentenced to time served. In his hopes to cash in on his 'murder', he took umbrage at news outlets using the staged photograph without his permission. As his wife took the picture on her own camera, copyright remained with her. 'Now the photo of me being dunked isn't mine,' he said of his torture prior to murder. 'Me being dead is.' He claimed to have knocked back thousands of dollars for the photograph, and eventually came to a settlement.

Ross Ulbricht has been moved to the maximum security prison in Colorado where he is to serve out his sentence. The double life sentence without possibility of parole was handed down partly because the prosecution was allowed to lead with evidence of Ulbricht ordering six murders for hire, despite no evidence of any murders ever having taken place, nor Ulbricht ever being charged with anything relating to murder. Had there been sufficient evidence to charge him with attempted murder, or conspiracy to commit murder, it stands to reason the government would have done so.

Murder for hire is not for the faint of heart. It has, however, become just one more service that has moved online thanks to the dark web. While the potential victims of the Dread Pirate Roberts lived to tell their stories, others were not so lucky.

PART II

Darker

A death in Cottage Grove

On 13 November 2016, the Cottage Grove Police Department was called to an address on 110th Street, home of Stephen and Amy Allwine, to attend an apparent suicide by gunshot wound to the temple. The victim lay near the door of the marital bedroom, not yet cold, in a pool of blood.

On 17 January 2017, a Minnesota resident was arrested for murder. The eleven-page complaint revealed startling evidence of a murder plot hatched months before the death, with $13,000 paid in Bitcoin to dark web hitman-for-hire website Besa Mafia. The contractor used the pseudonym 'dogdaygod'.

I knew the name dogdaygod. I had read the emails between dog-daygod and the administrator of the murder-for-hire site and traced the Bitcoin paid for the kill into Besa Mafia's account.

I knew that the FBI also knew about the murder plot. How the hell had it happened?

Three weeks later, Chris Monteiro was in his south-east London apartment having soup on his sofa, within an arm's length of his bank of
computer screens, when he heard a noise at the door. He'd barely had
time to stand to investigate before the door was kicked in and half a
dozen armoured police stormed into the small space.

'Hands in the air!'

Bewildered by this unexpected visit, Monteiro complied.

'You're under arrest for incitement to commit murder'.

Hitmen: myths and stats

Hitmen, also known as contract killers, murder-for-hire, mercenaries, fixers, mechanics; they hold a fascination for us. They have been
immortalised in novels—think Mack Bolan in *The Executioner*—and
in TV and movies from the early days: Lee Marvin in *The Killers* or
Charles Bronson in *The Mechanic*. Those who prefer a more immer-
sive experience can play one in the smash-hit Sony game, *Hitman*.

The idea of a hitman is both frightening and fascinating. We
imagine they are either men with no morals—mercenaries to whom
only the money matters—or justified vigilantes, who only kill evil
people in revenge for heinous crimes. They are often portrayed as suave,
sophisticated characters, such as Tom Cruise's psychopathic Vincent in
Collateral or George Clooney as Jack in *The American*. James Bond,
with his licence to kill, is the epitome of the suave, principled hitman.

A recurring theme is that the job necessitates these outlaws be
loners (and lonely), like Jean Reno's Léon in *The Professional*. On the
other hand, Angelina Jolie and Brad Pitt starred as husband-and-
wife assassins in *Mr. & Mrs. Smith*, and John Travolta and Samuel L.
Jackson were best-buddy hitmen in *Pulp Fiction*.

Sometimes we are allowed to laugh at them. In the 1977 satirical cult classic *Andy Warhol's Bad* a middle-aged housewife ran an
electrolysis business from her home in New York, from where she

recruited her all-female murder-for-hire contractors. More recently, John Cusack played an unusual assassin with neuroses in *Grosse Pointe Blank*, as did Bruce Willis in *The Whole Nine Yards*.

But to what extent, if any, do these depictions resemble the real-life hitman? Very little, if 'The British Hitman: 1974–2013', a study by three British academics, is to be believed. 'Media portrayal often presents the hitman as a "professional", acting on behalf of an organised criminal network, or, indeed, as part of a government agency,' they wrote. '"Hits" within these various fictional genre inevitably seem to take place within smoky rooms, bars and casinos frequented by gangsters and are well hidden from everyday members of the public.' The study concluded that when it comes to hitmen, life rarely, if ever, imitates art.

For one thing, the vast majority of hitmen only ever had one victim. That is, 'hitman' was not their profession (or they were caught very early in their profession). Of course, some would argue, studies like this don't—can't—examine hitmen who were never caught or identified. Perhaps *those* hitmen are more like the ones we see in movies or TV. It makes sense, doesn't it? The report acknowledges this, saying 'those hitmen who remain at large might present a very different profile from those whom we have described here'.

What's more, the report goes on to say, 'might it be the case that there are some hitmen who are so adept as killers that the deaths of their victims do not even raise suspicion and are, instead, simply thought to be the result of natural causes?'

The very fact that there is this unknown gives us an opening to believe in the hitmen presented to us by popular culture. Academics can't study them because they are too good to get caught. The hitmen who evaded capture may be significantly different to those languishing in prison.

Nevertheless, there was at least one occasion in which life imitated art all too closely. In 1983, Paladin Press published a book written under the pseudonym Rex Feral, called *Hit Man: A technical manual for independent contractors*. Feral purported to be in the business of murder for hire and the book was written as a how-to manual for aspiring hitmen. The writing style is almost whimsical, reminiscent of a 'tips for housewives' article in a 1950s magazine. 'Let's not forget reading for entertainment—with the right attitude and an open mind, almost any good mystery or murder story can provide some ingenious new methods of terrorizing, victimizing, or exterminating,' the book advises in the section on preparing to become an assassin. 'Chuckle through the trenchcoats and warped personalities but test out any new theories you come across.'

However, the book warns, 'The use of cigarettes and alcohol in moderation is acceptable, although undesirable, but use of any kinds of drugs is suicide.'

At one point in the book Feral describes an assassin ejaculating in excitement when torturing a victim to get them to talk. 'You may threaten, bargain, torture or mutilate to get the information you want, and you must be prepared to use whatever method works.' The author also suggests a 'hefty additional sum' should the job include body disposal.

In 1993, musician and Motown Records producer-engineer Lawrence Horn hired former Detroit street preacher James Perry for the sum of $3500 to kill his former wife, their intellectually disabled eight-year-old son, and the child's nurse in their Maryland home. Horn was in debt and stood to gain $1.7 million from his son's malpractice lawsuit trust fund if the boy and his mother died.

Perry had become a self-styled mercenary for hire after purchasing *Hit Man*. He used advice from the book to inform his solicitation of Lawrence Horn ('one should solicit business through a personal acquaintance whom you trust') and negotiations ('get all expense money up front'). He chose the recommended AR-7 rifle from which he drilled out the serial numbers exactly as the book instructed. He made a disposable silencer using materials the book said were available in any hardware store, and hired a rental car, replacing its licence plates with stolen out-of-state ones.

Continuing to follow the book's instructions, he shot Mildred Horn and the nurse, Janice Saunders, using the method ('in the eyes, if possible') and calibre of gun recommended by Feral, then suffocated the child. He ransacked the house to make it look like a burglary gone awry and was sure to remove the ejected shells from the crime scene.

Afterwards Perry disassembled the gun, filed down its components, dumped the pieces by the side of a road and fled the scene in the rental car bearing its stolen licence plate. All in all, he followed the instructions in the book almost to the letter. Unfortunately, the book was silent about communicating with the person on whom suspicion would naturally fall—the husband—and telephone calls were traced to Perry's rooms at the Days Inn and Red Roof Hotel, where he had checked in under his own name.

Perry was sentenced to death for the murders, commuted to three life sentences on appeal, which became moot when he died of an illness in 2009. Lawrence Horn was found guilty on three counts of first-degree murder and is serving out a life prison sentence.

A US Appeals Court ruled that *Hit Man* was not protected by the First Amendment and Paladin Press could be held liable for the triple murder. Paladin Press settled out of court at the behest of its insurance company, for an undisclosed sum paid to the family of the victims, and pulped the remaining copies of the book.

Rex Feral, meanwhile, was exposed as a suburban Florida-based housewife, who had never killed anyone. She had originally written the book as a novel, but the publisher was impressed with the depth of her research and changed it to faux non-fiction as a marketing strategy.

In another incident, Brazilian politician and TV presenter Wallace Souza had to stand down from his true-crime program *Canal Livre* over extraordinary allegations. Police had become suspicious that Souza's TV crew was always the first to murders involving car thieves and drug dealers, often even beating the police. In one particular instance a reporter walking through a forest told viewers: 'It smells like a barbecue,' as he closed in on a still-burning corpse. 'It is a man. It has the smell of burning meat.'

On top of several other incidents, this was simply too much good fortune in terms of the program being in the right place at the right time, and Souza was accused of commissioning hitmen to carry out five murders to increase ratings and eliminate his opposition.

Souza denied any involvement in the deaths and died of a heart attack or liver failure while awaiting trial.

Hitmen online

As with nearly every product or service imaginable, it was inevitable that murder for hire would move online. The average person doesn't know any hitmen, and it is pretty intimidating to head down to the docks or a pub in the rough part of town, asking around if anybody knows of someone who will take cash in return for a murder. The most common form of hitman appears to be the established underworld figure, working for other established underworld figures, taking out rival underworld figures. The vast majority of us don't have access to that world.

Much easier, perhaps, to invoke private browsing and search online for people who might be prepared to carry out murder. And the most likely place to turn would be Craigslist, the behemoth website where products, jobs and hookups of all types are advertised in the millions. Craigslist had already proven popular for drug deals, with participants using coded language. Someone may be looking for a study buddy (adderall or speed), a hookup to take them skiing (cocaine), or they may offer to introduce you to Molly, Poppy, Gina or Tina (MDMA, heroin, GHB or meth).

There are also escorts available of every type imaginable, including those who are underage. Logically, other illegal activities could similarly take place. To many, it made sense that contract killing would move online, just as everything else had. But stories of people making enquiries, then being put onto somebody who turned out to be an undercover police officer seem to be more common than tales of those who are successful. The enquirer invariably lands in prison with their target happily still alive.

Twenty-three-year-old Megan Schmidt of Iowa discovered such pitfalls when she posted an advertisement on Craigslist for someone to do a 'one time job' for US$10,000. When people responded to the advert, she told them plainly she wanted somebody to kill her father. After exchanging emails with one person who agreed, she telephoned the person she thought was the right man for the job. Unfortunately for Schmidt, she was actually talking to an undercover officer. She was sentenced to 87 months' imprisonment.

In Michigan, mother-of-two Ann Marie Linscott tried to hire someone to murder a love rival by offering a freelance gig on Craigslist, and was similarly brought undone.

Rather than rely on Craigslist, Vegas poker dealer Essam Ahmed Eid set up a website, HitmanForHire.net to attract clients. While most who came across the website naturally thought it was a joke, some were hopeful that it truly did offer solutions to problems as promised. A woman in Allentown, Pennsylvania, hired Eid to kill the girlfriend of an ex-boyfriend in Woodland Hills for US$37,000.

As the *Los Angeles Times* reported:

His clients may have thought they were emailing a veteran killer, but his computer records painted Eid as a novice when it came to murder for hire. After launching the website a few months earlier, Eid appeared to have done what any modern-day neophyte would do with a new task—he turned to Google.

Between numerous searches for Clay Aiken—Eid's wife was an avid fan—Sotelo [the investigating FBI agent] found records showing that Eid had surfed the Web about his new trade. He looked up how to make a homemade silencer from toilet parts, attempted to place an Internet order for cyanide, and researched ricin—the castor bean-derived poison famously used in the 1978 assassination of Bulgarian dissident journalist Georgi Markov through an umbrella gun.

Despite his enthusiastic research, Eid never got around to killing anybody. Instead he blackmailed his potential clients, demanding a ransom of ten times the down-payment on his services to cancel the assassination. Ultimately he wound up behind bars in Ireland, and later the US, serving eight years on extortion charges, before returning to his native Egypt in 2016 to become a cattle farmer.

As with other crimes, the ability to remain anonymous was key, and it was here that the regular internet could not deliver.

The dark web and Bitcoin, once again, provided the answer.

Dark web hitmen

You give us a picture; we'll give you an autopsy report!

– C'thulhu: Solutions to Common Problems! dark-web site

Drugs, hacking services, stolen financial and personal information and fraud-related services are the staple products of the darknet markets. But there have always been websites offering far more sinister wares—poisons, human organs, sex slaves and hitmen. Such sites are overwhelmingly amateurish, poorly worded fakes, designed to separate the gullible from their Bitcoin. Hitmen-for-hire services have been offered on the dark web for at least as long as the commercial darknet markets.

Contract killing services were a natural progression for the dark web. All the elements were there: both customer and hitman could remain anonymous from one another, payment could be made in virtually untraceable cryptocurrency, and arrangements could be made away from prying eyes thanks to encrypted text messages using anonymous email providers.

It was not surprising that these services started appearing on the black markets. Silk Road refused point blank to allow hitmen to advertise on the platform. Others, such as Black Market Reloaded, allowed murder-for-hire advertisements in the early days, but soon all darknet markets banned these services from listing, partly because it was a bad look and partly because there were too many complaints that the services were scams.

The assassins turned to their own websites to advertise their services. Many were multi-faceted—they offered not just murders, but beatings, rapes and other types of 'problem-solving'. They came up with names like The Fixer, C'thulhu (named for H.P. Lovecraft's monster), Unfriendly Solutions and Hitmen Inc., or names stolen from movies like *The Jackal* or *The Mechanic*. Because their strengths lay in being able to kill a man twelve ways with their bare hands and in weapons procurement rather than web design, the results were invariably disappointing: simple text sites with a Bitcoin account and a TorMail or Safe-mail or whatever the anonymous email provider du jour was.

Most rational-thinking people were sceptical of the claims, but others either believed or desperately wanted to believe. It made sense, the argument went. The dark web offered the safety of anonymity and plausible deniability. The customer could choose to be out of the state when the murder happened, and many services offered to make it look like an accident anyway. There would be no trail of evidence leading from the customer to the murder, from the hitman to the victim or from the customer to the hitman. The dark web erases all such evidence. It obviously worked for drugs, they said, so why not for hitmen as well? Surely it was the same premise?

The problem with this logic was that drug dealers typically rely on building up a strong client base of happy repeat customers, whereas hitmen are unlikely to achieve this because people usually order murders as a one-off. It is pretty rare that the person who orders the murder of their spouse decides, 'that worked well, I might take out my asshole boss as well; maybe I'll get a discount on follow-up hits'.

With rumours swirling and the veracity of the hitmen a hot topic in the early days of the dark web, I decided to try and engage one. Fresh, untraceable TorMail address notwithstanding, I was nervous about contacting my first hitman. I concocted an elaborate plan of obtaining fake ID to open a PayPal account to purchase the requisite Bitcoin to pay the hitman, so that I would have a believable story if my selected hitman was prone to questions.

Next I made a list of the killers-for-hire who were advertising their talents on the Hidden Wiki, the Underground Market Board and Black Market Reloaded. These advertisements for contract killers were invariably badly written, though this could be attributed to the hitmen having English as a second language, with most claiming to originate from Eastern European countries.

'I will "neutralize" the ex you hate, your bully, a policeman that you have been in trouble with, a lawyer, a small politician . . . I do not care what the cause is. I will solve the problem for you. Internationally, cheap and 100% anonymously,' promised Unfriendly Solution.

Hitman Network hoped I would recommend their services to a friend after I was successfully rid of my nemesis: 'Tell others about this shop, and earn 1% from every purchase they will make.'

Some hitmen refused to kill children (one wouldn't kill women) though they varied with the age range of what constituted a child. Others had higher prices for politicians, famous people and, bizarrely, journalists. That last one made me feel a little better, knowing that, should anyone want to take a hit out on me, at least they would have to pay a premium.

I fired off emails, fiendishly disguising myself as semi-literate, which is harder than it should be. 'Hi can you get rid of someone in Australia my ex husband is abusive and is still allowed to see my kid.' I thought this was a perfectly plausible reason for wanting somebody whacked and might even be considered somewhat righteous, should I come across a hitman with a conscience.

Two never responded. One wrote back and apologised, saying they did not service Australia. This implied they weren't scammers, but I placated myself by deciding they were a law enforcement honeypot and I was outside their jurisdiction. Another response was in such mangled English, I couldn't understand it.

The most promising response came from the best-known contract killing advertisers on the dark web, C'thulhu: Solutions to Common Problems! 'We are an organized criminal group, former soldiers and mercenaries from the FFL [French Foreign Legion], highly-skilled, with military experience of more than five years. We can perform hits all around the world.' Hits could be arranged 'from as low as 6000 euros' and they would take care of things within two to four weeks, making it look like an accident when possible. 'We would be happy to service your request. 20,000 Australia dollars. Our terms are half the payment by transfer up front.'

They needed a target and an address, so I sent them a photograph of my former partner (who was already well and truly dead, just in case), along with an address in another state that Street View assured me was a vacant lot. C'thulhu promised me the deed would be done within two weeks of them receiving the initial deposit. I was impressed by the efficiency with which they responded to queries. They understood I was reticent to provide such a large sum up front and eventually came down to $2000 for passports and travel expenses.

I tried to extract some useful information, but my hitman was having none of it. 'We cannot share such information like past activity and ID makers,' he told me. The whole exercise did not give me any great insights into the life and times of a contract killer, but strengthened my belief that there were no genuine murder-for-hire sites on the dark web.

A slightly different beast was the Assassination Market. This site based itself upon an elaborate scheme described in the 1995 essay 'Assassination Politics' by Jim Bell, where he imagined anonymous benefactors could order the killings of government officials and those who were seen to be violating citizens' rights.

Normal hitman sites offered to kill someone in return for a certain price, paid by one person. Targets would usually be an ex-husband/wife, a business partner or somebody else who had personally wronged the client. The Assassination Market was a crowd-funded market for assassinations of prominent people. The names of the targets were public, and anybody with a bit of Bitcoin could donate to the pot (or 'dead pool'). When a person added funds to the pool they would also provide a prediction of the date and time of the person's death. The prediction would be cryptographically linked to a Bitcoin address, and whoever correctly 'predicted' the death would 'win' the pool. Once the pool was large enough, somebody would invariably 'predict' the date and time of death and carry out the assassination then, thus winning the pot.

Although the idea was not new, the dark web and Bitcoin offered anonymity to donors and the opportunity for anyone to check the pool address and confirm that the money was still in the pot. When someone in the dead pool was killed, anyone could check that the Bitcoin was transferred to the wallet of the person who correctly predicted the death, all without revealing the identities of the people involved.

There were dead pools for a number of prominent people, including President Obama. The largest pot was dedicated to Ben Bernanke, head of the Reserve Bank (and who many believed was responsible for the Global Financial Crisis)—it was around $60,000 at the time.

The Assassination Market went offline some time in 2014. Nobody knows what happened to it. What we *do* know is nobody on the list has been killed, and all of the Bitcoin donated is still sitting in the donation wallets. Nobody has taken the Bitcoin and run. With the increase in Bitcoin value, the amount in Mr Bernanke's pot alone is worth well into the millions of dollars, but there is no way for new bets to be placed.

Once Donald Trump became president of the United States, another dark web 'solutions' site, CrimeBay, started up a similar initiative. 'Donald Trump is an extremely difficult target,' the site acknowledged, 'however, he is neither a God nor immortal, and CrimeBay enjoys a challenge.'

Silk Road hits

After the arrest of Ross Ulbricht and his succeeding trial, much was made of the Silk Road mastermind allegedly ordering murders for hire. Dread Pirate Roberts apparently ordered six hits on people, but not only did these never eventuate, there were unbelievable twists in these tales, recapped briefly here.

Hit 1 was ordered on Curtis Green, Silk Road administrator Chronicpain aka Flush. DPR ordered the hit after Green apparently botched a very large drug deal and was apprehended. DPR ordered it (a) because he was afraid Green would provide information to law enforcement and (b) because an account operated by Green stole hundreds of thousands of dollars from customers, which DPR had to pay back.

But the person DPR hired to carry out the hit, drug dealer Nob, was actually an undercover police officer, Carl Mark Force IV. He and fellow officers faked the murder, sent pictures of 'proof' to DPR and got paid for it, keeping the payment as evidence. It also later turned out that Force's colleague Shaun Bridges was the one who actually stole the money in the first place—it was not Curtis Green after all.

Hits 2–6 happened when a user, FriendlyChemist, began trying to extort money from DPR by threatening to release details of Silk Road's customers. Another anonymous user, redandwhite, contacted DPR out of the blue, hinting he represented Hells Angels and offering to 'deal with Friendly Chemist'.

When redandwhite reported back that the murder of Friendly-Chemist had been successful, he claimed FriendlyChemist had let slip where they could find Silk Road's biggest scammer, Tony76. DPR requested a murder for hire on Tony76 and his three colleagues. Redandwhite eventually reported these hits had taken place and payment of approximately $300K was made.

Again, no such deaths ever occurred and it appears redandwhite was, in fact, Tony76 himself, pulling yet another scam.

Whether or not any of the above really happened is hotly debated but, in any event, the hits were not ordered through a darknet market or a dedicated murder-for-hire site, but rather arranged privately between 'trusted' individuals.

With no deaths that could be attributed to dark web murder-for-hire sites, it seemed clear that hitmen in cyberspace were yet another myth.

That is, until Besa Mafia turned up on the scene, along with at least one very dead body.

The arrival of Besa Mafia

Thank you Besa Mafia for doing the hit promptly and as per the requirements. I was able to cash out the insurance money with no problem and police did not suspect anything as I was out of town at the date of the murder.

– Darkyman testimonial for Besa Mafia

Besa Mafia opened shop on the dark web in December 2015. Unlike the static pages advertising the services of hitmen previously, Besa had a slick and professional fully functional site. Previous sites had offered the services of a single person to carry out jobs in the US or Europe (further afield if the customer would front the expenses); Besa Mafia had a different approach. Borrowing from the success of the darknet markets, Besa promised to match buyers and sellers of services. Two tiers of membership allowed someone to either sign up as a potential customer or to offer their services as a potential killer, hacker, thug or loan shark. When a customer posted a job, Besa would assign a nearby operative, holding the money in escrow until the job was done to the customer's satisfaction.

While earlier dark web hitman sites had tried to convey the impression they were the suave, shadowy figures of popular culture, Besa Mafia admitted outright that their hitmen were gang members and drug addicts; stupid, but willing to murder a stranger provided they were paid.

When we fantasise about getting rid of an unwelcome or irritating person in our lives, we want it done perfectly. We want the highly skilled, proficient and efficient Jackal-type to carry out our bidding. We certainly wouldn't trust the job to some tweaker or junkie who is likely to screw it up and then squeal our names to law enforcement in return for a lighter sentence. Unfortunately, we are much more likely to come across the latter types in our day-to-day lives and never have the appropriate contacts to introduce us to the former. Even if we did, we probably couldn't afford them. They always seem to wear such nice suits, and those leather gloves probably don't come cheap.

The dark web provided a solution to this conundrum. The murder itself would be carried out by the dime-a-dozen gang member hitters, who were willing to do so for as little as $5000 (a bargain, when the average cost of a hit reported in the UK was £15,180, with £100,000 being the highest amount offered, according to the 2013 study

'The British Hitman: 1974–2013'). If the thug got away, great—it would probably look like a mugging gone wrong, or a hit and run. If they got caught, however, it posed less of a problem to the purchaser of the hit, because the killer had no idea who they were. All they could provide was a dark web address from which they had received their instructions.

Besa Mafia claimed to be the digital arm of a mob of Albanian organised crime figures, with employees and operatives all over the world. The website was developed to be similar to other online shopping platforms, where users could browse, order and pay with Bitcoin. One page was dedicated to testimonials from satisfied customers:

> This was the third time my husband cheated on me. I got tired of his beatings and threats, thank you Besa Mafia for the perfect opportunity and smooth murder. It was all made to look like an accident and now I don't have to be afraid ever again. He was threatening me that he will kill me if I submit for divorce papers. Now he is the one who is dead.
>
> – Happywomen

Similar testimonials popped up on clear-web sites, with personal stories of successful hits. Redditors would claim the others were fake, but Besa was the real deal. Believers would stubbornly insist they knew someone who knew someone who hired a contract killer and paid them in Bitcoin through the site.

Like any commercial service, Besa Mafia could only be profitable if the site had customers. Whereas one would usually think that contract killers would want to remain under the radar, the administrator of Besa Mafia, Yura, was happy to answer questions sent by email and looked forward to seeing his company featured on the Newswire. He was willing to talk about the business to anyone who asked.

'Our hitmen are mostly gang members from various states and countries who know how to use computers,' he said in one such exchange. 'Drug dealers, who do a lot of criminal activities. But we do have several hitmen that are ex military soldiers and have combat experience, they have sniper guns and fighting training, they can kill targets that have bodyguards with them, like business men, medium actors or musicians.' Those specialists were far more expensive to hire. Prices started from as low as $5000, but would increase with difficulty, particularly if the job had to look like an accident or if the victim had a high profile. 'We don't have the logistics or planning power to kill presidents of big countries,' he admitted.

Potential hitmen would open up an account on the website, where they could monitor orders from customers in their area. When an order in their geographic region matched their skill set—whether that be beating, rape, arson or murder—the hitman could apply to have the job assigned to them.

Yura insisted that most of the victims listed on his site were guilty themselves, people with many enemies, drug dealers or members of crime families. 'We don't ask the motive about the service because we don't care,' he said. 'If a customer pays to do something, he has a reason to do it.'

The business was international in scale with members ready to carry out crimes in most countries, although most enquiries came from the US or European Union. 'Only small countries like Nepal or Malaysia do not have members,' Yura said, 'but we do jobs there with hitmen that want to travel using fake IDs. However the price is usually $30000–$40000 when is involving traveling.'

The majority of orders placed with the site identified a male target, and most of them were what Yura described as 'scum bags; normal family people do not upset anyone to the point of getting them killed'. When the target was female, the motive usually involved cheating, divorce or cashing insurance. The site would not take orders to kill children.

In Yura's experience, this usually meant one parent was trying to get the ultimate revenge on another, and the child was an innocent victim.

Yura ran a tight ship, and in the few cases when a hitman failed after accepting a job, his account would be suspended and he would no longer be eligible to get further orders through the system. The customer would be offered a refund or another hitman.

New hitters were required to carry out a smaller job—usually arson—to prove they were genuine.

'We can not be fooled with fake evidence or photoshopped pictures or movies,' Yura stated with confidence. 'If he does the job, he is part of the team.'

A potential client would provide as many details as possible about their target, including photographs, links to social media pages, locations where they lived and worked, details of routines or movements and any other information that could be helpful. When a customer's order was accepted, the Bitcoin would be placed into escrow until the job was carried out. When all parties were satisfied, payment would be passed on to the hitman, with Besa Mafia keeping a 20 per cent facilitation fee.

'It is very profitable,' Yura admitted. The number of people willing to pay for beatings, property damage and murder was surprising, even to him.

Pirate.London

Chris Monteiro was rarely without a screen in front of him. The 34-year-old systems administrator from south-east London lived and breathed computers. During breaks or quiet times at work, he could be found administering one of the niche wiki sites he had developed, or updating his personal website, Pirate.London, which covered political activism, cybercrime, computer and information security, digital rights, transhumanism and the sociology of futurism.

Chris liked to trawl Wikipedia for stories related to the dark web. When he found misinformation he would correct it and if there was something missing that he thought significant, he would add it, sometimes creating an entire new page.

That's how I first met Chris; he made a Wikipedia page for my website, All Things Vice, and tweeted me about it. We soon found we had many aligned interests and stayed in touch, sharing anything we found that might be of interest to one another.

What kept Chris busiest in his spare time was his volunteer position as chief moderator of reddit's 'deep web' subreddit, where he posted under the moniker Deku-Shrub. Reddit brags that it is 'The front page of the Internet'. As a news aggregator, discussion board and social media platform, reddit is continually in the top ten most visited sites on the world wide web. It is community-run, with members submitting news, links, opinions and information or misinformation about every topic imaginable.

Reddit is divided into thousands of subreddits, essentially topics of interest in categories such as educational, humour, entertainment, science and technology, self-improvement, porn and image-sharing. The deep web subreddit (the name 'dark web', which would have been more accurate, was taken, though in little use) was where over 38,000 users shared stories and experiences of what they found when exploring the dark web.

Chris prided himself on being a realist and spent much of his time debunking dark web myths, misinformation and rumour. He was the scourge of sensationalist YouTubers and authors of detailed stories, known as creepypastas, about the horrors that could be found on the dark web. 'Red rooms are fake,' he would tell anyone who questioned him. 'There is no such thing as the "Shadow Web". Mariana's Web does not exist.' He was quite the spoilsport when it came to discussions of the salacious parts of the dark web.

Naturally, Monteiro firmly maintained that all hitmen advertising their services were shysters out to separate the gullible from their money. One day, he noticed somebody had edited his RationalWiki page about dark web assassination markets. Although all the others were fake, the edit said, Besa Mafia was not.

His interest piqued, Chris started digging further. He quickly discounted the notion that the site was genuinely the digital arm of an Albanian Mafia family. But he couldn't help but be impressed with the design and layout, which was significantly more sophisticated than any of the previous sites had been.

Around the same time, there was an influx of posts to the deep web subreddit claiming to be testimonials and success stories of people who had used the Besa Mafia website. Whenever a person posted asking about the legitimacy of Besa Mafia, an army of shills, all using similar broken English and odd turns of phrase, would respond in the affirmative.

Yes, the sad truth is that they are legit.

Besa Mafia is a well known criminal organisation, and they have extended to Deep Web to get more business from the onion [dark web address], after the Silk Road was closed.

They do have lots of business outside the Internet, but as Deep Web growed to move millions of $$ around in drugs dealings and killings many mafia organisations have moved in.

I do hope Police is able to shot down their site as they did with Silk Road back in 2013.

Chris was having none of it. He grew tired of what he said was misinformation and rumour-mongering being spread by Besa shills.

He responded to every post that claimed the services offered by the website were real with a rebuttal and even interviewed the site owner, then ridiculed him on his blog, Pirate.London.

I was also fielding questions about Besa Mafia at the time and I, too, responded that I was absolutely sure the site was nothing but a scam. Chris and I would exchange the stories and messages that we received and laugh at the gullibility of those who believed that you could really hire a hitman on the dark web.

Rational people knew this site was a scam, just like all the others. Probably some geeky kid with too much time on his hands and too many hours spent on PlayStation having a laugh.

Then something happened.

On 10 April, Chris Monteiro emailed a private crypto group we are both part of with a link to a video he'd received that day. 'I am freaked out by this,' he wrote. 'Any advice?' The amateur video showed a car being torched, with a chilling touch. The arsonist held up a piece of paper in front of the burning car that said: 'gang member for besa mafia on deep web—dedication to Pirate London 10 April 2016.'

Trainee hitman

John Smith liked marijuana and money; the order of his preferences changed depending on how much he had of each at any given time. At seventeen years of age, however, he was more often than not without either.

Not academically inclined, John had dropped out of school before finishing, but had found even shitty jobs hard to come by in his home state of California. He liked to tinker with cars and fancied himself a bit of a mechanic, but nobody was interested in taking him on.

One day, while sitting around with some friends, John bragged that he planned to join the US Navy and eventually become a 'covert operator'. Neither John nor any of his friends knew what a covert operator was or how to become one, but it sounded cool. John figured it would probably involve having to kill people and he was pretty sure he could do that.

Methods of earning, or otherwise acquiring, money were a frequent topic of conversation among the young men. They had little regard for whether the methods were legal or not. They were all thugs to one extent or another, and aspired to gain reputations as local tough guys. 'Hey,' said one of them, 'I heard that there's hitmen for hire on the dark web. They don't just kill, they beat up people and burn cars and shit too. Maybe you could do that.'

The lads had all heard of the dark web, of course, thanks to Silk Road and the other markets where you could buy drugs and guns as easy as shopping on eBay. Everyone had a friend of a friend who had used the dark web for one reason or another and there had been plenty of news reports that confirmed it was legit. But nobody among John's group was clear on exactly how to access it.

John was intrigued. He was not as familiar with computers as most of his generation, but had nevertheless grown up with them, so he knew how to google stuff. He went home and searched 'dark web hitman' and was pleased to discover several blogs and posts which confirmed that, although most of the murder-for-hire sites were scams, there was one that was the real deal: Besa Mafia.

He checked on Quora, a reputable question-and-answer site, and found that a 'distinguished and educated' professor of research had vouched that Besa Mafia was a genuine dark web murder-for-hire site.

Yes, Besa Mafia is real.

Besa Mafia hitmen don't wear black suits like hitmen in movies, and don't go in the houses of victims to do the killings; they wear normal clothes and do the killings on street, usually from a car after which they drive away.

Besa Mafia is a Dark Marketplace that focuses on body harming services; that means they beat up, set cars on fire, kill people. Here is some video proof posted by some of their members

I can post more video proof that their members have shared on the net, like beating up, acid attacks, shooting people, but these are too disturbing and might not be allowed.

I don't support or recommend them, but I do want them to be taken seriously and shot down by Police.

All people claiming there are no hitmen on Deep Web are fat lazy cops who want to discourage people from doing it. That is ethical good; but legally wrong, you should move your lazy asses out to the street and catch criminals instead of lying that there are no body harming services on deep web.

Wow, these guys seemed pretty serious! A bit more googling led John to the Tor software and finally he was able to launch the browser that let him in to the dark web. A couple of the articles he'd found even provided the URL—ending in .onion instead of .com so he knew it was a proper dark web address—for Besa Mafia.

A thrill ran through John as he read through the details provided by the website. There were photos of hits they had carried out, and testimonials from happy customers:

When I first found Besa Mafia I didn't thought they were real. How could someone get hitman orders on Internet? I thought to myself. But then I learned about how Deep Web works, and how sites are protected by Tor and have a hidden IP, making them safe from shutdown by Police. I used their services to kill a bastard in my family and cash the insurance money. Thank you guys.

Holy shit, it was real! Of course, it made sense that if something like Silk Road (which John heard made over a billion dollars), could run for years out in the open selling drugs, then a hitman service could too. Silk Road got shut down because of a dumbass mistake by the owner, but Besa Mafia was fucken mafia. Proper organised crime, not some amateur who thought he was a kingpin. They would be much more careful and hard to catch, for sure.

The FAQ explained how a potential hitter could sign up to the service and start earning big bucks. John chose 'ThcJohn' as his username and carefully noted the requirements to apply. It was like a job application and he didn't want to mess it up.

'I am offering the following services in USA west coast: beat up, cut, break bones, hand kill, sharp object kill,' ThcJohn wrote by way of introduction. 'I can use firearms with military proficiency but do not have any.'

He wondered if he should tell this little white lie. Hopefully they wouldn't check it out too carefully, but he made sure to put in the bit about not having any firearms so they wouldn't immediately put him on to a shooting job. John glanced down at his feet, where his faithful pitbull Rex was curled, and had a great idea, one that would surely make him stand out from the crowd.

'Also I have an attack dog so I can provide the dog bite service,' he wrote.

A bit about his motivation seemed in order. 'I am offering my services because I am broke (of course) and am looking for quick cash. I have military training (US Navy).'

Well, he *would* have military training when he got into the covert ops section of the navy, and he had seen enough movies and TV shows, played enough combat games on his PlayStation to fake it for a while.

The application form suggested that he name his price for different jobs. He didn't want to price himself out of contention, but he also didn't want to look too cheap. Eventually he came up with prices that seemed fair and reasonable for the different services:

- dog bite: $800
- cut, break bones: $1500
- beat: $750
- arson (small target car, 1 story house, small office): $1200
- arson (large target): to be discussed
- hand kill, sharp object kill: $7500
- small caliber short range kill: $6000
- long range kills are to be discussed as there are many variables

John sat back and surveyed his work. He'd never been so pumped to apply for a job, and now he was on a roll. 'All prices are basic and special circumstances are subject to higher price. Any kill job is subject to declination based on personal morals.' Hmm, he didn't want to look like a pussy, so added: '(I don't have many)'.

He wrote a couple more explanatory lines about his ability to travel and expenses and then signed the application off as politely as he could: 'I think I covered everything but don't hesitate to ask for more specific information.'

Now that it was time to hit the Send button, John felt his bravado slipping away. He'd had some small-time thug life experiences, but this was on a whole new level. This was a huge organisation of real, sophisticated criminals. This was big time. Was John really ready for it, considering he hadn't yet turned eighteen?

They won't know who I am, he thought to himself. He'd been careful not to give too much away, plus there was that misinformation about the navy that would throw them off. The same tools that protected them from detection by the long arm of the law protected him from them. They were sure to start him off small and he could always decline if he didn't like the sound of the job.

John decided to sleep on it. The next morning, he'd made up his mind. He needed the money and he wanted to be part of something important. This was his chance. No more excuses. He hit Send.

He didn't have to wait long. Later that evening, he received a response from the administrator of Besa Mafia. It got right to the point: 'Hello, we can send you a test order, if you do it you will get paid for it, and we give you more orders. The first order is to set fire to a car, is that ok?'

John was relieved. Torching a car he could handle, provided it wasn't some rich dude's BMW locked up in a garage in a gated community. He responded eagerly. 'Yes I will comply but is there a certain car that you have in mind or just any car?'

The administrator assured him it was just a test, so pretty much any car would do, but he would need to provide proof that the job was done. 'You need to video record the whole process, using a smart phone, and you need to write down [the following] on a piece of A4 paper'.

gang member for
besa mafia on deep web
http://oiiuv2gwl2jhvg3j.onion
dedication to pirate london
10 april 2016

John was ecstatic. There were plenty of cars around that were easy pickings if he was able to choose any one he wanted. This was easy money and well within his comfort zone. If he could pull this off to the mob's satisfaction, who knew where things could go?

Having copied and pasted the exact wording and printed it on his home printer, in the early hours of the morning, John Smith stole out and found a small white sedan parked alone in a lot in Woodland Hills in the San Fernando Valley, just north of LA. It was his hometown, but John didn't think there was any reason he would be a suspect and he planned to make it look like an electrical fault. John carefully drilled a hole into the underside of the gas tank, then using his tablet, he recorded himself holding up the sign and setting the car alight, just as he'd been told.

John replied to Besa Mafia as soon as he got home. 'How can I get the video to you?' he asked. Besa Admin suggested he go to a café with public Wi-Fi and upload the video to a popular filesharing site, Vimeo. John knew the quality was rubbish, but he hoped that it would be good enough to get him on the payroll.

He passed! 'We will pay you $200 for the test order, because this is easier than burning a specified car at a given address,' Besa wrote. 'Hope this is ok. We will start giving you orders from customers and we will pay as per your prices that you specified in your previous messages.'

John was a bit miffed, but emboldened enough to request payment of $300 to the Bitcoin address he supplied to the hitman. 'You are a good negotiator,' the hitman said. '$300 is on its way to you.' Besa also had some suggestions for future filming: 'when video recording, please keep the phone at 90 degrees, so that you record panoramic view instead of vertical view; phone should be held like this [__] instead of like this [].'

The next day, Besa Mafia sent John his first real client: $750 to beat up a 44-year-old man in Georgia.

John Smith was well on his way to becoming a hitman.

Meet the Allwines

Stephen Allwine stood in the modest lounge room as his wife Amy fiddled with the camera on the phone. A mishmash of furniture—a two-seater next to a three-seater couch; a single chair accommodating an oversized teddy bear—was pushed back against the wall to make room for what was to come. There were two televisions on the corner TV stand: a family-sized one at eye level and a smaller one close to the ceiling. The wallpaper was beige stripes and there was a large landscape on one wall. It was the cosy home of a family comfortable with its clutter.

'Okay, basics,' Amy Allwine announced. The music started and the heavyset woman in her thirties, skipped up to her husband, who took her in the classic dance pose.

Both the song and the dance steps had been through rigorous evaluation by Stephen and Amy in order to be approved for use in the Christian dance class they taught for church winter camp. 'We want to be confident that we are providing good music with good messages,' the Allwines wrote on the webpage where they collated approved music for pastors and church elders to use for dances. 'There is a lot of Christian music out there, but we also want people to realize that there is mainstream music that is OK to enjoy, as well.'

Songs talking about love had to be about love between husband and wife. Songs that included lyrics about sexual relations or illegal activities, or used 'bad words', or took the Lord's name in vain would not be approved. Even if there was a 'clean' radio version of a song and a 'bad' album version, it would not be approved in case someone who enjoyed the clean version inadvertently downloaded the naughty one to enjoy later.

Any songs that spoke to the occult, suicide or drug use would fail the test. Even if a song passed all the tests, if its video was objectionable it would not get played at a church dance, as the Allwines believed that videos 'provide insight into the mind of the artist'. Such was the case for Justin Bieber's *Boyfriend*: 'Video: inappropriate touching for boyfriend relationship. Not approved.'

Sometimes a song would be approved, but flagged for further review. In *When I Was Your Man* by Bruno Mars, the Allwines were concerned that 'the song does not indicate that they were married when she left, so assume dating'. *Interlude* by Attack Attack!, it was noted, 'has the ability to get out of control. We are to be in control of our bodies and emotions.'

Stephen and Amy stepped smartly back and forward to the sounds of *I Want to Know What Love Is* by Foreigner, he gazing lovingly into her eyes. As the demonstration of the simplest dance moves finished, Amy spun away and Stephen smiled after his wife. 'That's pretty basic,' he laughed.

Amy may have been already marked to die.

———

Stephen Allwine met Amy Zutz when they were both students at the now defunct Ambassador College, a liberal arts college run by the Worldwide Church of God, in Big Sandy, Texas. Not so much an educational institution as a training ground to prepare youth for life and service in church, the colleges had a motto: *Recapturing True Values*. The pair worked in the IT Department together and got to know each other through church socials, where they would always choose each other as dance partners. After college, Steve moved to Amy's hometown of St Paul, Minnesota and soon after they married, when both were in their early twenties. Amy's father, Charles, placed Amy's hand into Stephen's. 'Take good care of my little girl,' he said.

Both Stephen and Amy were deeply committed to the church. God and religion played a central part in their life together. The United Church of God (UCG) is an evangelical congregation that believes in the imminent second coming of Christ and adheres strictly and literally to the teachings of the bible, including those of the Old Testament. In some circles, the small religion, also known as Armstrongism, is defined as a cult. Its teachings draw on some of the more extreme elements of Mormonism, Jehovah's Witnesses and Seventh Day Adventism. Members are not permitted to marry outside of the faith, which meant, according to a former member, 'the pool was very small.'

Stephen and Amy did not observe Christmas or Easter, as the UCG teaches that these are pagan celebrations: 'We do not teach or command the observance of Christmas because of the silence of the Bible on this topic. Christmas has its roots in pre-Christian and non-Christian traditions and was never observed in the Bible by the apostles or early Church.' The Allwines attended services every Saturday at a modest building in St Paul that the UCG shared with the Methodist Church, which held its services on a Sunday. They would arrive at around 12.30, a good hour before the service began, and would stay for all the activities afterwards, not leaving until the evening.

Stephen and Amy spent most of their spare time together, and the bulk of that time was devoted to church business. They travelled extensively serving congregations around the world and taking part in humanitarian efforts. The two were ordained as deacon and deaconess of the United Church of God in the spring of 2006, Stephen a month before Amy. A year later, they adopted their only child, a son, Amy bringing him home when he was just two days old. It was an open adoption, and the Allwines stayed in touch with his birth mother. The desperately-wanted child became part of the family and joined the tradition of Friday night dinners with Amy's parents and brother. On those nights, Amy's mother would put out the good china and silver-ware, while her father prepared the food. Amy always brought dessert, and often that would be her mother's favourite, strawberry pie. When he was old enough, their son would join Amy in picking the biggest, juiciest fresh strawberries they could find to make that pie.

To all who knew them, the Allwines had an idyllic marriage. Nobody ever saw them fight and they both participated in bringing up their beloved son. 'They were loved as a couple, and loved individually,' one friend said.

But even the happiest marriages have weak spots and even the most religious people can be led into temptation.

Ashley Madison

Ashley Madison was a dating website like no other. Rather than matchmaking singles looking for love, it catered exclusively to those who were seeking an extramarital affair.

Men had to pay a fee to join, while for women it was free. When one party found another that they liked, they could initiate a conversation only after purchasing 'chat credits' from Ashley Madison. Once the initial chat was paid for, the two could exchange messages and decide whether to meet for an illicit affair. Not surprisingly, the site came under considerable criticism for its unabashed advertising: *Life's short. Have an affair.*

In July 2015, Ashley Madison was hacked. The hackers had discovered that Ashley Madison did not remove client details from its database even after the client had paid a fee to the company to do so. They also claimed to have evidence that Ashley Madison's database was comprised overwhelmingly of males—some 95 per cent of members—and that Ashley Madison hired people to pretend to be women to string the men along, providing them hope of a real-life meeting that would never eventuate, but would ensure the men kept paying up for their chat credits.

The hackers, calling themselves The Impact Team, demanded the parent company, Avid Life Media, take down its cheating website or suffer the consequences. When Avid Life Media failed to act, The Impact Team released their entire database, with details of thousands and thousands of customers worldwide on the dark web. They released a statement with the dump:

> Avid Life Media had failed to take down Ashley Madison. We have explained the fraud, deceit and stupidity of ALM and their members. Now everybody gets to see their data.

> Find someone you know in here? Keep in mind the site is a scam with thousands of fake female profiles . . . Chances are

your man signed up on the world's biggest affair site, but never had one. He just tried to. If that distinction matters.

Find yourself in here? It was ALM that failed you and lied to you. Prosecute them and claim damages. Then move on with your life. Learn your lesson and make amends. Embarrassing now, but you'll get over it.

It did not take long for data enthusiasts to extract the information from the data dump into a user-friendly searchable database, where anyone could enter an email address and find out if the person who owned that address was signed up to the Ashley Madison website, and thus presumably having an affair.

Worldwide fallout included public shaming, broken marriages, extortion and blackmail, suicides and, maybe, murder. Buried somewhere deep in that database was the name Allwine, from the town of Cottage Grove, Minnesota.

An order for Besa

BESA MAFIA Order No. 30312

ORDER BY: Dogdaygod

TARGET: Amy Allwine

LOCATION: La Quinta Inn Molina Airport 5450 27th St, Moline, IL 61265

PICTURE: http://www.allwine.net/travellog/hawaii/P1020057.JPG

DESCRIPTION: She is about 5'6", she looks about 200lbs. She should be driving a dark green Toyota Sienna Minivan

This bitch has torn my family apart by sleeping with my husband (who then left me), and is stealing clients from my business.

I want her dead. That is the 13 bitcoins, if it can look like an accident then you can have the rest.

Amy Allwine

Amy (Zutz) Allwine grew up dedicating herself to her faith and to helping others. Born to a couple who were adherents to the Worldwide Church of God (WWCG), Amy was the middle child, with an older sister and younger brother. The children were not allowed to take part in extra-curricular activities at school, nor did they have any friends from outside the church. Nevertheless, Amy had a happy childhood, and enjoyed sleepovers with her two best friends, the three girls staying up well past their bedtimes, giggling and telling stories.

Amy attended Woodbury High School, but her participation in school life was limited to lessons. She could not form any meaningful relationships with her schoolmates, some of whom considered her odd, especially when they noted she did not celebrate any of the usual holidays the rest of the class looked forward to.

That's not to say Amy had no social life. She was an enthusiastic cheerleader for the WWCG basketball team, and put a lot of time into putting together dance routines for the girls on the squad. There would have been no skimpy outfits or suggestive moves in Amy's choreography.

In the mid-nineties, the WWCG leaders introduced changes that substantially altered the fundamental doctrine of the church. This led to some members forming breakaway organisations, including the United Church of God (UCG), which maintained the fundamentalist beliefs and goals of the original WWCG. Amy and her family joined this new church.

Well known and loved for her generosity, Amy travelled to the Ukraine in 1999 on a church medical mission, distributing glasses and assisting dentists and medical professionals in treatments, diagnoses and flu shots. Over the years she would travel often to spread the word of the church and do what she could to help the less fortunate. The entire family—Amy's parent's, siblings and husband, and later their son—would travel overseas every other year for the Fall religious festival of their church, the harvest feast.

Amy's primary passion outside the church was dogs. She had been a dog lover since childhood, but in 1999 she started taking dog agility training more seriously and quickly became an active and popular member of the dog training and competition scene. Before long, her Australian shepherds were frequent competition winners, thanks to Amy's talent for training.

That knack with dogs saw Amy turning her hobby into a career, training dogs to compete in agility trials and competitions. She registered a new organisation, Active Dog Sports Training. As the sole owner and operator, Amy threw herself into the business of dog training in a way one friend described as being consistent with her values. 'Whatever she taught, she would offer at the "just for fun" level or the competition level,' her friend said. 'She would treat both types of clients equally. There was no pressure to compete when you trained with her. If you wanted to do it just for fun your whole life, that's what she would do and she would support your decision. If you wanted to compete, she would support that. She never pressured you one way or the other.'

'She could bring out the best in all of us,' a customer of Active Dog Sports told FOX 9 Investigators. 'We'd make crazy mistakes with our dogs, and she'd find some funny way for us to learn something about ourselves. And us as a team. She was great.'

Despite her growing success, Amy's first priority continued to be her family and her church. Everyone who knew her would confirm she had just three things in her life: church, family and dogs, and she excelled in all three. She was anointed deaconess of the local chapter of her church, she was a devoted and involved mother and wife, and her reputation as a dog trainer and her popularity among that scene continued to grow. When a new sport emerged from California, nosework, Amy was a pioneer. Again, this was born as much out of her desire to help people as her love of dogs. She recognised that agility training was out of reach for some people due to its high intensity for both dog and human.

'Amy started nosework because it was a sport that any dog and any human could do, no matter their age or fitness level,' said her friend. As with everything Amy touched, she shone, soon becoming a leader in the field, travelling all over the country for competitions and trials, which were judged by the K9 division of the police departments.

She was known for being relentlessly positive, outgoing with a sunny disposition. 'She always had that huge smile,' her friend said. 'She was a very friendly, positive person. She was never negative, never judgmental and never gossipy.'

It wasn't long before Amy's business outgrew the house the Allwines lived in at Woodbury. They found the perfect piece of land in Cottage Grove, Minnesota. The 28 acres (11 hectares) held a large barn that had been used for a small manufacturing business, but no house. They decided to rent out the Woodbury house, buy the land and refurbish the barn for the dog training business, Active Dog Sports. They rented out the land they weren't using for truck gardening.

Steve did not share Amy's passion for dogs, but the Allwines decided their money was best invested in Amy's business. They bought a prefab home that was shipped in pieces and assembled on their property, the idea being that they would build the house of their dreams later.

The Allwines' house was the epitome of 'worst house in the best street'. The street is long, semi-rural, with very large blocks. Neighbours were not close enough to complain if the dogs got a little rowdy from time to time. The Allwines had the last house on the street before a tiny carpark led to the Grey Cloud Dunes sand-gravel prairie. The prairie was popular with walkers and often sunset-watchers would sit in parked cars, enjoying the view.

The house was no shack, but the simple dwelling could not compete with the significantly larger and more elaborate homes of the neighbours. It comprised four small bedrooms, an open-plan kitchen/living area and three bathrooms. An attached double garage provided an alternative entry to the house via a mud room that doubled as a laundry. Stephen's office was in the basement along with another bathroom.

The dog training shed just a few metres away was three times the size of the house and Amy made sure it was kept immaculate. Active Dog Sports grew to be a respected and successful business offering an array of dog-related services. Amy became a certified nosework instructor in 2013, later co-hosting Minnesota's first canine Odour Recognition Test. Her sunny personality and genuine love of dogs— all of her training was by positive reinforcement—saw her friendship group among fellow dog-lovers grow to become second only to her church group.

Despite her faith, Amy was not evangelical to those who did not share her beliefs. According to those who knew her in the competitive dog circles, Amy was wonderful and well loved by all, and one of her most outstanding attributes was her empathy. Part of that empathy was her ability to imagine how she would feel if someone were to impose any beliefs she did not have on to her. 'She rose above it with character and integrity,' a friend in the dog world said.

Amy exuded success. She owned multiple businesses, travelled the world to help disadvantaged people and co-founded scholarships for her local communities. She created and nurtured a large and loving community dedicated to dog training and travelled extensively with her own dogs, entering competitions and trials all over the country. She had a husband she adored and a cherished son, who was also showing interest in the dog scene. If there was one thing she was perhaps not satisfied with, it was that she weighed more than she might have liked, and was constantly on one diet or another in an attempt to get it under control.

Amy appeared to have it all. But appearances can be deceiving.

Stephen Allwine

Stephen Allwine was not a fan of dogs. He had little interest in the canines that surrounded Amy, much as she tried to include him in her passion.

Eventually he announced he would like a Newfoundland, which could do cart-pulling on the large property. Amy didn't particularly want such a large dog and knew that all of the training and care would fall to her, but she decided she would indulge her husband and hoped that it would be the beginning of his entrée into the dog world. Bolson the Newfoundland joined their little family.

Steve started out with some interest, but in no time at all, he backed off and Bolson wound up being very much Amy's dog, along with George, the Australian shepherd. Although Amy liked having them in the house, Stephen was not so keen, so the dogs had kennels in both the mud room and the fenced-in yard that could be accessed from the patio door.

Stephen was not as outgoing and gregarious as his wife. He was quiet, cerebral and intellectual. Some of Amy's friends said they never felt comfortable with him. His love—outside his church and family—was reserved for computers. With his two work-from-home jobs, one for an insurance organisation, and the other for an IT company, Stephen remained the main breadwinner. He put in long hours in the basement, which was cluttered with technology. Computers, monitors and peripherals filled the small space.

The handling of the family's technology naturally fell to Stephen, who was more comfortable with it than Amy. His mind worked methodically; he sought out getting solar panels onto their house after figuring out, to the cent, the cost savings they would receive on a daily basis. As a result, their home was energy efficient, keeping the bills low.

Like Amy, the UCG was one of the most important influences in Stephen's life. After becoming a deacon, he rose to become an elder, with responsibility for counselling married couples, giving sermons at church and anointing those who fell ill.

But it was Amy who seemed to have it all—a fulfilling, successful career, close family, dozens of friends and a real zest for life. As for Stephen, according to one source: 'He wanted to be the star in the relationship. He wanted to be important in their religion. He wanted to be somebody and she WAS somebody.'

Perhaps it was living in Amy's shadow that made Stephen respond to a Backpage advertisement to purchase two overnight dates with an escort in 2014. Perhaps it was living in Amy's shadow that sent him to the Ashley Madison website, where he trawled for casual lovers.

Perhaps it was living in Amy's shadow that made Stephen no longer want to be married to her. The ultra-conservative United Church of God would expel him if he sought a divorce, but the status of being an elder mattered more to him than anything else. Stephen needed to find another way out of his marriage.

Secrets and lies

As an IT specialist for over twenty years, Stephen Allwine knew that nearly every service available could be found somewhere online. He turned to the Ashley Madison website to find partners who would be discreet. His first attempt, dinner at the Legends Golf Club, ended abruptly when after the meal his date, Autumn, said she had to go to the bathroom, and kept going. Stephen nevertheless messaged her twice more, suggesting they try again. Autumn blew him off.

His next match, Michelle, proved to be more successful and they entered into a relationship in 2015 that lasted well into 2016. Their trysts would usually take place at her house, but he also took her on two work trips: one to a charming B and B in Hartford and the other to Syracuse.

Michelle, who was suffering with anxiety and depression, appreciated Stephen's kind and polite demeanour. He was dependable and predictable, although she was struck by how little emotion he showed in any situation, no matter how stressful. He never spoke of his faith, so she was surprised to find links to his sermons when she googled him.

When Stephen decided Amy had to die, he once again turned to his computer. After all, a man of God in Cottage Grove does not have many opportunities to meet with the kind of person who could do that sort of job for him.

Stephen had first visited the dark web in 2014. There were many things Stephen wanted to hide from his wife and church group, and his IT background meant he became aware of Tor as a way of masking his IP and ensuring anonymity.

Once he entered the dark web, however, he discovered there was much more to it than just covering his tracks when logging on to the Ashley Madison website. One thing that intrigued him was the many goods and services that could be bought, seemingly without intervention by law enforcement or government, on the black markets.

Drugs, guns, counterfeit notes, stolen goods and fake identification documents were all a simple mouse click away. There had been a lot of mainstream media attention on the big markets and there was no doubt they were genuine.

But then there were smaller, more niche markets hidden even deeper. These ones offered illegal pornography, human slaves, exotic animals. And even hitmen.

Of course, many people said that the hitmen sites were scams, and most of them certainly seemed to be. But there was one that was getting a lot of publicity, and hundreds of people were posting on various sites that they had used Besa Mafia for beatings, arson and even murder. There were testimonials popping up all over the web in a variety of forums. There were no people claiming to have been scammed out of their money—the only people still saying the Besa Mafia website was a scam were bloggers and journalists, who simply assumed it. Obviously they had never tried to hire a hitman themselves.

On 14 February 2016—ironically, Valentine's Day—using Tor to mask his IP, Stephen signed up to reddit with the account name dogdaygod. His first post was to a subreddit called DarkNetMarketsNoobs, a forum dedicated to people who were new to perusing, buying or selling on the darknet markets. Stephen had done some homework and used the abbreviation LEO he had seen in other threads to reference law enforcement officers.

'New to the markets, but I assume that there are LEOs posing as sellers in the markets. How do I identify a LEO vs a real seller? Any tips would be helpful,' he wrote. The few answers he got were vague, but reassured him that he didn't need to worry about law enforcement honeypots, although they assumed he was talking about vendors on the drugs markets rather than murder for hire.

Apparently happy with this, Stephen signed up to Besa Mafia and on 15 February 2016 sent his first enquiry. He used the same username as he had on reddit—dogdaygod.

Stephen was no doubt aware that in the case of the suspicious death of someone, the spouse was always the first person the police would look to. Hiring a hitman to do the job was the first step towards taking the heat off himself—he could be sure to be out of town when it happened. But another problem was obtaining the requisite amount of Bitcoin without raising suspicion. Bitcoin was still relatively novel, and large purchases often pointed to illicit activity. However, he was sure a reputable contract killing service would have come across this issue before and would have ways around it. His first query to the site sought to address this.

'I am looking to hire you for a hit, but what is the recommended way to convert cash to bitcoin anonymously? If I pull $5000 out for a hit, after the hit I would assume that the police would see that draw and wonder where it went, so even if the bitcoins are not traceable, that missing money would raise suspicion? Is there a way to make it look like I am buying something and end up with bitcoins, so that the money looks like it is going to something tangible and not cash to pay for a hit?'

Stephen already had $10,000 readily available if he needed it. In two separate transactions, on 7 January and 11 February, he had taken a collection of silver coins, then some silver bullion bars, to Great Lakes Coins & Collectibles. The pawn shop had paid him $5600 and $4200 respectively for the silver, which Stephen kept in the safe behind one of the screens in his basement office.

The response from Besa Mafia was swift and helpful. The customer service administrator provided him with the names of a couple of Bitcoin traders that did not require identification and suggested there were several ways to hide the true purpose of the Bitcoin. He could, for example, claim to have purchased a gaming server (Besa could provide him with access to one they used for money laundering for a limited time, that he could claim as his own), or say he invested it, used it for training or consulting or purchasing a car, or simply lost it gambling online.

Stephen was eager to put a plan into action, but wasn't going to rush into anything. He would exchange as many emails with the Besa Mafia customer service team as necessary to ensure all his questions were answered. He thought that, rather than arrange something to go down at home when he just happened to be out of town, it would be better if the hit took place while Amy was travelling, and better again if it looked like an accident. That way, he could be the bereaved husband and nobody would ever suspect a thing.

Stephen knew Amy was due to attend one of her dog trials soon, but didn't know where. He used his MacBook to search for 'K9 Nosework' and clicked on the trial calendar that came up for the address.

'The target [Stephen started using proper hitman-speak in his communications so they would know he was serious and knew what he was talking about] will be traveling out of town to Moline, IL in March,' he wrote. 'What is the price in BTC for hit and ideally making it look like an accident?'

He soon discovered that hitmen have add-ons for anything other than a straightforward gang shooting, and staging an accident was considerably more expensive. A $5000 hit, he was told, was by a low-level gang member 'using a turtle neck and a handgun'. This would usually happen in a parking lot as the unsuspecting target was getting in or out of their car. An accident would usually cost an extra $4000. However, there was a cheaper option that happened to be available in Illinois: 'Our gang members can wait at the location and run him over by a stolen car, or run into his car to the driver side, making it look like an accident. This costs $6000,' Yura wrote.

Perfect. 'That would work fine. So can we say 15 bitcoin for hit with a car and ensure fatality?' he asked. Yura assured him it was a deal.

The very next day, Stephen Allwine investigated Bitcoin services. Even those who work in IT can forget to erase all of their digital footprints. Stephen didn't notice that each of those services had stored some cookies on his Samsung Galaxy S5.

On 3 March 2016, Stephen withdrew $7000 from the TCF bank account he shared with Amy. Rather than purchase Bitcoin via an exchange, Stephen found LocalBitcoins, a site that allowed person-to-person transactions. He met with a man named Ryan at a Wendy's burger joint, where Stephen exchanged a wad of cash for a scan of a QR Code that deposited Bitcoin into his wallet. He may have been nervous, because he locked his keys in his trunk and had to call Liberty Mutual Roadside Assistance to send someone to open it for him. He kept his date with Michelle, however, and told her about his purchase and the key mishap.

Stephen may have been overthinking his potential alibi when he made his next move. In case he ever had to explain the silver-to-cash-to-Bitcoin transaction, he walked into the Cottage Grove Police Department where he made a report to the officer on duty, Jenna Kroshus, that he had been defrauded in a Bitcoin transaction. He said he had entered into a transaction with an individual known only as 'Mark' to purchase Cisco training and test preparation materials for $6000 in Bitcoins. Stephen advised he acquired the Bitcoin and trans-ferred it to 'Mark', but never received the goods. He became suspicious that he may have been defrauded when he noticed that 'Mark had used an untraceable guerrillamail address in his email of 3 March 2016 confirming the transaction.

The Cottage Grove police were not familiar with Bitcoin and didn't really know what Stephen was reporting. In any event, he didn't seem too concerned about the police following up on the crime. 'We just took the report and kind of filed it away,' said Sergeant Randy McAlister. 'Didn't really do any investigation on it. So, that was about it.'

Yura sent Stephen messages every few days to his dogdaygod email address, asking whether he had any questions and prompting him to seal the deal. Stephen decided he would feel more comfortable using an external escrow service. There are several third-party services that will hold Bitcoin payments for a transaction and only release them to the seller once the buyer has confirmed they have received the services and they are satisfactory. Stephen nominated bitrated.com as his preferred escrow provider. However, it needed details of the product or service being offered in the case of arbitration. 'Any recommended thoughts on wording?' he asked the hitman. 'I assume you have worked through this before, so you probably have better ideas.'

Yura responded quickly that he did not think bitrated would work as it was a reputable service, unlikely to be happy about brokering a murder-for-hire deal. 'If our gang members claim they did the job, escrow should be able to verify that the person is dead,' he said. There would be obvious difficulties for the escrow service deciding a dispute.

Yura went on to explain that Besa Mafia itself was in essence the escrow service. The website brought killers and customers together and held the money until the job was done, at which point they would transfer it to the killer after taking a 20 per cent cut. But if Stephen insisted on adding yet another party (and another party's fees) to the mix, 'Please find a reputable escrow that allows illegal things, like drug trade, prostitution, organs traffic, murder for hire, unregistered guns, and then tell what escrow you want to use,' Yura advised.

Stephen had reservations. 'Can you explain to me how your escrow service works, because all I see when I go to deposit money is a bitcoin address, which could be a personal address?' he said. 'I want to trust you guys, but I do not understand how I have any control over the money once I send it to you to ensure that the project is done. I assume you can understand my concern.'

Yura patiently explained that the Besa Mafia system was fine; it was the system Silk Road and other successful markets were built on. At some point, you have to trust someone with your Bitcoins. Besa relied on good reviews, recommendations and repeat custom, so would arbitrate if there were any issues between hitman and customer.

Finally reassured, Stephen transferred US$6000 worth of Bitcoins to the Besa Mafia Bitcoin wallet. 'OK, I did some research and everything that I read says that you are real and can carry out what you say you can do,' he wrote. 'They say that Besa means trust, so please do not break that. For reasons that are too personal and would give away my identity I need this bitch dead, so please help me.'

The dogdaygod persona claimed to be female, a jealous former wife of a lover of Amy's. Not even Besa Mafia could be trusted to know that it was, in fact, her husband arranging the murder. However, for someone so tenuously connected to Amy, dogdaygod had a lot of detail about her. Besa Mafia was provided with a URL of a photograph that had been taken on a church trip to Hawaii and which happened to have been uploaded to the Allwine's family website that very day. Dogdaygod also provided details of Amy's height and weight, as well as the route she would be taking to Moline, Illinois. She would be staying at La Quinta Inn, Moline Airport on the night of Saturday 19 March and would be participating in a dog trial at Quad Cities Christian School on Sunday 20 March. She would be driving a dark green Toyota Sienna Minivan.

'I want her dead. That is the 13 bitcoins, if it can look like an accident then you can have the rest,' dogdaygod said. 'She will have a companion with her, but no one that I care about.'

Besa Mafia assured dogdaygod that they had a hitman available in the area and the job would be carried out during the evening of 19 or 20 March.

On 19 March 2016, Amy Allwine kissed her husband goodbye and set off with fellow dog trainer Kristen in her dark green Toyota Sienna Minivan to a dog trial at Quad Cities Christian School, Moline, Illinois.

More warnings

ThcJohn could not take on the Georgia job—Besa Mafia would not front him the money to travel the 2200 miles (3541 kilometres) from home. John was surprised that Besa didn't have someone in the Atlanta area, but Yura assured him that it was an error on his own part—he wasn't from the US and thought the job was in California.

Instead, Yura put him to work torching more cars. This time he wanted the destruction dedicated to Fox and Pinochet, the administrators of Hidden Answers, the dark web's censorship-free version of the Quora question-and-answer forum. Hidden Answers, and Fox and Pinochet in particular, had also regularly ridiculed Yura and the Besa Mafia site.

ThcJohn had no idea who Pinochet and Fox were or why he was dedicating his vandalism to them. In fact, he assumed that they, and Pirate.London, were upper management of the Besa Mafia family, who wanted to use the videos in marketing. Yura had mentioned needing to have the videos uploaded long enough that his 'bosses' could see them and verify them.

John needed the money and the credibility with the service, so he took on the jobs. Yura was somewhat more specific in his requirements this time as the first video had been shaky, dark and had barely passed muster.

For the first order, Yura demanded another random car, 'but this time use a small light to show spilling of gasoline,' he said, 'and please make sure you record the car burning at least 10 seconds with the paper shown on camera while flames on background.'

For the second, ThcJohn was to choose a random car in an isolated area—'not too cheap, not too expensive'—approach it in daylight ('but make sure there are no people around,' Yura suggested helpfully) and shoot it 10–15 times, making sure the holes were visible. 'Then run away,' Yura counselled, 'and the car should be empty, we don't want to kill anyone in this order.'

The specifics frustrated John, who negotiated Yura down to letting him torch the car by drilling a hole in the gas tank again (it could be explained away as an electrical fault) and beating the car with a baseball bat rather than shooting it, which Yura agreed to, provided he damaged windows, mirrors and lights, and spray painted 'Besa Mafia' all over the car's carcass.

Yura promised he would pay the going rate for the cars this time ($1200), but John relented a little. 'Since you are letting me pick random targets, I'll do 25% off, which comes to $900.'

They had a bit of back and forth about the sort of gun Yura would source and supply to him—it would be a major brand (a Glock or Colt, not some Chinese shit that jams for a Besa hitman) with a silencer. 'After we get you a gun you can do shootings of cars and people for us,' Yura assured him.

This time Besa Mafia was considerably more difficult to deal with. John burned the first car as ordered with a much better video (filmed in landscape instead of portrait as requested) and asked whether he would be paid for the first job right away—Bitcoin, after all, was all about instant payments. Yura told him that the two jobs were scheduled in the system as a single one to be paid together.

'I don't mean to be any fuss,' said John, 'but from what I understood they were to be two separate orders.' Yura assured him that the system was such that he couldn't do anything about it, but John would be paid after the second job.

The first car John trashed for the second job was an old piece of shit according to Yura ('it looks like you dragged it from a car cemetery') and not good enough for a warning; John would have to do it again.

John got a valuation on the next car, which he trashed and set alight by throwing gasoline over the seats and putting a match to it. A 2008 Mercedes-Benz E350—worth almost $17,000 according to the Kelley Blue Book valuation John included.

Yura agreed it was good enough.

'You'll be paid shortly,' he assured John.

Twice a day for the next couple of weeks, John followed up that payment. 'Sorry to be a bother,' he would say. Next time 'Sorry to flood your inbox . . .'

John needed the money badly, but Besa Mafia seemed to be having technical difficulties at their end.

It was annoying, but he would wait it out. He'd never had the prospect of so much easy money before.

A series of hitman errors

Stephen was also finding Besa Mafia's customer service and efficiency lacking.

A couple of days before Amy left for the competition, Besa Mafia had contacted Stephen and reminded him to ensure he was constantly surrounded by people on the 19th and 20th so he would have a solid alibi for when the job was done.

Stephen made sure to be seen in several places over the weekend. By the evening of the 20th he was keen to know whether he could relax yet. 'Haven't heard anything, do you know if its been done?' he messaged.

It had not. According to Yura, the hitman on the spot had called in to say that Amy wasn't the type to speed or put herself into vulnerable situations while driving. He could not put his chance of success at any better than 60 per cent.

There was another option, which was to engage a sniper whom Yura knew to be within a two-hour drive of where Amy was. The issue was, snipers were expensive—$30,000 was the going rate—but they had a100 per cent success rate. Because Stephen was already a customer and had been let down, Yura said he could give him a massive discount—just $12,000. 'Let me know if you are interested to upgrade to the sniper hitmen option for 10 bitcoin with 100% success rate, or if you would like to proceed with the current order for existing 15.5 Bitcoin paid, accident murder,' Yura said. 'Either way is fine with us; a third option, if you want to cancel the hit, we can send you the bitcoin back, as our customer satisfaction is the most important thing for us.'

Amy was on the way home by this time and Stephen didn't have the cash readily available. He held on to the hope that an accident could still be staged somewhere on the long drive home. 'If she stops and he can get her there then do that. If not, then I will take a refund and place a new order when I find out her new travel arrangements,' he said.

That evening Amy returned from a successful trip to Illinois happy and intact. There had been no car accident, nor any near miss as far as Stephen could tell.

Stephen lost no time getting back on to the computer in his basement. He was irritated, but mistakes happen and when you're talking about murder, it is better to err on the cautious side. As he fired up Tor and logged in to his hmamail account (hmamail stands for 'hide my ass' and promises anonymous email, but using the Tor browser added an extra layer of anonymity) he was already thinking ahead to Amy's next venture out of town.

Over the next few weeks, Stephen and Yura stayed in almost daily contact, discussing various options for murdering Amy. Stephen set up appointments for the hitman for at least five different days. Amy went travelling again (and Stephen gave into Michelle's curiosity and let her visit him at the marital home), but again arrived home unscathed. At one point the Allwines had a piano for sale, and Stephen suggested the hitman call to make an appointment to see it and do the job then. Each time, something prevented the hitman from getting to Amy.

During one conversation, Yura surprised Stephen with a question, 'We don't usually ask this, because we are not interested in the reason for why the people are killed, but is she your wife or some family member?'

Why would the coordinator of hitmen want to know something that personal? The whole idea of a dark web hitman was that none of the parties—hitman, Besa Mafia and client—knew who the others were, so if one was caught they could not point the finger at another.

'If she is your wife or some family member,' Yura went on, 'we can do it in your city as well; making it look like accident or robbery. Doesn't have to be away from home, you can leave the city too, when we plan to kill her at home.'

'Not my wife,' Stephen assured Yura, 'but I was thinking the same thing. How much would it be to kill her at home, and then burn the house?' Stephen went on to describe when Amy would be home or away, with an astounding amount of detail for somebody who was not her husband. He provided exact time slots for different days, and added, 'I know her husband has a big tractor, so I suspect that he has gas cans in the garage, but I do not know that for sure.'

He knew for sure.

Yura advised him that a murder plus arson at the Allwines' house would come with an additional ten Bitcoin cost, but assured him that, unlike the cheap option with a local thug, the plan had a 100 per cent success rate. Dogdaygod transferred $5000 worth of Bitcoin the next day, confirming by email that it had gone to Bitcoin address 1FUz1iECnhN2Kw8MUXhZWombbw1TCFVihb.

Yura appreciated the tipoff that there could be gas canisters in the garage—very helpful for the hitman, though he would bring his own just in case.

'We schedule the hit on Thursday at 12 PM,' Yura said.

On Thursday Stephen was out and about, making sure people would remember where he was and that he had definitely not been at home. Cottage Grove was not a particularly large town and news of a blaze big enough to encompass an entire house would not take long to spread. He heard no sirens, nor any gossip.

Unable to get to his basement and on to the Tor-protected computer, Stephen fired off messages from his phone: 'Do you have an update? I suspect the kid and dad will be home about 4 and then we will need to hold off.'

When Besa Mafia didn't reply, Stephen ventured home. Neither Amy nor her car were there and the house was standing with nary a puff of smoke in sight. The gas containers in the garage appeared untouched. Perhaps she hadn't come home and the hitman had waited in vain.

A call to Amy confirmed that she had, indeed, been home at the allotted time and all had been normal.

Stephen became exasperated. After all, he had paid out over $11,000 and he expected to be rid of his wife by now. Their son was now on spring break, which meant fewer opportunities to catch Amy alone. It looked like he might have to wait until the kid was back at school before trying again. He fired off a surly email to Besa Mafia, subject line: 'What Happened?' In the message he outlined his frustration.

Besa was contrite. They hadn't responded earlier because they were trying to get in touch with their man on the ground. 'I apologise he could not do the hit today, he had some problems with getting to the location,' Yura wrote. He insisted that the job was still live and next time, he was sure it would be done properly and dogdaygod would not be let down. 'Our customer satisfaction is very important for us; and we can give you a refund if you are not happy, but I do hope that you will provide us with a new date and hour . . . Sometimes things don't go as we want them or expect, but with perseverance we will do it; we just want to get it right.'

Stephen may have been frustrated, but he was getting into the territory of sunk costs now. Even though the money was being held in escrow, how sure could he be that it would be returned to him? Anyway, that still wouldn't fix his problem of a very alive Amy.

Remembering that Besa Mafia did not know his relationship to the 'target' he responded, 'Yes, I do want it done, but I have to pretend to be her friend to get this information and it's driving me crazy to be nice to her. I am also afraid that if I dig for information too many more times that it will look strange.' Nevertheless, he said he would find another day and time for the hit to finally be carried out.

'It looks like Monday might work,' he wrote later that day. 'It sounds like the dad is taking the kid somewhere. If so, early morning would probably be most likely for her to be home alone (8:30–10 or so). I will try to get more specifics on times, but let's plan that tentatively.'

'Ok, Monday morning is set,' responded Besa. 'This must work.'

Where's my money?

ThcJohn was getting more and more agitated. Not only had Besa Mafia not yet paid him the $1800 it owed for three more destroyed cars, it had failed to strip the audio and metadata from his videos before using them for its marketing. Instead, he was seeing his work circulating around the clear web with the incriminating evidence intact.

His entrée into the world of contract killing was not nearly as smooth or profitable as he had hoped. All he had to show for his work was $300 in Bitcoin, and some of that got lost in fees when cashing out.

He was still polite with Yura—after all, you probably shouldn't fuck with professional hitmen too much and Besa Mafia also employed expert hackers—when he chased up his payment. 'Sorry I don't mean to be rude, the time difference is complicating things. I will wait to hear back.'

Yura assured him that he would have his money soon and that his bosses at Besa Mafia were very pleased with ThcJohn and looked forward to working with him further. But his responses were taking longer to get to ThcJohn each time and the excuses were becoming less believable.

The next thing John knew, he was locked out of his account.

More delays for Stephen

Monday came and moved into night, with Stephen Allwine's house standing strong and Amy still happily busying herself with her dogs, church and community work. As she cooked the family dinner, Stephen stomped down to the basement, muttering about having to work overtime.

'Yes, this did not happened this morning,' Yura said, stating the obvious. Apparently, the most annoying thing had occurred; on his way to carry out the murder, the hitman had been stopped by police for a routine driver's licence and registration check. As luck would have it, the car had been reported stolen and the hitman was taken in for questioning.

Fortunately, the hitman's lawyer was able to come in and convince the police that the car had been purchased with good intentions and without the knowledge it was stolen property. Nevertheless, the hitman had to stay around to provide more statements, and would have to postpone the job for three or four days.

Alternatively, Yura had a different hitman in the area he could assign to the job. This time he would recommend that the contractor buy a cheap car rather than stealing one for the job. 'They don't use their real cars because if someone sees the license plates while they drive away, they could give it to police and they could just go pick up the hitman,' Yura explained.

The alternative hitman Yura had in mind also had an unregistered sniper rifle, and Besa Mafia could arrange for a fake ID for him with which to buy the car. However, it would come at a cost—an extra eight Bitcoin; four to buy a used car and four for a second hitter to help and ensure the job gets done.

If Stephen didn't want to do that, he could just wait for the other hitman to get released from custody and do the job 'in a week or two'.

Somewhat reluctantly Stephen elected to wait, but he was seething. He toyed with whether or not to express his feelings to Besa Mafia; he certainly didn't want to become a target himself. But Amy was sure to start to wonder why he was suddenly so interested in her exact movements every day, no matter how casually he worked it into the conversation.

Stephen decided it was time for a firmly worded letter. He spent a couple of days crafting the letter to ensure the right tone and to pepper it with just enough misinformation that Besa Mafia would still not know who they were dealing with:

Hello,

I was very disappointed that the hit did not happen Thursday and Monday as it was expected to. I realize that things happen, but this bitch has torn my family apart by sleeping with my husband (who then left me), and is stealing clients from my business. I have had to continue to act like her friend to get information and I cannot do it any more. I have gone out of my way to try and get you good information. I feel that I am at risk of being suspected if I ask too many more questions. You have had three good attempts at her and none of them have worked.

I liked the idea of shooting and fire, because I think it would look like a robbery and cover up, but I am at the point that I do not care how it is done. I believe that if I go about my regular routine that I will not be a suspect, if I stop asking questions and just act normal.

So, I would like to suggest that you have until May 1st to do it in whatever way works best for you and your people. Based on our previous conversations, if it is a straight shoot and kill then it is 13, if it looks like an accident then it is 15, and if it [is] a robbery and fire then it is 25. If it is not done in someway by May 1st then I would like my money back. Does that sound like enough time for you? I cannot get my hopes built up again like I did this weekend by having a date in mind and then have those hopes torn down when it does not happen. So I do not care about date or method, you have her picture and address, so you can tail her or do whatever you need to do to get the job done. I ask that you only get her and not the dad or kid as the kid is a friend of our child's and I do not want to leave him orphaned.

. . .

Thanks for your help with this, I need her out of my life, so I can move on.

Besa Mafia was sympathetic and did not seem to take offence at the tone of the letter. 'I am really sorry to hear what she did. Yes she is really a bitch and she deserve to die,' soothed Yura. He assured Stephen the hit would be done by 1 May and that he should stop digging for information—they had enough to go on with. He was sorry, but that was the price of doing business with low-level drug dealers and gang members. Unlike the movies, real hitman services rarely had military-trained hitters. 'For 35 Bitcoin we can assign the job to a ex-military from Chechnya. He has moved into the USA 4 years ago, and he does occasional murders for us, he use explosives and he is an expert in hand to hand combat. He is not hesitant like other gang members; he can kill with cold blood with guns or with bare hands; he doesn't think twice as other people do,' Yura said.

Stephen knew better than to throw good money after bad. 'We should stay with the current hitman and plan,' he said. He had little choice but to wait for the hitman to do his job.

Hitmen hacked

On 25 April 2016, shortly after the Allwines' house should have been burned to the ground, Chris Monteiro did his regular Google search for mentions of Besa Mafia on the internet in the preceding 24 hours. He was expecting the usual posts or articles from Besa Mafia's army of shills claiming that the dark web contract killing site was real and dangerous, or perhaps even another car torching video.

Instead, today, he hit the payload. Quietly uploaded in a pastebin was a file called 'Besa Mafia'. Pastebins are sites for storing text files, often used to share lines of source code among geeks. They are also popular for sharing the results of hacking activity in what are known as 'dumps'. Whoever had uploaded this particular dump, a hacker going by the name bRpsd, had not notified any websites, nor boasted in any forums of the job done.

As a teaser, the plain text dump listed what it claimed to be user-names, passwords, email addresses, dates of registration and account type (customer or killer). At the bottom, the post linked to additional files: victims.zip, msg.csv and orders.csv.

Chris was still not convinced that Besa Mafia had landed in his lap so easily. Victims.zip contained 59 images of potential targets. But it was the .csv files that yielded the most of interest. They opened into Excel spreadsheets. One file contained all of the emails sent to and from besa@sigaint.org, the official email address of the Besa Mafia website. The other contained details of orders placed through the website. Peppered throughout were details of Bitcoin transactions.

Even better, according to the pastebin, Besa Mafia's administrator's login details to the main website were:

username: admin
password: fucked.

Chris knew I would be interested in the dump. We had worked in tandem, our paths crossing often as we went about the task of disabusing the public of the notion that hitmen really operated on the dark web. Between us we wrote blogs and articles, responded to questions on reddit, and wrote essays on Quora, the popular community-led site where questions are asked and answers ranked according to the utility of the response and the expertise of the author. We would gang up on YouTubers spreading misinformation and pull apart tabloid articles that were big on hype and short on facts. We really were the buzzkills of the dark web, debunking myths of red rooms, gladiator fights to the death, snuff movies, murders for hire and dozens of other creepy stories that circulated the internet.

Chris shot me an email pointing to the dump. 'There's thousands of messages to go through,' he said, adding that he'd already informed the police, but nobody else yet.

As we combed through the emails looking for evidence of Bitcoin transactions, which we could cross-reference with the blockchain to confirm they were real, the magnitude of the operation began to dawn on us. We needed to get going quickly if we were to be the first to break the news of the true story behind Besa Mafia.

Stephen writes a review

Stephen couldn't believe the bad luck he was having with what should have been a straightforward hit. Useless cheap gang junkies who couldn't pull off a simple car accident. Lazy bastards who just didn't turn up to work on the day.

He was still reading rave reviews on reddit and other sites about the success people were having with Besa Mafia. He read about a big-time drug dealer who was busted and imprisoned thanks to evidence from his former partner. When he was released after four years, he wanted revenge, but didn't want to get his hands dirty. 'The same day I had specified for them to kill him, I got a message with a picture of his body shot dead,' the lengthy review said. It linked to a news story about the death of the target.

Another testimonial was from a disgruntled employee who had a hit taken out on the boss who fired him. There was the young guy who got beaten up by the jealous boyfriend of a girl he was dancing with and retaliated by getting Besa Mafia to give the bully a harsher beating. According to the accompanying news story, the guy had to have face reconstruction surgery.

Then there was the reddit testimonial that started with 'This should have been a great day, but instead was a horror day; my girlfriend was raped by a Giovanni, a colleague and a scum from her workplace . . .' Besa Mafia came to the rescue and Giovanni will not be raping anyone ever again.

There were also sites dedicated to fighting Besa Mafia, unmasking their operation and shutting them down. On these sites, law enforcement officials and academics talked about measures they should take to stop the killings; they were most concerned that murder for hire used to be available only to the select few who were willing to enter the criminal world, but was now available to anyone.

Thanks to the internet, innocent wronged people had their own opportunity for the sort of revenge usually only available to hardened criminals.

Besa Mafia rocks. My daughter was raped 1 year ago by a jerk who managed to get minimum jail time with a good lawyer. After he came out from jail he was harassing my daughter again and threatening he would rape her again. I would have killed the bastard myself but I didn't want to get caught and do prison time leaving my daughter unprotected. I hired a killer from Besa Mafia and he did the job with no incident.

Stephen was frustrated that everyone except him was having great experiences with Besa Mafia. He decided it was time to set the record straight and wrote a post on reddit under his Besa Mafia username dogdaygod, criticising the service he had received from the most profitable dark web contract killing service that ever existed.

A few hours later, when Stephen logged on to the dark web, Yura had already seen the review. One of his staff had brought it to his attention.

Yura remained polite with Stephen, but firm. Delete the comment or there would be consequences.

Sifting through the data

Chris Monteiro and I, working on opposite sides of the world, set to work sifting through the thousands of messages sent to and from the Besa Mafia website.

We read applications from men who claimed extensive military training and wanted to become hired guns for Besa Mafia. OnionKiller stated in his application that he had served five years in special forces as a weapons sergeant, had served in every military hotspot in the world and had 50 confirmed kills; he also had a cache of unregistered weapons at his disposal. As well as being willing to kill anyone, even if they were accompanied by an army, he claimed his grandparents were Albanian, in the hope it would give him an extra edge.

OnionKiller wasn't particularly happy to be given a test job of shooting up a car ('I understand you are not some punk teenager from the streets,' Yura told him, 'however it is our internal policy to give a simple test order to all applicants').

They came from all over the world, and most had far less impressive resumés than OnionKiller. There was Gegren from Moldova and Gostman from Indonesia. TriggerMan was looking for work in Norway: 'I am good with my hands and with a knife but I can also use long ranged weapons. I do not have any military training, but I am quite good at different tactics. I can provide a quick and clean death for anyone, but not children under the age of 16, and any top 10 politicians. My prices can be different, but not less than about $3000 for a kill, and about $200 for a beating.' Others were succinct and to the point. 'Countries: Spain in Catalonia; services: killing and beating; Price: Minimum 100. I have no military training,' wrote equalizer1938.

Locks67 of London, England, wanted to start off with beatings only, and wasn't ready to take on any jobs involving killing 'at this time'. Bettercor would take on jobs in Hungary, Germany and Austria, and was an expert at hiding the body afterwards.

On the customer side, we read tales of jealousy, greed and revenge from the hundreds who signed up to the site hoping for a unique fix to their problem.

There was the guy who wanted to kill somebody who was currently in prison, and the other who had read the FAQ and wanted to know just what qualified as a 'kid'—would they kill, say, a fifteen-year-old for the right price?

Junkie900 in Canada asked for a price on a murder that would look like an accident: 'It is an old woman with a heart condition,' Junkie said, 'she goes around the neighborhood and talks about us. She is a hater and she is very bad woman.'

A frightening number of people requested information about acid attacks, and those often seemed particularly sadistic: 'The strongest acid you can obtain in the largest amount possible should be thrown at her directly in the face. She has to be severely deformed, unrecognizable . . . Please make this attack really ruin her life that she will never be able to function normally again and be undesirable to any man.'

One fellow in India, Hero, wanted to kill the person who was the 'reason my sis died' but was a little cautious. The last three hitmen he tried to hire ran off with the money he paid up front: 'I understand your concern,' he told Besa Mafia as he tried to negotiate for payment after the fact, 'but you also need to understand my point as well. As already said I have already wasted my hard earned money 3 Times as people fooled me as they said they will completed job but after taking the money they ran away.' He had previously tried to hire two hitmen from hiredkiller.wordpress.com and one from LinkedIn. All of them emerged untrustworthy, so it meant he was a little more reticent to front the cash (or Bitcoin). He eventually relented and paid for the hit to be carried out by the reputable firm of Besa Mafia.

Some people used anonymous Tor-based email accounts like Sigaint, but others were happy to provide their Yahoo or Gmail addresses. Nobody used PGP encryption, the most basic security precaution of anyone trying to procure illegal services on the dark web.

We saw the orders for the car torchings carried out as warnings to bloggers and site administrators who had disparaged Besa Mafia. I thought it interesting that the hack had come hot on the heels of the torchings dedicated to Fox and Pinochet, the joint administrators of Hidden Answers. Hidden Answers was a popular corner on the dark web for users to seek to hook up with hackers, or to get small illegal jobs done. I wondered if the timing was coincidence.

'The hack was carried out by a Hidden Answers user,' Pinochet said in response to my message to him. 'No admins were involved.' As an aside, I pointed out that his site still ran paid advertisements for Besa Mafia. 'Anyone is allowed to put an ad up on the site, as long as they pay for it,' Pinochet told me.

One of the most striking stories was that of dogdaygod, a lady who wanted a hit carried out on a woman who 'tore my family apart by sleeping with my husband and is stealing clients from my business', and wanted it to look like an accident. She had paid approximately $13,000 so far, the most recent instalment just a couple of days ago, but the hit was yet to happen.

I had several articles lined up, ready to be published as soon as we got word from the law enforcement agencies around the world that

Chris and I had contacted, or somebody else came across the dump and found the story, whichever happened first.

Amy lives on

Stephen was getting frustrated, but he was no idiot. He took down the negative review as per Yura's instructions. 'Comment is deleted, but I NEED you to be successful,' he said belligerently. He promised Besa Mafia there would be an extra 25 Bitcoin—over $20,000—after the fact if the murder was done soon ('if you could get us 10 now and 15 after . . .' said Yura). Increasingly desperate, Stephen sent over another four Bitcoin and said he would try and find the rest, but insisted the job be done as soon as possible.

Two days later, Amy was still alive and blissfully unaware she was the target of her husband's greed and hatred. Stephen, meanwhile, decided another firmly worded letter was in order, this time documenting exactly what had gone wrong with his experience with Besa Mafia so far:

> Orginally on Feb 16 (over 2 months ago) you said that it would be 13 btc to have a close range shot (shot going to or coming from her car)

> Then you said that hit and run would be 15 btc.

> "Yes, 15 Bitcoins for hit with a car and ensure fatality."

> You then ensured me that this would happen on Mar 19th

> You indicated that she was being followed, but he did not have an opportunity with the car. The accident was a secondary objective not the primary objective. It is hard to believe that in

that weekend there was not some opportunity to do the close range shot.

You then recommended a sniper and I said that was fine.

You said it would be an additional 10 btc

"Let me know if you are interested to upgrade to the sniper hitmen option for 10 bitcoin with 100% success rate"

At the time I did not have it, but I have since added that and more.

You followed that with the option of the home

"To kill her at home, and burn the house afterwards would be 10 extra Bitcoins, and the success rate is 100%."

Indicating that both of these are 100% success rate.

We have a 0% success rate now with 2 different teams, and being at this for a month.

Mar 22nd was a fail

Mar 26th was a fail—you said our guy will be ready at 8:30

You had from then until April 12 to follow her and do a close shot

You indicated "So 13, 13 or 14 is the date when she will die." (I think you meant the 12)

April 12 was a fail

April 13 was a fail

April 14 was a fail

You said "however if you could get us 10 now, and 15 after, I am sure I could assign a different team on the job that would get the job completed tomorrow"

You were sure you could get someone that could do it on the 15th.

I did not have 10, but I had 4+ and you were going to cover the rest to get us to that mark of 10 to get someone that you were SURE could do it on the 15th

You said "yes this should be done today or latest tomorrow"

April 15 was a fail

You said "[i]f you can add the difference of 5.6 Bitcoin; as you sent 4.4 and about 10 was the difference to get this excellent team assigned, i can get them assigned and they would do the job within a day guaranteed"

Based on our previous agreement you were going to front the 5.6 btc to get the 'excellent' team, but apparently that did not happen.

Again on the 18th you claimed "Yes, we will be succesful"

You said that you asked your team "to make a good plan this time to succeed without any trouble or delays" and "I asked them to complete it in max 24 hours"

Yet here we are at the end of another day with another broken promise.

Please remember that the house, the accident, etc is all secondary goals. The primary goal is her and has always been her. I think people are getting so tied up in the secondary goals that they are forgetting the primary goal.

I do not care how it is done, but based on our discussions over the last 2 months, I believe that I have added enough for

– close shot

– hit and run with car

– sniper

– burn house

– better team

– excellent team (with you filling in the other 5.6 as we discussed)

And yet it is still not done. What are you going to do to get the job done and get it done right?

Yura finally seemed contrite. 'I need to apologise. You are right, this has been dragging quite a long time, and needs to be completed asap.' Yura launched into a lengthy litany of explanations and excuses for the dismal customer service. 'So, long story short,' he finished up, 'the failure so far was because the teams so far did not have a lot of experience, and because maybe your target was lucky.' Dogdaygod had three options: continue to wait for the inexperienced team to get their shit together; cough up more Bitcoin for an expert team; or take a full refund.

'This is an easy job, which is why I do not understand why it takes so long,' wrote Stephen. There was no reason, he thought, that the basic team couldn't get it right. Maybe they just needed more explicit instructions.

'She has a class from 9:00–10:30, there is something at her son's school at 11:30 (so she would be home from 10:30–11:30 . . . your guy could watch for all the cars to leave and then follow her back to the house), she has to be back for a class at 1:30 (which means that she should be home about 12 or so, he could sit at the end of the road and watch for her green van to pull in the driveway and do it), then she should be home about 3 or so in the afternoon (once again, sit at the end of the road and watch for her van). She said her husband is out running errands tomorrow.' There. He couldn't be more explicit than that.

Before hitting Send he added: 'I want her gone, I NEED her gone. Please help me.'

The truth about Besa Mafia

Chris and I waited, and waited. In the meantime, we snuck into the site via a back door created by an acquaintance of Chris after gaining initial entry to the site using the information in the dump that the administrator's password was 'fucked'. That meant we were able to watch new messages come and go, adding to what we had already seen thanks to the original hack.

By 14 May, three whole weeks after the initial leak, Chris had received no news from the law enforcement agencies he had contacted. He had tried LAPD general enquiries, and was bounced from section to section until he was finally put through to their detective division. The detectives referred him to a local cyber support division that said it was unable to help. He tracked down the LA computer crimes unit, and finally found a person who was interested in the unusual murder conspiracy component, but felt this was better dealt with via the FBI. Chris tried FBI cybercrime, where an associate in the LA field office seemed sympathetic and competent, but suggested it would be better routed via the NCA (National Crime Agency) or UK law enforcement.

Meanwhile I had seen links to the hack pop up on reddit and a couple of other sites, and I knew it was just a matter of time before the media got hold of it and ran a story. 'Now that it's been reported in a few places, I'm going live with my blog,' I told Chris.

I had received a response from the Australian Federal Police to my email to them about the Australian targets within the leak. They could not have been less interested. 'Your questions would be best placed with Scamwatch,' they wrote.

It was a fair call, because when I hit 'upload' for my article, 'The Curious Case of Besa Mafia', the whole truth was revealed.

Besa Mafia was a scam.

Nobody had been killed. Nobody had been raped or beaten up. Nobody had ever been refunded his or her money. The only criminal activity carried out on behalf of Besa Mafia was the torching of four cars by someone called ThcJohn. And even he had been scammed; Yura had only paid him for the first one at the discount rate of $300.

The scam was carried out in a way that would make a Nigerian prince proud. Anyone who provided Bitcoin was strung along for as long as Yura could manage, upsold on services and fleeced of increasing amounts of money.

Poor old 'Hero' was scammed again—a fourth-time loser. He handed over money and even provided his phone number, which was kept in the logs. Others lost varying amounts before finally understanding that they had been conned. Many were yet to realise the truth. The thousands of emails were full of people either clinging to the belief that their order would be fulfilled, or confident they would receive their money back guarantee. To his credit, Yura was ingenious in the excuses he came up with and prolific in his responses to customers.

When one customer, kbgmkn, suspected after half a dozen attempts that the hitman wasn't really on site, the customer provided the address of a gas station and wrote: 'I want a picture of the cornwallis street sign showing the intersection with a very small portion of a finger showing on the right hand side.'

Yura obliged with a picture, but kbgmkn was less than impressed: 'Ok . . . this is obviously a Google Street view with a photo shopped finger added in.' Unperturbed, Yura went with it. The hitman had fooled him as much as he had fooled the client, but he would get a new team onto it right away. He used the opportunity to try and upsell kbgmkn to the sniper option 'to ensure 100% success'.

The only other people to ever get paid by Besa Mafia were from Yura's army of freelancers—cheap labour employed to write testimonials and stories verifying the legitimacy of Besa Mafia, which they placed all over the web. They were recruited through online content mills, such as Upwork and XBTFreelancer (which accepted Bitcoin as payment). Of course, Yura did with them what he did with ThcJohn: paid for the first piece of work and then commissioned much more, for which he never paid.

Like any good dark-web service, Besa offered incentives to bring in potential customers. If someone came to the site using a particular referral link, Besa said they would pay the referrer 10 per cent of any money received for hits. That enticed people to spam forums with their referral links but, not surprisingly, no such money was ever paid out.

In addition, if anyone wanted to sign on as a hitman, they needed to pay one Bitcoin into the Besa account to prove they weren't 'kids playing a joke'. But if they couldn't afford that, they could earn credits instead by either torching cars or touting for Besa and writing stories on high-traffic websites about their personal experiences in ordering successful hits.

Another potential thug, 'Joe', also recorded himself setting a car alight dedicated to Besa Mafia. 'Im able to kill so good, i do this job for over 8 year. i wait to know something. Think that this car is inside an house parking during the night. Tell me if i need to do others . . .' He managed to get some good shots of the very distinctive tattoos on his hands. He was still waiting for his first job.

Everything pointed to Besa Mafia being an operation run by a single person somewhere in Eastern Europe, most likely Romania. The server had leaked a Romanian IP and, with Yura's track record for security, it was doubtful that he had spoofed it to throw people off the scent.

What was also apparent was that this scam was extremely profitable. Because of the nature of Bitcoin, we were able to check the blockchain to verify if payments were made to the wallet addresses supplied by Yura to customers. In less than six months, Besa Mafia had taken in well over $100,000.

I understood Australian authorities not being interested, because there was no evidence that anyone making enquiries about Australian targets had gone so far as to pay Bitcoin. Most people never got beyond the enquiry stage, and it was reasonable to assume that a good proportion of people who contacted the site were curious about the murder-for-hire claims and had no intention of ever placing a hit on anyone.

In other countries, however, people paid real money hoping for real hits to be carried out, and some of the amounts were substantial. That had to mean that the targets in those situations were in real danger. We could only assume that the applicable agencies in the countries in question were investigating and had no intention of sharing any details of those investigations with a couple of bloggers.

Stephen gets suspicious

Stephen should have been ready to throw in the towel right around the time of the hack. By this time, he had over $13,000 in Bitcoin held by the site. Yet again, there was no murder and nothing but excuses from Besa Mafia, but he persisted. 'OK, it looks like nothing was done on it today,' he said after the hitman failed to find an opportunity during a week when Amy was home alone while Stephen and their son were away. 'If it is not done tomorrow (Thursday) then I want some evidence either picture or description that proves that they made an effort and that they have been tracking her. I am not convinced that anyone is actively working on the order.'

Stephen checked in halfway through the week and then again the night before he was due to return home, reminding Besa Mafia that it had just one more day within this particular window of opportunity. He lamented that the promised 24/7 support was lacking and it didn't look like Yura was forwarding all the information Stephen was providing to the hitman on site.

'I just talked with her, which means it is not done yet. NOT GOOD, but it looks like the husband was slowed down and will not be in until about midnight, so it looks like there is a little more time, but not much,' he wrote. Yura assured Stephen he would forward that information to the hitter who was watching the house.

When Stephen came home, Amy was as alive as ever. There were no suspicious or unfamiliar cars at the end of their dead-end street. Finally, Stephen had had enough. 'That's it, your local guys suck,' he fumed, and advised he had initiated a refund request through the site. 'I expected more from you and the people that you contract with.

I am not impressed with your organization's ability to hire quality individuals to do an easy task.' He left the window open for a future engagement, providing he could get the funds to hire the high-quality people, but in the meantime, he needed his money back. 'I hope you guys have not screwed my business by letting this bitch live,' he said.

That would show them!

The next day Stephen received a response to his refund request.

Hi,

I am sorry to dissapoint you.

Unfortunattely, this site has been hacked. We got all customer and target information and we will send it to to law enforcement unless you send 10 bitcoin to this address 1H1pNNP6dqWuk9H3EKfGjFTc7grasd9D2X

We injected mallware and javascript into the site and are able to dox the customers (find out who they are) by expert IP and proxy analisis and this hacked site uses javascript to extract personal information from the user computer.

If you want to avoid us give your info and target info to law enforcement, please send us 10 Bitcoin to the address above

Once we receive the additional money, we will delete your account, all messages, and all information about you and the target.

If you don't send the additonal money, we will send all information to law enforcement and you might be arrested, ordering murder and paying for murder can get you in jail for a long time you have one week to send the money to the above address, or you go to jail, we have extracted everything from your computer and have complex info on you along with all proofs that you ordered the hit, purchased bitcoin, sent bitcoins to the address of besa mafia, and provided target details, this should get you in jail if you don't pay up

if you say you don't have the money, please borrow it, if you can't borrow it then you go jail

please do not post anything about us blackmailing you anywhere, if you do, we will immediately send your information to law enforcement

let me know

Adding insult to injury

'We don't usually ask this,' wrote BesaAdmin to every person who seemed serious about carrying out a hit, 'because we don't care why you want a hit, but are you the target's [husband/wife/jilted lover]?'

Sadly for the hapless would-be killers, once BesaAdmin felt they had drained as much Bitcoin as they could get from them (or if they placed an order without paying), they passed on the details to law enforcement, using the email address janeblondiesexy@gmail.com. Many of the email exchanges contained enough detail to identify both victim and the person who wanted them gone.

User 'xtyndtu1QWdg' was a Texan who contacted the site with a request to kill a woman that he claimed was his wife. The details provided included the fact that 'She is alone in her car in a small town consistently of Friday nights,' after her shift ended at a party supply store known for its terrible customer service. He provided the number plate of her tan-coloured 2010 Nissan Murano. The marriage was over, he said, and his wife was now abusing their two little ones. She had also frozen all of their accounts, he claimed, so he would not be able to withdraw the money until after the 'accident'—however, he didn't think that would be a problem, as Besa Mafia obviously would be able to identify and find him if he failed to pay and he would never be stupid enough to do that.

Although this person claimed to be the husband of the woman targeted, the details were so unnecessarily explicit—a simple Google search immediately brought up the full name, photograph and address of the person who it would appear was placing the order—that it could have plausibly been a frame-up job.

Yura tried his usual tactics to extract money—any money—from the Texan, including reducing the amount required up front and suggesting sources for loans. Or, he said, 'you can pretend to be depressed and go to a casino, buy chips for $2000 ... play $200, cash out the remaining when going out of the casino, drink some bears [*sic*] and claim to have your wallet stolen in some public place.' The Texan stuck to his guns and insisted no payment was possible while his wife was monitoring the accounts. He also said he was in contact with other 'individuals who would benefit the same' if he could not come to an agreement with Besa.

Yura reduced the price to $500 up front, but xtyndtu1QWdg advised that he would use a local alternative.

'Don't use local alternatives. All local alternatives are undercover cops, you will be arrested,' warned Yura. The Texan said he would be happy to meet Besa Mafia's hitter in person—'we could pre-script a conversation, but not discuss the job'—but still would not put forward any money up front.

Obviously, as Yura had no hitman to send, they were at an impasse. Yura wished him luck, told him he had erased all traces of their conversation, and gave him a few tips on working with a professional hitman:

I wish you best lock [luck], and make sure:

- he is not an undercover cop

- he has an unregistered guy [gun]

- he cleans the guy and bullets with a cotton cloth against fingerprints and any dna traces

- he has a getaway stolen car; witnesses could see his car model and collor if is not stolen and could be traced back to him

- he is not seen by witnesses while he waits in the car to see her

- he has good aim to hit from first shot, because after shooting everybody has the reflex to hide down and seconds shoots might be harder to hit

- glass might deviate the trajectory of low caliber bullets so if he shots through glass at an angle and not perpendicular on glass he might miss

- he should have somenone to help him and make sure there are no accidental police in near in the area, you might even do a fake call from paid phone to 112 reporting some crime to a different address, to have local cars of police going to that direction, away from your place

Because when shooting happens, you might have police cars coming to place very fast, if he doesn't have a silencer

Very soon afterwards, Yura received an email from someone called 'Guido' who was using an email address from Tor-protected anonymous email provider Sigaint, claiming to be FBI, and further claiming that the local Texas police had forwarded them intel about a potential murder-for-hire plot in the town where xtyndtu1QWdg lived. 'Can you provide us with the customer's intent, his contact information as well as his validity in meeting your fake hitmen,' the email said.

Yura was quick to comply. 'We receive orders to kill people from all over the world,' he explained, 'however our site is fake and we don't have any hitmen. We forward the orders to police departments where the targets are located … We are a team of computer programmers living in Europe, and we made this website as a honeypot for criminals, to fight crime and criminals.'

He provided Guido with the email address used to sign up to the site, the name, address and photo of the target, and the information that he had already forwarded everything to the local Texas police.

Yura then asked Guido for an official FBI.gov address, so that he could forward all future details of Texas hits directly. 'Unfortunately the "official" e-mail addresses use our real names, which we're not going to provide on here,' Guido responded. After more prodding by Yura, Guido provided a generic Dallas FBI address.

Yura had a lightbulb moment: FBI would be unlikely to use a Sigaint address (unless they were pretending *not* to be FBI). 'Guido' was most likely xtyndtu1QWdg checking whether Besa Mafia had really erased all of his information. Yura shot off another email to Guido:

I am a former member of Besa, and ex-member of their cyber team.

I don't work with them any more, but I still have access to their system from a backdoor, the other cyber team members miht find it and remove it soon.

Please notice that Besa is doing real killing for hire, but they are also working with law enforcement to keep it looking like it is fake with the purpose to avoid the site being tracked down.

Their strategy is to do real murders for customer who pay, while giving in customer information who don't send payment to law enforcement, to claim they are fake and that they give all information in.

Hitmen can also sign up, those who send deposit of 1 BTC get real orders, while those who sign up and don't send deposit are given to law enforcement.

They are keeping in touch with several police departments and law enforcements, from several countries, I am sending out this message to all known accounts on Besa Mafia to be of law enforcement

Please be aware that only information from customer who do not pay are given to police.

Customers who pay have their orders completed, with 80% going to hitman and 20% to besa mafia marketplace

They claim they work with law enforcement and that they are fake, but they advice customers not to give their real info and not to meet hitman.

They only give out the stupiest customers to law enforcement, those who are stupid to provide lots of info and who don't pay, this way they mentain the look of fake service that works with law enforcement and this way they don't get stut down.

Hope this message gets to be read by all law enforcements who have accounts on this site before my access gets removed.

I moved out from them and am on a runaway from them, if Besa Mafia finds me they will kill me

Stephen has a new idea

Stephen was done with Besa Mafia. He realised he would not be getting his refund, but he wasn't stupid enough to stump up a further ten Bitcoin to pay the ransom that Besa Mafia had tried to extort from him. He was confident that he had peppered his communications with enough red herrings that the trail would never lead back to him.

He was now out of pocket a substantial amount of money and his problem—Amy—was still alive and under the impression her marriage was as happy as the rest of her life.

Despite his bad experience with Besa Mafia, Stephen still had faith in the dark web. He used reddit to research the current major darknet markets and settled on one of the biggest, Dream Market. Dream was the main competitor to market-leader AlphaBay at the time.

Stephen was used to being dogdaygod now, so he used the same handle to sign up to the Dream forums. His first post was in the Marketplace discussion forum:

Looking for drug dealer physically located in Minneapolis area

Looking for a partner for a job, need to be willing to stay anonymous and be paid by bitcoin.

As he waited for a response to his request, he made a second post in the same section:

Scopolamine

Does anyone have Scopolamine for sale?

Scopolamine is a drug used to treat motion sickness, but is dangerous in large doses. It is sometimes referred to as the 'zombie drug', as it is said to induce amnesia when too much is ingested. It can make the user so drowsy that they are incapacitated, and is said to make unsuspecting victims highly susceptible to suggestion.

Although Stephen didn't get a public response to his first request (good hitmen are hard to find, even on the dark web), he received two replies to his request for Scopolamine. The first anticipated that it was to be used for no good:

There is a seller, but avoid that shit mate. It's dangerous as fuck and you WILL kill someone.

However, the second response provided Stephen with the name of a seller of the drug:

Yeah bro try [vendor] p3nd8s on dream but be careful that shit will make you gladly hand over your kidneys and have no idea where why or who to when you come back to reality

It is unlikely that Stephen intended to gain first-hand knowledge of the effects of the drug. He had a source now. He had a backup plan.

A message from Besa Mafia

I probably should have known that even a fake hitman would not be very happy with losing a source of income that was bringing him in hundreds of thousands of dollars simply for writing some emails.

It was a dream job, the kind of riches that all those 'work from home' advertisements promise but never deliver. Yura was not about to let it slip away without a fight.

I followed up my initial blog post—which received a lot of attention from the mainstream media—with three more posts going into different facets of the Besa Mafia operation. Meanwhile, the UK's *Daily Mirror* interviewed Chris Monteiro, who supplied the newspaper with the entire database. The news spread about the dark web murder-for-hire site that was scamming its customers.

Yura went into damage control. He set his army of shills onto the various stories, writing rebuttals on all those that had a commenting feature, saying that the leak, not Besa Mafia, was fake. Yura himself bombarded reddit, Quora and my own site in an effort to discredit Monteiro, me and the hacker who leaked the information in the first place.

What he didn't know was that we were still being fed information by the hacker who was monitoring Besa Mafia's email account. As far as Yura was aware, we only had information up to the date of the database leak. We were one step ahead of him the whole time.

Yura was fighting an uphill battle. Not everybody was aware of the hack, but some of his potential customers got wind of it and those who had paid money started demanding refunds. In between emails looking for his services, Yura had to field trolls laughing at him for being exposed.

One day I received an email to my public email address from an unfamiliar name. The grammar and syntax, however, was unmistakable. Yura was reaching out.

'Please do not publish this email, is intended only for you,' it started. 'Yes, Besa Mafia is a scam. However, I consider that is not morally wrong to scam criminals who want to hire hitmen.'

He had a point. As the American showman P. T. Barnum famously said, you can't con an honest man. Yura's income came solely from would-be murderers. Yura had obviously spent some time on this email, because it was long and listed the benefits of his site, numbered for ease of reference. His argument boiled down to this: he was stopping crime by depleting the resources of would-be murderers. 'Our policy is to ask more money and more money and more money until they have none left,' he told me, in case I had missed his business strategy. In reality, he reasoned, his murder-for-hire site was saving lives, because he took all the money that might otherwise go to real hitmen.

'No human being or animal has been ever hurted by our site,' he said, but admitted, 'a few cars have been burned to make the service appear legit'. He told me that my articles would help criminals get away with murder and implored me to take them down. 'One guy sent us $20,000 to have a kid of 16 years old killed,' he said, offering to send proof via the blockchain. 'If he paid $20,000 to some gang member in his neigberhood, some desperate gang member in debt, he might have got the murder done. Because he sent the money to us, the kid who is the target will not be dead.

'You are stopping scamming, but you are helping murder and murderers. Scamming is not ok, but murder is not either. Which is worse?'

Again, he had a point and I was softening to this earnest, polite plea to my better nature. He told me he passed on information about the people who signed up to commit murders to the police. He also told me it was irresponsible of me to make public the sort of money he was earning, because it might encourage somebody to start up a similar site for real if they saw how much money there was to be made.

'I kindly ask you to remove your articles and allow us to keep scamming bad people who want to do murder,' he concluded. 'Go expose those who do credit card fraud, or fake shops, or teach people how to be secure from credit card and phishing if you want to help. But leave the fake hitman online alone, they are actually helping.'

He signed off with a request I get back to him as soon as possible.

Meanwhile, Yura was still doing damage control, firing off emails to the customers who had found out about the leak. He decided the smart thing to do would be to lay the blame at the feet of those who were most adamantly reporting on the scam:

Hi,

Please know the previsous message was not from me, it was from a different admin.

I will tell you the truth.

We were 3 admins and founders of this project, me (Yura), Eileen O from allthingsvice.com and Chris Monteiro from pirate.london.

When we first started Besa Mafia, I wanted to make it real marketplace where hitmen can join and provide services; but I asked Chris Monteiro by nickame of Deku-Shrub from pirate.london to do the programming of the site as he had deep knowleage of deep web

He did the site, and we also asked Eileen O from Australing, blogger allthingsvice.com to help with promoting she hired army of shills to promote on freelancer.com

I wanted to have things for real, have killers, gang members, and everything real, but Eileen a girl saith that we should just scam people, and Chris also wanted beating and fire but no murder

So, we got lots of customers and lots of gang members signing up, gang members wanted to do murder for money so we gave them orders from customers

In february when the first murders hapened, Eileen and Chris got afraid and wanted to quit on the project, so they published an old version of database with important customers removed, all murders removed, etc, to say is scam to backoff police and to appear that they are against

Your money are stuck, you can ask Eileen and Chris to unblock it, but they refuse to admit they are fonders of the site . . .

And they have access on the site and pretend to be hacker and they ask for more money.

don't send.

The FBI comes to Cottage Grove

In the spring of 2016, the FBI contacted the Cottage Grove Police Department with the startling news that an individual had attempted to procure a hitman to kill Amy Allwine.

Threat reports were pretty common in state police departments, especially via anonymous text messages or the internet but not hit-men-for-hire. On 31 May 2016, Cottage Grove PD's Detective Terry Raymond accompanied FBI Special Agent Silkey on a visit to the Allwines' home. Amy was not at home at the time, so they made arrangements for her to attend the police station the next day.

Stephen and Amy Allwine were shocked. They had no idea who might be threatening her; Amy had no enemies. She never even had disagreements with anyone, personal or business.

The FBI made some discreet enquiries of people who knew Amy, to find out if there was anyone who might wish her harm. The overwhelming response was that she was a lovely person, open and friendly, with not an enemy in the world. Everyone they spoke to was adamant that there was no way Amy was having an extramarital affair.

The police left it at providing Amy with their business cards and advising her to install security measures at her residence and report any suspicious activity. Stephen, ever the attentive husband, set about installing an alarm on the secluded house, and put new codes on the garage door.

They became more vigilant about their surroundings and in June 2016 Amy called the police to report a suspicious blue van parked at the end of the street. Police attended, but it turned out to be somebody who worked nearby taking a nap.

Apparently concerned about the FBI visit and unanswered questions, Stephen decided on a further, more drastic measure. Although the Allwines already had a shotgun and two rifles, on 22 June 2016, he applied for a permit to purchase a handgun and received his permit to carry on 10 August 2016. He and Amy went shopping for personal protection and settled on a Springfield 9mm. They kept the gun in a handgun case under Amy's side of the bed, and the key inside a cupboard next to the bathtub in the ensuite bathroom.

As often happens with these things, Stephen and Amy soon became lax in setting the alarm codes. They resumed their day-to-day lives, Stephen still private, quiet and spending time in his basement and Amy filling her life with family, church and dogs. Although she confided in her best friend and the two of them puzzled over who could possibly be behind the plot, Amy kept the incident to herself, or downplayed its seriousness to those who knew. From the outside, nobody could tell anything was wrong. Amy continued to be the same bubbly, happy person when she attended her regular meetings with the dog community. She still had a marriage that was the envy of many. Inside, she was devastated that, as she put it to her sister, there was someone who thought the world would be better off without her. And she had no idea who.

Yura and me

After his initial email, I asked Yura if he would be open to doing an interview with me. I would not, I told him, remove the article I had written, but would be happy to give him the opportunity to state his case. There was some merit in his claims of providing a community service and, as far as we could tell, all of the targets on the Besa Mafia site were alive and well.

Yura and I started up a civil dialogue. The Besa Mafia brand, he conceded, had taken a hit that it would not be able to recover from. However, he had an idea for a new site: 'It will be a darknet marketplace where gang members can signup to provide services, and customers can purchase hitmen services,' he said, apparently oblivious to the fact that he was describing an exact replica of the Besa Mafia site. 'Of course, it will be a fake one; because I do not support killing or harm to human beings, nor to animals :)'

Yura offered payment to take down the articles I had already posted and promised to make it lucrative for me if I were to work with him and write new articles stating that both Besa and his new site were real, and that I had been fooled with a fake hack. 'I cannot change my articles as you wish, not even for money,' I told him. 'All I can offer you is your chance to participate in an interview where you come clean.' I was somewhat sceptical that any cash would be forthcoming for my efforts even if I had been inclined to play along.

We reached an impasse. Yura had been making a tidy profit from his scam and he was not at all happy to have the golden goose stop laying. The email messages became more frequent and would vary wildly between trying to convince me he was doing a noble thing, to denying the site was fake at all, to veiled threats.

After I posted another article about one of his scammed customers, I received an email that said: 'Thank you for a nice article. I hope you won't mind if we publish several articles like this one.' Yura linked me to a newly created site, "Besamafiamurderforhireblog" which I couldn't resist clicking on:

Besa Mafia admins exposed, after FBI closes on them

Chris Monteiro aka Deku-Shub and Eileen Ormsby, the owners of Besa Mafia are trying to appear clean claiming that the site is just a scam, with no harm intended or actual kiling done

The article claimed Monteiro and I were part of the original Besa Mafia team, made a healthy profit from it, but decided to split following an argument with our other partner, Yura. True to his word, Yura began posting his fake news prolifically around the internet, with over 30 sites popping up over a couple of days, dedicated to telling 'the truth' about Besa Mafia ownership.

'Haha that's awesome! I have tweeted it and put it on Reddit for you :)' I told Yura after the first one.

'Good,' he responded. 'I am considering donating the website [Besa Mafia] to some new owner; he might not be so "against harming people" as you claim that the old owner was.' For the next couple of weeks, Yura proudly sent me links to the blog posts, articles and threads he started with his accusations.

Yura's intention was to push stories about the hack and scamming from the first page of Google searches. Unfortunately, his search engine optimisation (SEO) skills were lacking, so mine was still the first site that came up in a search for 'dark web hitman'. Meanwhile, he still had no idea that Chris and I were getting fed daily information on the messages coming and going through the Besa Mafia website. Occasionally I would tease him with snippets of things that I knew. 'So is it true you are now blackmailing your customers with threats to go to the police?' I asked him after seeing his message to some customers, including dogdaygod, to do just that. He assumed that his clients had contacted me, rather than that I could see his emails.

He remained defiant. 'It won't be long and you will have the police at *your* door, especially after they link the car burns and the murders to you,' he said.

In the background, he set about rebranding. He sent off an email to all those who had signed up to provide services to let them know the hack was fake, the site was real, and he would be reopening a new site under a new name. The recipients included ThcJohn, who was sympathetic and naively optimistic. I shook my head as, unbeknown to Yura, I read ThcJohn's reply to him:

'Are you aware if the hacking attempt was by authorities or private party?' he asked before getting to his real point. 'Also I'm not trying to be rude and I do realize the reason for past and possible future delay but I still have not received payment, no problem like I said I understand but I'm sure you understand that I just don't want to be forgotten when you get this please send an email to the provided address.'

Yura and I continued to message each other. He played on my concerns that by publicising how much money he made as a fake hitman site, I could entice someone into opening up a real hitman site. It gave me pause to think, but all of the old reasons that a real hitman site would not be practical online were still there, so that did not worry me.

Okay, Yura said, he would start a new site, 'probably called something like Murder Bay', and would purchase the servers in my name. It would be 'like freelancer.com but for body harm services on deep web'.

'Also, I will make accounts in your name, Eileen Ormsby and also in your friend Chris Monteiro and I will advocate the new site really hard, make it look like you are dedicated supporters . . . And the new site will be real,' he warned. 'Thank you for destroying the scam, and preparing the road for the real thing. I would have preferred the scam, but now the real thing is fine, as I have learned a lot from it, and you proved that the real thing is profitable.'

Yura went into details of how he imagined the FBI would come after me, break down my door and they would be bamboozled by his cunning, foolproof plan.

'Have fun and welcome into the game, switie!' he signed off. And then, just in case I thought he was clueless, he added a postscript: 'PS. I know there is no FBI in Australia, but I am sure you will be asked questions from some law enforcement too there.'

When I didn't respond, he wrote again. And again. And if possible, he started to sound even more unhinged.

'The next gang members who signup I will ask them to do something bad, from your name with dedication to you . . . and publish it on the net. I am sure there are many crazy fucked up dudes who will do it . . . :) so nice watching your name Eileen on some live burned dogs or cats . . .'

TheJohn gets confused

'Hello I have been waiting over a week for payment with little response from you I understand that you suffered a hacking attempt but that's not my problem I was told 24 hours max and it's been over 168 I don't know if a supervisor has approved my payment or not,' John wrote to Yura, 'and all I hear from you is I will receive it shortly or we will send it shortly I'm not mad just a little impatient and would like better communication from you because of the fact that it's been over a week.'

'Hi, Sorry for the delay on replying, but we were very bussy with lots of questions and our programmers implemented several improvements on the site,' Yura wrote back. 'The delay in your payment was that our boss decided to change several things around the site and we credited your wallet directly with the amount. You should be able to see 4 Bitcoin into your wallet this is about $1800 as we agreed. The programmers are working on the withdraw feature and this should be ready soon, and you will be able to withdraw payments directly from your account on besa mafia to any wallet you want soon.'

'Well thank you,' responded a placated ThcJohn. 'I thought I was being ignored for some reason. Let me know when I can withdraw.'

Several weeks later, after multiple attempts to find out 'when the withdrawal feature would be fixed', ThcJohn finally began to get suspicious. It was not just some obscure blogs and reddit reporting on the Besa Mafia scam, but more mainstream news services, too. John decided to get tough. 'Okay so now that we know you're fake you should know that I am not xactly as advertised and I will only ask nicely once. Pay what you owe please.'

Yura's response was to deny that he had written the most recent messages to ThcJohn, and to claim that they had in fact come from the 'other owners' of Besa Mafia: Chris and me. He explained to John that he wanted to make it a genuine hitman site—'real killers, real gang members', but 'Eileen being a girl saith that we should just scam people, and Chris also wanted beating and fire but no murder'.

So with the three owners in disagreement over the way the site should be run, once the first murders happened, Chris and I apparently became afraid. We quit the project, then manufactured a fake hack so that people would think that Besa Mafia was a scam.

In conclusion to his convoluted and unbelievable tale, Yura told ThcJohn, 'Your money are stuck, you can ask Eileen and Chris to unblock it, but they refuse to admit they are fonders of the site . . . I am going to send you the money as I want to keep you aboard; but please give me some time so sort out this mess.'

John was sceptical. 'I appreciate your honesty but find it hard to believe that your being truthful since your telling me your colleagues names if youre being honest then send my payment to

12grUFYjNMXpzjopQyU7AQDENnH8WLhUob within a week and we wont have any problems,' he said. 'Tell you what I'll settle for $700 because I need the money and these jobs were fun.'

Yura replied with a similar, but slightly different version of his previous story. He and John were well matched in their capacity for delusion.

Hi,

Let me tell you the full story here.

We have been three guys on this project. Me, I am born in Albania, but lived in many countries in Europe, and curently live in London.

I am using many proxies, socks and http to hide my real IP, I use IPs from Germany, Finland, Sweeden, Albania, Romania, India and other countries.

I have hired Deku-Shrub as the programmer to do the site; he built the platform and the site as he is an old programmer and know well deep web. He has a blog, Pirate London

He worked with OzFreelancer, she has a blog allthingsvice. com to develop ideas of how to keep the site safe as she knows well Silk Road and she wrote a book about it.

When the site was first launched, Deku-Shrub wanted to be a scam. However, more and more gang members signed up.

Some gang members were not real, but other gang members like you were real.

The site become more and more dangerous; and more and more jobs were done.

We paid you for the first job, remember? The site was running fine at that moment. We were getting jobs, we were getting gang members, jobs were done, etc.

Deku-Shrub decided to stop the site. We had a fight and I wanted to lock him out of the server.

He is good technical guy, he blocked all bitcoin wallets, he took an old version of database, exported it to text, edited it in notepad to remove completed jobs.

He removed many gang members and many completed jobs, and he added new messages to make it look like there were incomplete jobs

He also added messages about FBI

He then released the fake database dump by some name of hacker bRsub or whatever, and claimed the site was fake, to kill the site.

We had internal fights to get access on the site and wallets.

Right now, I don't have access to the wallets to repay you.

But I created new wallets and I am working to rebuild the reputation of the site. As soon as new customers come and order jobs and send money to these wallets, I will be able to pay you. And also to send you jobs.

You are not the only gang member in this situation. There are many other gang members waiting payment.

You will be paid soon, and if you can help us rebuild the reputation of the website; I will be happy to pay even more money.

Basically the site has 3 components:

– the customers, who pay, the more, the better

– the gang members, who do services and orders

– the admins, and internal system server and site

I am albanian, and I have been involved with drug dealings, etc within local albanian mafia.

So, the site can be called Besa Mafia for a purpose.

However, all kind of gang members are accepted.

If you have any suggestions on how to improve the site, please let me know

For now, I am focusing on repairing the reputation damage on the site; and then repay the gang members who are waiting money

Let me know

ThcJohn followed up forlornly a couple more times and in response, Yura changed his story yet again, seemingly unwilling to just let John go. His desire to ensure there were no first-hand reports of his scam was strong and ThcJohn was perhaps best placed to blow the lid on the scam completely.

> Hi
>
> Let's make some money. I am going to be very honest with you, and you can earn good money with this.
>
> Besa Mafia is a scam; basically it was made by me, Chris Monteiro and eILEEN Ormsby .
>
> We scammed customers who wanted to do murder, out of their bitcoins.
>
> We also asked gang members to do test orders to be able to look legit
>
> The problem is, Chris and Eileen and me had a dispute and they manage to block the wallets on the site.
>
> I have been locked them out of the server, and got full control. But I can not access the wallets and bitcoins without their passwords. So I can replace the wallets with new wallets, where I have full control, but they are empty.
>
> I can't send you your 4 Bitcoins unless I get money from customers.
>
> This is where I need your help. I need you to help me do some videos to prove the Besa Mafia legit, but WITHOUT killing anyone.

I am not a murderer and I don't want anyone be murdered.

So this is my plan; I will search for someone who has been shot recently in the street by some unknown killer. And, we will claim that we did it.

I want us to do some video of shooting some person that appears to be the person shot in the news papers.

We can publish the video and say Besa Mafia real killers for hire, and they see how we shoot some guy and then how the guy is in the news as dead. This way I can get a boost of customers ordering murders and paying with bitcoin.

They usually send $5000 or more for each order, so if we get 10 customers that is $50 000.

I can give you 20% of that, if you do the video for me. To do the video, you need to get some gun, and load it with blank amunittion, that is no bullets. You can buy some replica gun or some gas gun, or whatever

Then you need to have a friend appearing to come out from the home, you will then record the paper saying gang member for besa mafia, oiiuv2gwl2jhvg3j.onion, Murder Order Id #1032 or something saying is a murder order for besa mafia. You show the paper to the camera, then you go behind the person coming out from his house and shoot him with the blank bullets . . .

The guy will pretend he falls down, and you shoot a few more rounds to be sure and run away.

We will distribute the video. I think we can get a lot of customers if we can do this convincing

Police will know that our video is fake, because your friend will not fall exactly in the position of the guy who was killed, also many other things that police will find about the person killed won't match our video. So they will know is fake, but public on internet won't

I am sure we can get easy 10-20 customers after this video so we can scam $50 000 or $100 000 or more easy, and you get $10 000 or $20 000 or more just by doing a fake murder video

How do you know I will pay?

Because if I don't pay, you will tell everybody the video was fake and I get no customers

So, we can do a video for this murder

http://www.nbclosangeles.com/news/local/Man-Found-Dead-Rowland-Heights-Home-380233571.html

or this one

http://www.vvdailypress.com/article/20160515/NEWS/160519806

Both people were shot on aleys in the park, so you can do in the same location and do a video while simulating that murder in a realistic way that people would belive if viewing on you tube

I am sure that our video will be caught by big news sites and we will get good customers

So let me know, do you want to be part of this scam?

Your advantage: you can make a lot of money in a short time just doing videos for me.

Risks: zero, as no real murders will be done, if we get caught we risk to be accused of scamming and fraud, as we don't intend to do any murder or body harm

Lets work something out and I can guarantee you at least $10 000 for every video that you do, that looks like murdering someone

we will need to release constant videos from now to get customers but no murders should be done

let me know

ThcJohn was interested, and wrote back to Yura with a suggestion of his own.

i think we can do this also i thought of an idea to settle our debt i assume that you could get a gun for cheap if you can get me a kimber .45 preferably a TLE II but as long as it is a full size model ill be happy ill also settle for a glock 17, 19 or 21 and if its not too much a threaded barrel w/ suppressor if you can get me this then i will be more than happy to make BOTH these videos for you and when your site has issues which it does alot contact me at thcjohn2@sigaint.org

Besa never provided ThcJohn with the gun, but sure enough, someone made a video, a link to which was posted onto my own site.

Amy hears from Jane

Since the visit by the FBI, Stephen realised he would have to step up not just the security on the house, but his own computer security if he were to continue with his plan. He had to make sure that nothing that the police would be likely to see could incriminate him. He went to the website radaris.com, a comprehensive public records search engine for information about people, properties and businesses. In the search bar, he entered first Amy's name, then her parents'. The details that were returned had some errors, which was perfect for his purposes.

Still using the username dogdaygod, Stephen also enquired on reddit.com about 'Tails', an operating system designed to preserve the user's privacy and anonymity, and that will erase all computer artefacts and searches as soon as it is unplugged.

A week later, Amy received an email from an anonymous email address, jane@gmail.com:

> Amy, your family is in danger. Last Sunday you received an email with the solution to this problem, and you have not done anything about it yet. Are you so selfish that you will put your families lives at risk? If you did not see the email then you check your junk mail soon.

Amy checked her spam folder, and sure enough, there was an email from the same person, dated 25 July 2016:

> Amy, I still blame you for my life falling apart. I do not know how a fat bitch like you got to my husband, but because of you he left, and my life has become shit. I am sending you

this email, because it looks like you already know about me. I see that you have put up a security system now, and I have been informed by people on the Internet that the police were snooping around my earlier emails. I have been assured that the emails are untraceable and they will not find me, but I cannot attack you directly with them watching. Here is what is going to happen. Since I cannot get to you, I will come after everything else that you love. I know about your son, your husband, and your business, but thanks to the internet (www.radaris.com) I see you have a mother and father in Woodbury, a brother in St. Paul, and a sister in Yardley, PA. I have been busy researching topics on the internet, and have found that if you inject water into the brake line, then you will cause them to fail. What would happen if the brakes on the truck failed when your husband was hauling a heavy load? I found how to blow up a gas meter and make it look like an accident. I know that the meter on your house and on your business are on the east side, and the meter on your parents' house is on the south side. I am still watching you and your family. While, I did not see your son this week, I saw last friday he was wearing a bright pink shirt. I see that you moved the RV. Here is how you can save your family. Commit suicide. If you do not, then you will slowly see things taken away from you, and each time you will know that you could have stopped it, which will eat you apart from the inside. By the time I am done you will want to end it anyway, so why not do it now and save them. Based on lasthope.com the best ways to do it are shotgun to the head (which you might not have) cyanide (which you probably do not have) gunshot to the head (which you might not have) shotgun to the chest (which you might not have) explosives (which you probably do not have) hit by train jump from height (a lot of bridges around) hanging household toxins (anti-freeze, ammonia and bleach) inhaling gas (carbon monoxide) slitting wrist or throat. I know about this website, because I have thought of this option many times. Remember if you do not get it right the first time, then you will likely be committed for mental health issues, and you will lose your business and possibly your family. so I would pick a reliable method. I think it is an easy choice. 1 life to save 6 lives. Your family does not need you, but you can save them. DO NOT tell ANYONE about this email or this deal is OFF and I will come after your family. You have seen that the police are not able to track my earlier emails, but I was informed of them searching. They will not be able to track this either, but I will know if they look into it. Unless you are a heartless, selfish bitch then I expect to see your obituary in the paper in the next couple weeks.

Amy was understandably upset when she forwarded the email to the special agent at the FBI. Through a number of email exchanges, Amy was eventually placated by the opinion that a move from trying to arrange for Amy's murder to telling her to kill herself was an overall de-escalation of the situation. As to tracing where the email came from, thanks to the anonymity afforded by the dark web, there was little the FBI could do by way of linking an IP address to a real person.

Amy did not take Jane's advice to kill herself. Her family needed her and it would have been at complete odds with the teachings of her church.

A few weeks later, she enrolled in the eight-week Cottage Grove Citizen's Police Academy. Under the question on her application asking why she was interested in attending the academy, Amy wrote: 'I would like to learn more about the police department, what it does, and how it works. I would also like to see what I can do to support them better as a citizen.'

When it came to the four-hour ridealong with an officer that was part of the academy experience, Amy naturally requested she be assigned to accompany the K9 officer.

Besa Mafia gets nasty

The threat to burn cats and dogs alive in my name was just the beginning. The emails began to come thick and fast, and most of the time without even waiting for a response from me.

'I am have the new site soon ready. What do you prefer? a nice dog or a cat to be spilled with gas and burned alive?'

I preferred neither, but Yura had all sorts of plans to punish me.

Anyway, what I will do is

step 1.

Publish some articles, that are signed Eileen O, where you are an dedicated advocate of silk road, drugs, and crimes online, and where you strongly fight all scams trying to scam drug dealers

step 2.

Publish some articles with videso of dogs and cats burned alive, dedicated to you, making it look like you ordered it, saying you love killing animals and torture them

step 3.

Publish some articles where you will promote your new murder site, saying is real

'You do realise you are laying out your evil plan in detail like a James Bond villain, right?' I asked him. The emails were bordering on comedic:

I am going to start filling the net with accounts on your name and picture, with description such as

'I love torturing animals, I hate cats and dogs, I hate flowers and I hate anything nice. I am a girl who is not the average pink loving girl, I love deep web, I love drugs, guns and child pornografy. I love criminals and I hope to be able to become a criminal one day to become history, without being cut.'

Much as I would have liked to use that as a Tinder profile, I was a little nervous about how unhinged Yura was becoming. I was now being bombarded with twenty emails a day from the would-be hitman.

And I am going to trash your reputation online.

I am going to post lots of articles on your name, where you will have a bad opinion about lots of things.

I have lots of free time and lots of money, and a good reason to fuck up with you :)

I will fill the gay sites with ads on your name and picture, looking for girls, and I will put your email address, and I will fill the classfields sites with ads on various things wih your name and picture

I will fill the net with things on your name and picture. I am going to make you look like a shitty girl in the eyes of the media ☺

***

I have lots of free time

I have lots of freelancers

I have lots of money in bitcoin

I do like to revenge

***

I am thinking what to associate your name with . . .

so when someone searches for eileen orms . . . the first pages
will be your blog and some of my blogs on your name, let me
know what you want me to put there

child pornography? I will say you support and recommend
child pornography and I will include some good links

Also I will put some links to wharez sites with pirated serials
and stuff

I will put some photos of child nudes

I will put some links where to buy drugs

I will make you the most lover of shit things on deep web,
recommending links to people

just watch

***

So you have 24 hours to remove your articles on besa mafia
or I will put up a blog on your name recommending all shitty
things saying you do it

from child pornography, to underage rape, animals sex, gay,
drugs, everything on deep web.. you will be the admin of a
nice link page

———

I asked Chris Monteiro whether he was getting any similar messages,
but it seemed Yura was concentrating on me for now. Chris was a little
concerned, which made me concerned. 'I hope this isn't getting to you,
let me know if it is,' he said. 'Remember, he knows very little about
what we know.' The deluge kept coming.

Maybe I should just pay thcjon? I owe him only 4 bicoins
while I got over 120 bitcoins with the site

so I can pay him and then I can pay him more to come to
australia and burn your car? he has experience with it and he
looks like he enjoy it and australia is a nice country, nice for
him to visit

or maybe he enjoy raping . . . maybe you want to be raped? :)

anyway.. on the next site that will be on your name; i could
give tests to australian gang membrs to rape a target and give
your name and addresss.. see if they manage to do it . . .

This is a dangerous game . . . will I ask freelancers on the new
site to rape eileen or not?

***

I have a proposition for you

We can be either friends or enemies

You can join me if you don't join me I will have no choise but to constant harrass you in real life with gang members from australia to get you off the tail

***

I am going to do the next version for real, and guess what . . . I am going to send lots of gang members after your ass.

Remove your article now, if you want to make peace with me.

You don't know my name, you don't know who I am, but I know your name and I know where you live.

I will make version 2.0 of the site under a new name, I will get gang members signing up, and I will send them to rape beat and destroy you

And believe me, it will be successful

Remove your articles now. All of them.

I won't go away and next version of the site will be your enemy.

I remained calm, having seen plenty of evidence that Yura did not want to hurt me, or any dogs or cats, or anybody else. I felt confident that I was not going to be beaten or raped, and also that nobody in the world would be fooled by Yura's clumsy attempts to frame me for murder, child porn or anything else he had threatened me with. I remained blissfully unscared until I received an email from an administrator of one of the dark web hacking forums I sometimes visited. This was completely out of character as our communications until then had been restricted to the forum itself.

Sending this by email as I don't know how often you check ALHQ. As you know Besa is back and dumber than ever. He wants promotion for his new site, security help and a few other things. He is currently trying to pay for car burnings and beatings. You and Deku are marked out for beatings. In his last of many dumb emails he is offering to pay for me to use my connections to get your info. Apparently already has people ready in Australia which sounds like BS. I have suggested he go after someone who isn't a journalist/researcher.

I think he might actually be serious this time as he wants favorable publicity for his new site.

Though still sceptical that any physical harm would come to me, I was grateful that Yura had chosen to try and hire someone I was on good terms with. I wondered what might happen if he managed to find a less friendly hacker.

The body in the bedroom

Around 8 pm on 13 November 2016, Detective Sergeant Randy McAlister was thinking about bed. It had been a nice, easy Sunday pottering around with his wife, but he wasn't getting any younger. With fall beginning to ease into winter, a nice warm bed became an overwhelming temptation once the sun went down.

Those hopes were dashed when his telephone rang. Cottage Grove always had a detective on call after hours, and on that Sunday it was Randy McAlister. On the other end of the phone was a clearly distressed Patrol Sergeant Gwen Martin. There was an apparent suicide, she told him, and he needed to attend.

McAlister was bemused. Suicides, while tragic, were a common enough occurrence for the Cottage Grove Police Department, and not one that required a detective to attend. Martin's manner also concerned him; the sergeant, who was also a trained paramedic, was abnormally distraught. As her voice choked, she handed the phone to her partner, Sergeant Pat Nickle. Nickle told him that the victim had been a recent graduate from Sergeant Martin's class in the Citizen's Police Academy, Amy Allwine.

Randy McAlister felt the stirring of recognition at the name. 'She was the one that was threatened on the internet that time,' Nickle filled in helpfully. The detective sergeant lost no time in getting dressed. He no longer felt like going to bed.

An hour or so earlier, Emergency Services had received a frantic call from Stephen Allwine. 'I think . . . I think my, I think my wife shot herself. There's blood all over.'

The operator, Victoria Herrmann, tried to get information out of him as he spoke to his anxious son simultaneously. He provided the address, as well as details on the number of guns in the house as the operator guided him through the important points. He had last seen her, he said, when he left the house some time between 5:00 and 5:30 pm. Herrmann eventually asked him to check on his wife to determine if she was still breathing.

'She is not breathing. I, I can't tell where she's shot. I don't know,' Stephen said, as Joseph sobbed in the background.

Herrmann thought it odd that Stephen's demeanour switched from manic to eerily calm and that the child was so close to the telephone. But what really stood out to her was when the little boy asked his father, 'Are you gonna remarry?'

Stephen laughed at that. 'I don't know, bud.'

Cottage Grove Police Department patrol officers arrived while Stephen was still on the phone. The smell of roasting pumpkin emanated from the kitchen. Stephen and his nine-year-old son were standing in the garage. Amy was on the floor of her bedroom, a gunshot wound to her head, a 9mm Springfield handgun on the floor beside her. She lay flat on her back, her arms splayed out to the sides, in a pool of blood beside her neatly-made bed. Her pants were undone and her red sweater slightly pulled up, displaying her stomach and underwear.

Gwen Martin was stunned to recognise Amy from the academy. The idea of suicide was implausible. On her class evaluation Amy had written, 'I would like to do this again in a few years'. She was passionate about her business, eager to learn during the Citizen's Academy, and future-oriented. Nothing in her demeanour suggested she was suicidal.

Stephen had been working from home that day, he told the police officers attending. Amy had not been feeling well, and he had checked on her throughout the day until she told him not to check on her anymore.

Amy's father, Charles, had come to the house that day to finish off installing a new dog door that would allow Bolson, the Newfoundland, into the garage when it was cold. Charles was a frequent visitor to the house and enjoyed helping the family with handyman projects. He put Bolson and George in their kennels so that they would not disturb him doing the job.

Stephen had advised Charles that Amy was feeling poorly and lying down, so her father did not bother her. He told Stephen he could let the dogs out now and left the house. Five minutes down the road, Stephen called to ask him to return and take Joseph, as Amy had decided to go to the hospital.

According to Stephen, Amy decided not to go to hospital, but to remain in bed while he continued to work from the basement. He said he looked in on her one more time, before he went to collect their son. Usually they would go to Ninja Warrior class, but they were running late because Stephen had stopped to get gas and then spoke to Charles about Amy's health for a while. Instead, the father and son went straight to dinner at Culver's, a fast food restaurant around a five-minute drive from their 110th Street property.

Upon arriving home, just before seven o'clock, Joseph entered the house while Stephen unpacked the car. As Stephen removed his shoes in the mud room, Joseph came back to ask, 'Why is Mummy lying on the floor?'

She was still warm, but there was no pulse, which was unsurprising given the blood and brain matter the officers found on the floor when they moved her head. The gun was near her elbow and one shell casing was near her right foot; the gunshot wound was in the right of her head.

When Detective Sergeant McAlister arrived, the knowledge that Amy had previously been threatened made him a little more on the alert for anything that looked out of the ordinary. It occurred to him that a woman planning on committing suicide was unlikely to be cooking dinner shortly before. There was also something not quite right with the blood in the bedroom and there was a film over the floorboards outside the bedroom as if they had been recently cleaned.

When Amy's parents arrived later that night and advised that Amy was right-handed, which did not fit the gun placement, that was enough for McAlister to want another set of eyes. He called the State Bureau of Criminal Apprehension and asked for one of its agents to attend the scene.

The placement of the gun near Amy's left elbow was merely odd. The blood was another story. There was a large pool on the carpet around Amy's head, which was to be expected, but McAlister was more interested in the drops to the left. He had seen many murder scenes over the years as both a paramedic and detective, and these looked out of place, as though they had dripped from something being suspended above the area. McAlister's experience told him that when somebody shot themselves in the head, they instantly crumpled in a heap, before bleeding could even begin.

What's more, blood from both Amy's nose and mouth had dripped down the left side of her face, despite her being flat on her back facing straight to the ceiling. The wooden floor area outside the bedroom appeared to have been recently cleaned, with smear marks still visible. The clean patch was at odds with the rest of the house, including the bedroom, which was messy with dog hair.

Stephen cooperated with all requests from the police—including searches of his personal phone (a black Samsung Galaxy S7) and work phone (a silver iPhone 6) and a test for gunshot residue on his hands, as well as DNA samples from both him and his son. The test for residue came back positive.

The medical examiner reported that Amy had Scopolamine in her system—40 times the recommended dose.

Stephen remained unruffled. The previous threats, he told police, had most likely come from a disgruntled dog owner through Amy's business. The local dog community could get surprisingly competitive and intense. It stood to reason that one of that community had probably murdered her.

A digital trail

Murders were rare enough in Cottage Grove; murder for hire was unheard of. The local police were thorough in their searches relating to the strangest case many of them had ever worked on. Five officers were assigned to almost full-time hours uncovering and sifting through the unusual evidence. The dark web and Bitcoin were not terms to which they were accustomed.

On 15 November 2016, the police searched Stephen and Amy's basement, where they found not only a sophisticated computer setup, but also five cellular phones. A Samsung Galaxy S5 used the same phone number as Stephen's Galaxy S7, which he had upgraded on 9 November 2016. The cell phone records from the numerous devices, and messages within countless email accounts, required the attention of two forensic teams.

For an IT guy, Stephen was sadly lacking in more than rudimentary methods of covering his tracks. As anyone regularly carrying out clandestine activities on the dark web knows, operational security is paramount, and stretches further than simply using Tor to visit nefarious websites.

One basic precaution of people using the dark web for illicit activities is never to use the same username on different websites, and certainly never to recycle a name that is used on the clear web. Stephen used dogdaygod for everything, from email addresses to reddit posts, to hitman orders and purchasing poison. Nor did Stephen use the most powerful tool a dark web criminal has: PGP encryption, which would ensure that any communications intercepted by police (or friendly hackers) would be unreadable and thus worthless.

Police executed and acted upon over 50 search warrants, with the lead detective, Jared Landkamer, executing 90 per cent of them himself. 'We got records for anything and everything,' he said. The technology that Stephen relied upon became the most damaging evidence against him.

A review of the video doorbell system determined that no person had rung the doorbell that day until the police did. Nor had it been turned off, as it was controlled by the Galaxy S5. The home security system data confirmed that nobody had come to the house from the time Stephen left until he returned, but somebody had opened the garage door three times during the time Stephen claimed to be working in the basement. If a disgruntled dog owner had entered the house, they somehow managed to avoid all monitored entry points, or else they subsequently erased all traces of themselves.

As a work-from-home customer care officer, all Stephen's calls were logged by his employer. According to information received from the Optanix system, he was logged in for work until he took his lunch break, but entered no further case updates after that. He did not log in to the Cigna system at all that day.

Although he had taken care to erase evidence of his Bitcoin transactions, pesky little cookies had been left on his Samsung Galaxy S5 that showed he had used that telephone to access Bitcoin exchanges. The history of his MacBook revealed searches for Bitcoin mining, K9 Nosework trials, a Maps search on Moline IL, browsing through a reddit thread about disposable computers, and names input to radaris.com. On 4 March 2016, the MacBook browsed Amy's Facebook photos and on 5 March a photo was uploaded to their family website, allwine.net. Forty-five minutes later, dogdaygod sent Besa Mafia the URL to that photograph.

Cottage Grove Police finally had the motivation to properly investigate Stephen's complaint filed all those months ago about a failed Bitcoin transaction. Nowhere on Stephen's computer was any evidence to support a commercial deal for $6000 of consulting services from someone called 'Mark'. There was, however, email correspondence between dogdaygod and Besa Mafia where the latter suggested consulting services could be used to explain a Bitcoin transaction.

The most damaging evidence against him came from a computer forensics search of deleted files from Stephen's computer. Among them was a backup of Stephen's iPhone 6, which included a note of Bitcoin wallet address 1FUz1iECnhN2Kw8MUXhZWombbw1TCFVihb deleted minutes after it was made. Dogdaygod had told Besa Mafia he paid Bitcoin into that address for the services of a sniper. This was a smoking gun; Bitcoin addresses are unique and it created the direct nexus between dogdaygod and Stephen Allwine's telephone.

At the time dogdaygod posted on Dream looking for Scopolamine, several cookies for reddit and dark-web search engines were installed on his phone.

Police knew they had to thoroughly investigate the claims by dogdaygod that Amy was a homewrecker, but exhaustive searches found no evidence whatsoever of an affair on the part of Amy. 'Nothing we came across from the course of the entire investigation even remotely indicated that she had any kind of extramarital affair,' said Detective Landkamer. 'Her life was literally church, dogs and family, that was it.'

They did, however, discover evidence that Stephen Allwine had been using the Ashley Madison website for illicit affairs. Police contacted a 45-year-old slim blonde woman by the name of Michelle, who confirmed that she had had an affair with Stephen. She also told them about the day Stephen had been running late for their date because he had locked his keys in his car when buying Bitcoin from someone near a fast food outlet.

Suicide was ruled out. The circumstantial evidence was mounting and it all pointed to just one person—Amy Allwine's husband, Stephen.

Yura opens CrimeBay

As we knew before being locked out of any more of Besa Mafia's communications, Yura was busy rebranding and upping the level of marketing for his murder-for-hire scam. His new venture was called CrimeBay and was identical in almost every way to Besa Mafia, including the design and the 'testimonials'. CrimeBay was run by 'the Chechen Mob'.

This time it also had a warning to any journalists who were thinking of writing about the site, imploring them to contact CrimeBay and ask first. 'Please refrain from publishing information that is false, misleading or intended to hurt our business.'

Yura also managed to get somebody (it is unclear whether it was ThcJohn or not) to stage a hit exactly as he suggested. The video shows the inside of a car, music blaring, as an assassin prepares. Donning black leather gloves, he checks his handgun, then trains the camera onto a note that states this is a hit being carried out on behalf of CrimeBay/Chechen Mob. The assassin pulls up behind an unsuspecting victim who is retrieving something from the trunk of his car. *Bang bang bang.* The victim falls to the ground and the car speeds off. Another successful hit by CrimeBay!

Yura (using the pseudonym 'deep-web-expeert'—yes, complete with that spelling) posted a link to the video (which he had uploaded to a site called dailymotion) on my website, with a comment stating that when the mob heard that someone made a six-figure salary by scamming people, they figured they could do ten—even a hundred— times more with a genuine murder-for-hire site. 'CrimeBay is a real hitman for hire site because they provide real proof', deep-web-expeert declared.

Unfortunately, by the time I got around to reading his comment, I was greeted with 'video not found'. Dailymotion had apparently taken it down.

'Hi Yura, missed you. Could you please post that vid somewhere else . . . it has been removed from that site. Ta', I wrote.

'You are not correct and fair, you remove video evidence that crime bay is real and legit. I hope that you are smart enough to remove your articles and leave the sites alone or you might get a visit. You are annoying the wrong people and it might not end up well for you.'

'How the hell do you think I removed something from a site that has nothing to do with me?' I responded. 'I WANT to see your evidence you goose!'

Yura was contrite. 'I thought you reported the video to dailymotion and they deleted it.' He reposted it for me oblivious that I had seen his messages to Thcjohn planning, the video. I immediately tweeted it out asking for a critique.

'Hi Yura, I'm not really an expert in the field, so I have tweeted this to get some feedback and reviews from my Twitter followers. It doesn't look like very good OPSEC though,' I said, pointing out the errors that the so-called hitman had made that could identify him to law enforcement agencies.

Yura was annoyed. 'Yes, this is not an expert hitman. He is an amateur . . . what can you expect for a $5000 hit . . .? He is some crazy guy with an amateur pistol shooting some person into the back. He is not even using a suppressor. But as you can see, there were many fucked up people who signup to do bad things for the money.'

Later, Yura contacted me privately, his latest video warning not having the intended effect.

You are pretty stupid

I don't think this can work out

it is clear that you are protecting murderers and want to help them be safe from scams.

If you expose any other hitman scam, all the killings of innocent people will be on you

Please also keep in mind that there are many people who signed up to provide services, they want to do murders, fires, beat up etc.

A real market is not hard to do. Don't push it. If you love murderers, you might get a real site as a result

If you write any more, is clear that you want to help murderers to be safe from scams, and it means you are a bad person,

In that case I hope you will be killed, and have your chid orphan just like that women

'Now now that's no way to talk to a friend,' I responded, adding in a sadface emoticon for good measure.

Look, I don't got many orders on the new site

So hold on, and stop helping murderers

Besa did a lot of money, but now if you search for hitmen deep web you find all sites posts about besa being a scam so people are afraid of ordering

Remove your article and I will get orders

I will send you info and thats it

I don't know why you love so much murderers to help them not be scammed

I quite liked the idea of getting the details of murder plots that I could pass on to police, but at his very first opportunity, Yura tried to scam me. I agreed not to write any more articles if he would provide me with details of people who paid for hits. He sent me the Facebook page of somebody in Australia, saying it was a target and that someone had paid $10K for a hit on that person, and I could contact them through his site 'pretending to be the killer assigned'. I asked for the blockchain verification; he refused. Of course, it was just more bullshit from him and I called him out on it.

Stephen gets arrested

Almost nine months after we first discovered Besa Mafia's dirty little secrets, and details of people who had paid significant amounts in Bitcoin to have someone else killed, Chris Monteiro finally felt like he was being taken seriously. Having spoken to local police, Metropolitan Police dark-web specialists, the LAPD, the FBI, a private security contact, UK counter-terrorism (and complained to many friends and acquaintances along the way), he found that it was after being interviewed by a journalist that the NCA finally decided to give him the time of day.

'This Wednesday I'll be meeting with an undercover NCA agent and someone from their cybercrime division in an office in central London to explain the Besa Mafia saga, with the goal of them actually opening an investigation for this, which will likely involve referring the case to the FBI who seem best place[d] to lead on this,' he told me in an email dated 18 January 2017.

The next day, he reported that the meeting went very well.

The very next day, 20 January, I opened an email from Chris that was short and to the point: 'FUCK FUCK FUCK!'

Below was a link to a news report stating that Minnesota man Stephen Carl Allwine had been arrested and charged with second-degree murder of his wife Amy and that there was an unusual twist to the story: someone had tried to arrange Amy's murder six months earlier on dark web hitman site Besa Mafia. He allegedly used the name 'dogdaygod'.

We both recognised the name instantly as being one of the more interesting cases that had popped out of Besa's archives. I had mentioned dogdaygod in the first of my articles on the Besa Mafia scam. We knew that the victim's name and address were among the files and that there had been significant contact between the would-be hitman and the client. The police had all of this information. How had someone been so bold as to carry out a murder after all that?

Stephen Allwine had lawyered up well before he was arrested at a traffic stop on his way home from dropping his son to school. His attorney, Kevin deVore, attended the interview he had with Special Agent Michelle Frascone of the Bureau of Criminal Apprehension two days after Amy's murder. Frascone had attended the Allwine's house at the request of Randy McAlister and had immediately noted things that were inconsistent with suicide. A spray of Luminol revealed a recently cleaned patch of blood in the hallway, and bloody footprints leading back and forth.

During the two-hour interview, Stephen was subdued and softly-spoken, only perking up when he spoke about his church. He said he had not heard of the dark web until the FBI visited. He offered up that he had no idea where Amy's dog trials took her, but her friend Kristen did. He said the email telling Amy to kill herself had some incorrect details of her loved ones, pretending he had no knowledge of radaris.com, where the details came from.

Despite the investigation having already taken two months, Stephen was charged with second-degree murder, which suggested a non-premeditated killing. This seemed surprising given that Stephen had apparently been planning his wife's death for nearly a year. As well as the digital evidence, there was a small matter of a $700,000 life insurance policy on Amy, the beneficiary of which was her husband.

Stephen soon posted the $500,000 bail, which had several conditions attached, including GPS monitoring and only supervised visits with his son. Joseph was taken to live with his maternal grandparents and Stephen returned to the home he had shared with Amy.

Yura blames me

Shortly after the news of Stephen Allwine's arrest broke, Yura pinged me on Google Hangouts. We had progressed to real-time chats, although we remained at an impasse when it came to me removing my articles (I pointed out several times that his intermittent commenting on them only pushed them up in the Google rankings) and joining his scamming team.

After the usual pleasantries (he always took the time to enquire after my health and what I was up to), Yura asked, 'so how do you feel about that poor wife being shot dead?'

'I felt sorry for her,' I said. We launched into a discussion about whether the FBI had contacted her and why more hadn't been done about it. True, dogdaygod had pretended to be a woman scorned, angry with Amy for destroying her marriage. But one would think this story would not have stood up to scrutiny. If the police had determined that Amy was genuinely clueless about anyone fitting the description of 'Jane', surely the most obvious suspect would have been the husband. In any event, it would have to be someone very close, as dogdaygod had significant knowledge of Amy and Stephen's day-to-day movements.

'You should have not exposed that scam,' Yura said. He reminded me of his modus operandi: 'It was a trap for murderers,' he said.

'Sure it was a trap but it was just to make you money. You didn't really help law enforcement catch them,' I said. 'You only told law enforcement about the ones that didn't pay.' I still hadn't told him that I had access to more information than what was in the pastebin dump.

Yura insisted this wasn't true. Besa Mafia had a secret back page, the login details to which he had provided to the FBI. And anyway, he said, he had held bigger plans for dogdaygod. He would have been scammed until he had either run out of money or refused to pay any more at which point, experience told Yura, he would insist on meeting the assigned hitman to prove that he was real. 'And the answer is "ok, we don't do this usually but you can meet the assigned hitman",' said Yura, warming to his story, 'and then FBI goes and send undercover cop . . . if you didn't expose Besa Mafia, that would have happened. You might feel better thinking it would have not, but it would.'

The 'secret back page' Yura mentioned did not exist, but he had embedded a message to law enforcement in a hidden file that said: 'If you found this file, it means you are investigating this server.' A lengthy message went on to say that the purpose of the website was to fight crime by depleting resources of criminals and that Besa was keeping all records of the 'wannabe murderers', even if they tried to cancel their account. 'This is because there is nothing to hide,' he wrote, 'except the identity of the owner.'

Just in case authorities were interested in determining the identity of the owner, Yura told them how he avoided their prying fingers. 'Regarding the identity of the owner, here is how this has been done. The owner has purchased a second hand mobile phone and a prepaied sim card with Internet access. The owner is also accessing various wifi networks that do not have a password or where he knows the password, public places. He uses a computer that connects to the Internet by the means above. All connections to this server are made from such IP addresses that are not related to his real information.'

Finally, he wrote: 'In the future, the owner of this website will consider working with Police to share the information of the targets if this website becomes very popular and used by criminals.'

'Can I ask you a question again?' Yura had taken to pinging me whenever he wanted a chat, and the topic of conversation was always the same.

Do you think scamming wanna be murderers is a bad or good thing? Morally? I mean, why did you choose to help murderers by exposing scams? Like, "hey murderers watch out this don't fall for it! Save your money and buy or gun or use another method." If you have any morality, I would suggest you to delete your article about Besa

It was fun

It was nice

It was smart

but if you remove it I could revive the Besa Mafia.

I was becoming almost fond of my scammy little hitman now that he had stopped threatening me with rape and murder. It was abundantly clear from several of the emails he had exchanged with those trying to order his services and those trying to supply them that he didn't really want to hurt anyone—he just wanted to extract a lot of money out of bad people.

Whenever he asked potential hitmen to do a test job of destroying a car, he always warned them not to hurt anyone in the process. Of course, the people accepting those jobs might not have hesitated to hurt somebody who disturbed them. I had begun to form the impression that Yura did not always think through the potential consequences of his actions.

When it came to people seeking his services, he seemed less inclined to scam money out of those who did not appear to be criminals themselves.

Hippie, a 45-year-old woman, desperately wanted a loan (Besa advertised loan sharking as well) for $30,000. On hearing that she would have to deposit one Bitcoin to 'prove she wasn't a prankster', she became desperate. Yura actually seemed to take pity on her and advised her not to use a loan shark.

She insisted she would come up with the money, until eventually Yura said bluntly: 'Our loan sharks usually give loans of 5000 max 30 000 and interest is about 10% per month; that is a lot and if you don't pay they kill you so leave us alone and go to a bank.'

He also showed something akin to compassion to a seventeen-year-old girl who wanted to kill the two boys who raped her. She said it had not gone to court 'because of my mental instability'. Yura simply said he was very sorry, but Besa Mafia could not help her.

However, in the end, Yura was out for a profit and was willing to lie, cheat and scam to get it.

'I would not work to support a scam,' I told him, 'but I am not planning on any hitman blogs for a while.'

'Ok,' conceded Yura. 'I am glad that you have a good heart and that you are a moral person. I don't support drugs and murderers. I feel really sorry for that wife.' He really did seem disturbed at the lack of action by the FBI. 'They saw the messages about dogdaygod,' he said. 'Why didn't they do anything?'

United Church of God statement

The United Church of God, *an International Association* (to use its entire formal name) is an offshoot of the Worldwide Church of God. They worship on Saturday. Fundamentalist in nature, they have strict requirements of obedience to the commandments in order to be saved.

On 20 January 2017, UCG Twin Cities called an emergency meeting to discuss the Allwine situation. Stephen Allwine was stripped of his eldership, and his sermons removed from the website, but the UCG expressed a desire not to 'take sides'.

The church released the following statement:

United Church of God officials expressed profound shock and sadness in learning of the January 17 arrest of Stephen Allwine on the charges of second-degree murder of his wife Amy Louise Allwine. Two months earlier on November 13, Amy Allwine had been found dead at her St. Paul area suburban home by police and paramedics following an emergency call from her husband.

Church officials and members were first stunned and grieved when they learned of the tragic death of Amy in November.

After hearing of the tragedy, Church President Victor Kubik and his wife Beverly immediately traveled from Ohio to Minnesota to be with family members and show support during a heart-rending time for the congregation. Allwine had served as a lay elder for several years.

President Kubik has called for renewed prayers for the families involved as details of the charges emerge. He said that the whole situation was 'tragic and singularly devastating.'

Area police noted in their initial public comments that Amy's death appeared 'suspicious' and promised that an expanded investigation would take place. Allwine was not arrested nor named as a suspect at that time. During the investigation local church officials positively cooperated with police and law enforcement officials.

Church teachings based on the Bible condemn murder, and the United Church of God follows the teachings of Jesus Christ about the sanctity of marriage and the importance of loving family environments. 'Given our biblical commitment and our love for our members, this situation deeply hurts and grieves all of us,' Kubik said. The Church president asked for prayers of comfort, healing and understanding for all.

Nevertheless, a large contingent of United Church of God attended Stephen's hearings in what observers said appeared to be a show of support for one of their own.

The Besa files

True to my word to Yura, I stopped writing articles about the dark web hitman services. Both Chris Monteiro and I were shaken by the news of a real murder and wondered about the safety of the other people identified as targets in the Besa Mafia order list. We had been relieved to read that the FBI had visited Amy Allwine when the hitmen had been hacked, but wondered whether there was any more we could have done.

Before the murder, it had been quite comical reading through Yura's efforts at scamming would-be killers. But now they took on much more sinister overtones, and the stories became even more bleak when it was brought home that real lives were being affected.

It was a matter of just two weeks before Stephen was arrested again, after Amy's parents reported to authorities that Stephen had tried to contact his son, with whom he was supposed to have no unsupervised contact. He had asked Amy's parents to charge up his son's smart watch so that Stephen could track his whereabouts.

The judge raised the amount required for conditional bail to $600,000 and ordered Stephen to have no contact with his son or Amy's parents. He once again managed to post bail and was free to return home.

On 24 March, a grand jury elevated the charge against Stephen Allwine to first-degree murder. The judge set Allwine's unconditional bail at $2 million and conditional bail at $1 million. This time, Stephen was unable to post it and he was remanded in prison to await trial.

NCA get their man

In many ways, Chris Monteiro was your standard London geek. The 34-year-old lived alone in a one-bedroom, high-ceilinged Victorian apartment in a building in south-east London. The usual single-bloke décor included a map of London that almost covered one wall, a couple of guitars that were not played often enough and a drone that wasn't working, but surely would be working again soon.

Perhaps a little less typical was the whiteboard covered in the complex array of numbers and multi-coloured arrows typical of complicated networking analysis, and the bank of computers in his living room, where six screens displayed aspects of the different projects he was working on.

On 11 February 2017, a Saturday, Chris was sitting in his 'chill place'—on the sofa, within arm's length of his computers—eating soup for lunch. The soup was comfort food as he recovered from a bout of flu that had kept him home from work the day before. In the background, one of his computers was seeding a file of the Freedom Hosting II database.

Chris had been working every spare minute analysing the Freedom Hosting II infiltration since the hack had been carried out a few days earlier, and details of the people behind its 10,000 Tor-based webpages leaked. Around half those pages were child pornography sites. Chris had been blogging and tweeting his discoveries incessantly over the past few days.

He heard a noise at the door. Wondering what the hell it was, he got up from the sofa, but had barely put one foot in front of the other before his door burst open and six or seven people surged into the room. The Metropolitan Police wore body armour. Two people in plain clothes, he soon discovered, were from the National Crime Agency (NCA).

'What's going on?' Chris gasped.

'Hands in the air! Hands in the air!'

Chris complied.

'Up against the wall!'

His first thought was that he had been 'swatted'—that somebody had called in a terrorist threat to the authorities, plausible enough for

them to dispatch a SWAT team. It was a service on the dark web that
had been used against security researchers previously.

'You're under arrest for incitement to commit murder.'

'What?' Chris had no idea what they were talking about. His mind
worked furiously as his rights were read to him and the unwelcome
visitors examined and photographed his electronics. The only thing
he could think of was that it must be somehow related to the Freedom
Hosting II hack. His brain refused to work properly and he was terrified as they cuffed him and sat him down on his sofa.

Chris responded to their questions about his computers, his
nerves making him extremely chatty. When they asked if he had been
in trouble with the police before, he rambled on about the time he got
stuck in his bedroom window and emergency services had to attend to
get him out. As they led him out to do the walk of shame to the police
van, cuffed and dishevelled, all he could think was *at least they didn't
take my weed*.

During the drive, one of the police officers made small talk,
noting that Chris had the game *Hitman* among his collection. Chris
wasn't sure why the officer thought that particular game was worth
mentioning.

After going through the sign-in process, providing saliva samples,
fingerprints and having his first-ever mugshot taken, a Met police
officer went through the formalities again, and said to him, 'So you
understand you're being arrested for incitement to murder to do with
a website?'

Finally the penny dropped. 'That fucking website? You're fucking
kidding me.' Chris was too stunned to mind his language. Surely the
NCA—the fucking agency in charge of national security—could not
possibly have been duped by Yura's ridiculous 'articles' pointing the
finger at him as being a part of Besa Mafia?

Unfortunately, Chris couldn't put that question to the NCA
officers as they had not come to the station, but would be coming by

some time later to interview him. Meantime, he was to speak to the duty solicitor to ensure none of his rights were being violated.

'I understand you're facing a murder charge,' the pleasant and efficient criminal lawyer said. 'Not to worry, I've dealt with this before.'

'I really don't think you have,' Chris said. 'But I appreciate it.'

After his lawyer visit, Chris was told he needed to undergo another quick assessment. 'How are you doing?' the officer asked.

'How the fuck do you think I'm doing?'

'Right, take his belt, guys,' the officer said.

Chris laughed, because otherwise he would cry.

He was placed in a holding cell and offered some reading material, which he eagerly accepted. A few pages into the dire prose of an autobiography of some professional golfer he had never heard of, Chris threw it down.

As the hours went by, he tried whistling, meditating and finally settled on rhythmic pacing, which was interrupted only by occasional offers of drinks and shitty ready meals. Time wore on, and he went to the darkest place he had ever been in his life.

Finally he asked his jailer for another book. 'I can't take it anymore, this golfer's autobiography is killing me.'

The officer returned with the most welcome sight Chris had seen in a very long time: Terry Pratchett's satirical *Going Postal*. He had read it twice before—Pratchett was his No.1 favourite author of all time—but he devoured it again, taking comfort in the absurdist prose that somehow mirrored the surreal place he found himself in.

At 1:00 am, when Chris had been in jail for twelve hours, he was told it was time for his interview with the NCA. Relief washed over him as he realised freedom was within his grasp—all he had to do was clear up the ridiculous misunderstanding arising from someone's overzealous Google search.

The two NCA officers were not the same as those who were at Chris' apartment earlier. They were reading from the warrant.

'You were arrested for the offence of intention, encouraging or assisting an offence, namely the offence of conspiracy to commit murder. Do you understand that?' the humourless NCA officer asked.

'I do now,' Chris said. 'It's taken a while though.'

'You said several things to the arresting officers. You said something about seeding a file,' the more technical officer said.

'I thought that's what you were breaking my door down for,' Chris said.

'You said there is an ongoing investigation in which you are working with the NCA about the Besa Mafia website,' the officer said. 'Tell me what you mean by that.'

Chris explained that Besa Mafia was a fake murder-for-hire website that operated like a classic 419 scam. He explained that debunking such sites was a particular hobby of his. He took them through the articles, the hacking, the burning cars, the intimidation, the owner spreading ridiculous rumours about Chris and me being the brains behind the original site. He rattled off a list of services Besa Mafia purported to provide in a sing-song voice, as though he were a walking advertisement.

'So tell me about your role at Besa Mafia,' said the officer.

'My "role" is primary antagonist.' Chris felt he wasn't really getting through to them. 'Let it be on the record I'm upset about my stuff being fucked with.'

The NCA officers were not amused. 'So the next person I want to talk about is Steve Allwine.'

'Who is Steve Allwine? Is that the Minnesota guy? I never really profiled him. I put him in the top ten most dangerous but never took it any further,' Chris said.

'Did you ever speak to him?'

'God no.'

'Who is dogdaygod?'

'That's him isn't it?'

'When did he first come to your attention?'

'When my fucking Google alert went off.'

Chris answered questions as rapidly as they were put to him, but his hopes of being released were dashed when all questions were exhausted and he was led back to his cell.

Chris finally fell into a fitful sleep at around 4:00 am. He had never had such low confidence in the criminal justice system. As he drifted off, his last thought was *I hear the Ecuadorian embassy is nice this time of year.*

Sunday saw Chris go through more questioning, but at least he was allowed to speak to his parents and get in touch with his lawyer. He was finally released on bail on Sunday night, after the longest day and a half of his life. Unable to face his trashed apartment, he spent the night at a friend's house.

On Monday, he called in sick to work, then phoned his therapist.

'I've been through some stuff,' he said. 'I need an extra-long session.'

ThcJohn apologises

ThcJohn must have seen the *Daily Mirror* article that called Chris Monteiro a 'cybercrime expert' because he wrote to Chris, apologising for dedicating a burning car to him. He said he thought that he was dedicating it to a member of the Albanian Mafia, and assured Chris that the cars he burned were all insured.

'hello i am the "thug" that eileen had burn some cars to try and scare you,' he wrote, still confused as to who was really behind Besa Mafia. 'i thought their organization was much bigger than it really was i was new to the deep web and naive also i was needing money and eager to make some i consider everything that i did for besa mafia a mistake.'

He went on to explain that he was really a scared seventeen-year-old who wanted to become an apprentice mechanic—the kind that works on cars, not people.

'i know nothing about programming or "hacking" other than its not nearly as glamouros as the media portrays it to be that being said you problably know where i live and maybe who i am,' he said miserably. But there was still a spark of hope left in him: 'i want to let you know that i have nothing against you or what you do acually quite the opposite and maybe you might have some work for me however i dought it please get back to me as to wether or not there are any hard feelings'.

Yura goes MIA

Early in May 2017, CrimeBay's hitman-for-hire website was replaced with a bright blue seizure notice.

> This website is under investigation and its data has been seized by the National Crime Agency and the Bulgarian National Unit for Combating Serious Organized Crime.
>
> If you have visited this website for the purpose of using its services, or have previously used its services, you could have committed a criminal offence, including soli[ci]tation to murder. In the UK, solicitation to murder can carry a penalty of life imprisonment.
>
> The NCA and international law enforcement partners are identifying and prosecuting the users of this website. The NCA will continue to pursue the users of services such as these on the dark or open web.

I wondered if Yura had finally been caught and his scamming operation shut down forever, but CrimeBay reopened shortly after and seemed to be operating as usual. I reached out to Yura through all our previous communication channels, as well as the CrimeBay site itself, but I got no response.

News reports trickled in of people being charged with doing business with CrimeBay. An Italian woman was sentenced to six years for ordering a hit on her boyfriend. An English man was charged with (but eventually acquitted of) plotting to murder a baby to avoid child support. A UK man wanted his financial planner dead after receiving bad investment advice.

By all appearances, Yura had been arrested and his business taken over by law enforcement, which was using it as a honeypot to catch would-be murderers. I felt inexplicably sad that the faux hitman I had grown fond of might be rotting in an Eastern European prison somewhere.

Then not long after Christmas, just before I left for Minnesota to attend Stephen Allwine's trial, I got pinged for an instant chat. Yura—or someone doing a very good impression of him —wished me luck on my trip. 'I wish I could have stalled him longer,' he said. 'He should have gotten a diforce. I don't like when religion make people kill people. Religion should cause people to forgive, let go, be happy.'

Meanwhile, he had created a new murder-for-hire site, and had paid 'people with guns' to make much better videos for him, using blanks of course. He was wondering if I would be interested in a job fixing his spelling and grammar, which he thought might be deterring some customers.

He understood if I wanted to be paid up front.

The trial of Stephen Allwine

On 23 January 2018, after six days of questioning fifty potential jurors, the opposing attorneys finally settled on a pool of eight women and seven men to decide whether Stephen Allwine had killed his wife.

Those who were chosen professed a working knowledge of computers, but no in-depth technical expertise. Three of them would hear all the evidence but be dismissed before deliberations, there only in case any other jurors could not continue.

In his final case before retirement, District Judge B. William Ekstrum presided over the most bizarre trial Washington County had ever seen. Prosecutors Fred Fink and Jamie Kreuser drew together the threads of evidence that pointed to Stephen Allwine being Besa Mafia customer dogdaygod, and the man who ultimately pulled the trigger that took Amy Allwine's life. Kreuser's disarming manner and polite, persistent questioning of witnesses elicited responses that cumulatively built an airtight case against the defendant.

Throughout the trial, the courtroom was filled to capacity with family from both sides, UCG congregation members and the professional dog training community. They treated attending media with open hostility and took their own notes, which they would compare during breaks and probe for inconsistencies in testimony. Stephen and Amy's pastor would spend breaks counselling family and friends who were trying to make sense of what had happened.

Stephen showed almost no emotion throughout the trial. He did not turn to look at his family and rarely acknowledged his own lawyer. Instead, he would read through every report and piece of evidence that was tendered and occasionally pour himself a paper cup of water. Sometimes, when it seemed appropriate (such as when the 911 call was played and photographs of Amy's body were displayed), he would appear to be sobbing; the box of tissues in front of him remained untouched.

This most unusual trial called for a most unusual array of witnesses, including an escort, a Bitcoin trader, Stephen's mistresses, a pawnbroker, neighbours, dog trainers and an array of forensic and medical specialists, as well as the law enforcement officers who had attended the incident and worked on the case afterwards.

The prosecution's case ended with a detailed timeline of the improbable coincidences between the actions of dogdaygod and the actions of Stephen Allwine. It was impossible not to draw the conclusion that both were one and the same.

Allwine's defence lawyer, Kevin deVore, did his best with what he had. There was a neighbour who may or may not have seen Amy around 5pm, when the prosecution said she was dead. There were the reports from neighbours and the dog trainers using Amy's facility that two cars had roared away from the property at around 5.45 that evening. There was the unlocked, unmonitored patio door that was never tested for prints (the Allwines relied on the dogs that were usually in the backyard to deter anyone from entering the house that way). The prosecution said Amy had been killed in the hallway and moved to the bedroom; however, there was no blood on the carpet between the hallway and Amy, nor had it been cleaned. Weighing around 240 pounds, it is unlikely the slightly-built Stephen could have carried her there.

With medical evidence ruling out suicide, the only alternative theory was somebody else had killed Amy that evening. The intruders would have entered via the patio door, with the dogs safely locked in their kennels, killed the scopolamine-dosed Amy while Stephen was establishing his alibi with receipts from the gas station and the restaurant, and then roared off in their separate vehicles. Unfortunately, with overwhelming computer forensic evidence that fingered Stephen as dogdaygod, all this theory did was suggest he had finally been successful in finding his hitman.

Either way, it took the jury just eight hours to declare Stephen Allwine guilty of the premeditated murder of his wife, Amy. They accepted that, having failed to hire a hitman, he had pulled the trigger himself.

At Stephen's sentencing hearing, Amy's family spoke of the hole left in their lives. Her parents had come to the trial with open hearts, hoping that Stephen would be proven innocent. They had provided Stephen with a home from the time of Amy's death until he was arrested, so they felt doubly betrayed when the evidence convinced them they had been housing their daughter's murderer.

For the first time, Stephen spoke. In a rambling speech, he maintained his innocence and love for Amy. He said he had been housed with drug addicts, child molesters and kidnappers, but that he was bringing God to them; three atheists so far had been turned and were now attending bible studies regularly.

Judge Ekstrum was having none of it. Addressing Stephen directly, he told him he believed he was a hypocrite and a 'great actor' who could 'turn tears on and off'. Stephen was sentenced to a mandatory life in prison without parole.

The UCG put out a lengthy public release that expressed concern about the potential negative media coverage the case could bring the church given 'the fact that Mr Allwine was technically a lay (unpaid) minister at the time'. It barely mentioned Amy.

Meanwhile, the notion that you can hire a hitman on the dark web remains a myth. But there are plenty of other horrors on the dark web that are all too real.

PART III

Darkest

Welcome Snuff Seeker!

You have reached the dark web's darkest and greatest Red Room

Very soon we will be bringing our 'roomie' into this red room and even though she has at this time not the faintest idea yet of what is going to happen to her, she will be tortured, and then she will die.

And you could be a spectator!

We will be streaming this astounding event via the TOR network with our high capacity servers at 1080P, which is the minimum screen resolution required to fully appreciate death and dying. High fidelity sound will also be included in this stream.

Take part in this once-in-a-lifetime experience!

To be present at this incredible, never-to-be-repeated event, you need to pay 0.5 BTC. Yes, that's right: for a mere 0.5BTC, you can be there and enjoy the spectacle of the bloody torture and inexorable death of a pretty young woman! Her being led into the room will be the first inkling she has that something is amiss, and you will already be in your front row seat.

This memorable event will last approximately 1 hour and will begin at 00:00 UTC, on Saturday, October 1st

Applications for entry to the September 24th event are now closed. Our next event will be held October 1st

Applications for the October 1st event are now open

– Dark web red room welcome screen

Snuff films—myth or reality?

> Snuff films depict the killing of a human being—a human
> sacrifice (without the aid of special effects or other trickery)
> perpetuated for the medium of film and circulated amongst a
> jaded few for the purpose of entertainment.
>
> – David Kerekes and David Slater, *Killing for Culture* (1994)

Ask anybody if snuff films exist and they are almost certain to answer
in the affirmative. It is one of those topics that people refuse to believe
is an urban myth. Just because there have been no verified examples of
snuff movies any time in history, they will argue, doesn't mean they're
not out there; humans are capable of all kinds of depravity—it could
happen, so it *must* happen.

There is something morbidly fascinating about the idea of snuff
films. Defining a snuff film is a bit like applying Stewart's test for
obscenity: you may not know how to define it but you know it when
you see it. The generally accepted meaning seems to be murder on

film, for the purpose of making a movie to distribute for commercial gain. Some people believe there must also be a sexual component to it.

Most people wouldn't consider accidental deaths caught on film to be 'snuff'. A greyer area is murders deliberately filmed, but not for the purpose of sale. Pre-internet, videos like the *Mondo* series and *The Killing of America* were popular, if somewhat underground. They are compilations of real death footage, but the killings involved were caught on camera by accident. They were not done for the purpose of the film and certainly not for commercial gain.

The first known use of the term 'snuff movie' was in a 1971 book by Ed Sanders, *The Family: The Story of Charles Manson's Dune Buggy Attack Battalion*. In that book Sanders relays a story about a stolen Super 8 camera that was used to film the decapitation of a young woman with short blonde hair on a beach. Such a murder was never verified, but Sanders coined the term 'snuff movie' to describe true murders on film.

The term gained wider popularity when it became the title of a 1975 low-budget horror flick, *Snuff*, a movie so bad it scores 2.8 on IMDb. Long before *The Blair Witch Project*, the director of *Snuff* had the idea of creating a film that would be passed off as real 'found' footage. In the movie, a filmmaker kills and disembowels his assistant, while being surreptitiously filmed by his cameraman. The makers spread the rumour that a movie had been made in which a genuine torture and murder scene took place, and many news services ate it up. The producer, Allan Shackleton, secured a showing at the National Theatre in Times Square and arranged a rent-a-crowd of 'protesters'. The stunt worked.

'A repulsive put-on film called "Snuff",' *The New York Times* said in an article headlined, 'Snuff is Pure Poison'. The journalist Richard Edar, wrote:

The main come-on—and put-on—of the picture, made by a group of people whose anonymity is deliberate, is a scene tacked onto the end. It depicts the director and the crew of a film-within-the-film getting so carried away that they dismember one of the actresses.

I didn't stick it out. When they took out scissors and cut off her fingers I put on my coat. By the time I'd buttoned the coat, they were applying an electric saw to her leg. By the time I was past a fascinated man on the aisle, an arm was off. I didn't turn around as I went up the aisle but I'm told a thorough job was done.

Although nobody was fooled thanks to the atrocious acting and special effects, the marketing worked, with the film earning many times more than it cost to make. It also made the term 'snuff movie' part of modern lexicon.

When you ask people about snuff films, most of them have an image or idea in their mind. It is generally that which Hollywood depicts—most notably the Nicholas Cage film *8MM* or the torture-porn *Hostel* flicks. It will involve the kidnap of a person, usually female, who will be tied up, perhaps blindfolded, in an empty room, unaware of her potential fate. We are often given the viewpoint of the viewer of the snuff film, through the eye of the camera that is making the snuff movie. The victim is tortured, often raped, then killed, all for the purpose of making a film, which is then sold.

Perhaps just as fascinating as the producers of these films is the idea of the shadowy super-rich, who are able to buy anything they want. Their desires get more and more difficult to fulfil, but the harder something is to procure, the higher its value.

In one episode of the 1990s series *La Femme Nikita*, 'Hand to Hand', Nikita is captured by a 'Talent Agency' where beautiful prostitutes are forced to fight each other to the death for 'the pleasure of perverted men', an audience of the super-wealthy. The fights are held in a luxuriously fitted-out bunker and the men who attend are rich, powerful and have shady, unexplained contacts that can get them entry to the show. Those who pay the most can choose from the bevy of beautiful women (who are kept in line with collars that can be activated to provide electric shocks) to determine the one who will fight the champion. Men in expensive suits sit silently in the shadows in their opulent theatre boxes as women in evening dresses fight to the death in a water-filled pit below them.

Despite these depictions of snuff films and the shadowy elite who purchase them, no verified examples surfaced over the years, although journalists and the merely curious continued to search for them.

The cover of a 1997 book by Yaron Svoray, *Gods of Death*, provided a tantalising suggestion that the former cop turned investigative journalist had uncovered the secret world of the snuff film: 'Around the World, Behind Closed Doors, Operates an Ultra Secret Business of Sex and Death. One Man Hunts the Truth about Snuff Films'.

The book details an investigation into the world of snuff films, which Svoray claims to have infiltrated. He claims to have seen several snuff films (including one in the company of a Hollywood A-list movie star, no less). However, the book is big on promises and small on delivery. It is notable that Amazon lists it in the 'humour' section.

There have been no credible examples of real snuff movies ever having been made, but they remain one of the most enduring myths. In an interview with culture website Spectacular Optical, researcher and author Simon Laperrière said that snuff movies are an example of an urban legend that grows and adapts to the world around it. David Cronenberg's *Videodrome*, he says, is an important movie because it 'allowed the urban legend to adapt itself to new technologies. Here, snuff films are no longer affiliated with cinema, but also with television and VHS. Such a switch from one medium to another allows the rumor to remain actual and appear real to an audience.' But an urban legend, nevertheless.

'According to [the legend], there's a secret network somewhere selling to rich individuals reels of films showing actual murders. As of 2013, we have no proof that such snuff films exist.'

The internet and blurring the lines

It is easy to believe that snuff films are nothing more than an urban legend when making one would necessitate large, expensive cameras and sound equipment, a director, and possibly even a crew. The movie would have to be made, and then physically distributed to viewers on film or a tape.

But what now, when every phone is also a camera? With half the world's population walking around with a camera in their pockets there is more chance than ever before of catching death and mayhem on film. Publishing it to the world takes a matter of seconds.

'The margins have become fudged,' wrote David Kerekes in an essay in *Snuff: Real Death and Screen Media*. 'The likes of the Dnepropetrovsk Maniacs, Islamic State and Magnotta were never a foreseeable part of the original "plan", goalposts change often in the new millennium.'

Kerekes said that the growth of the internet and ready availability of cameras meant he would need to revisit his book, *Killing for Culture*, the seminal text on snuff films. New technologies had rendered some material out of date.

Those cases Kerekes mentioned were the ones that came closest to bringing the myth of the snuff film into reality. The first is a reference to an amateur film dubbed '3 Guys 1 Hammer'. The video graphically depicts the murder of an innocent man with a screwdriver and hammer in the Ukraine in 2007 by two men known as the 'Dnepropetrovsk Maniacs'. The Maniacs killed a total of 21 people and there was evidence led at their trial that they had planned to distribute the video of the murder for profit, but never had the chance before they were caught. The gruesome video is readily available on 'gore' sites on the internet.

Islamic State terrorists harnessed the power of the internet by deliberately filming and circulating beheadings as warnings to those ideologically opposed to them and their message. The internet is now home to a plethora of films of the beheadings of both Western and Middle-Eastern hostages by Islamic extremists. Similarly, drug cartels sometimes circulate videos of their atrocities. One video shows a cartel member whose torture was filmed by a rival drug gang; he somehow remains conscious despite his face having been peeled off, his eyes gouged out and his hands cut off. Cartels have been known to use huge amounts of methamphetamine to prevent their victims from fainting, so they remain conscious throughout the ordeal. The man is eventually decapitated with a box cutter as upbeat music plays in the background. Although these are graphic murders on film, they fall shy of the definition of snuff as defined at the start of this part.

In 2012, Canadian Luka Magnotta tied naked Chinese university student Jun Lin to a bed frame, then tortured, stabbed and eventually murdered the young man with an ice pick. Magnotta dismembered the body, sexually defiled body parts, and went on to mail the limbs to two primary schools in Vancouver, as well as the headquarters of both the Conservative and Liberal parties. He edited together an eleven-minute video that featured the torture, stabbing, dismemberment and necrophilia, but not, apparently, the moment of death.

The video, which was provided to BestGore, a Canadian shock site (although it is not clear whether it was provided personally by Magnotta), came to be known as *1 Lunatic, 1 Icepick*.

Simon Laperrière studied the film. 'I came to the conclusion that while it's not technically a snuff film (it doesn't show the moment of death and was not made for commercial purposes), it is currently the closest thing we'll ever get to a real one,' he said in the Spectacular Optical interview.

What was disturbing was the appetite for viewing such material. Videos would turn up on websites dedicated to gore, with names like rotten.com, bestgore.com and ogrish.com, that encouraged members to scour the web and find the most graphic and disturbing images and films possible of murders, suicides, torture, mutilations and accidents. The sites were competitive and tried to outdo each other with their depictions of real violence. They get millions of visitors, with the most graphic videos garnering hundreds of thousands of views and being shared widely among snuff seekers.

People are provided the opportunity to comment on videos, and the lack of empathy, perhaps even psychopathy, evident in some comments is chilling.

This is a rip off. You don't even get to see him die.

What fun is it if the victim is too drugged up to fight back?

I love the sound when the hammer goes in and then when he's trying to talk after lol.

Thats kinda cool lol . . . fucked but sill awesome

I really don't care about the people he killed, I'm only sad about the kittens

This gave me an erection

Such incidents brought the snuff film closer to becoming a reality, but still nothing fit in with the popularly conceived notion of what a snuff film is.

However, they did open up the question of when something became illegal to own, download or share. The owner of BestGore, Mark Marek, was arrested when he failed to remove *1 Lunatic 1 Icepick* after it was verified to be a genuine murder. He was charged under Canada's obscenity law with corrupting public morals, to which he pleaded guilty and received three months' house arrest followed by three months of community service.

The gore websites remained popular, but were restricted by laws that meant they could not host illegal material. Although the appetite for more extreme, violent and genuine material continued to grow, the sites were stymied by the fact that any website operating on the internet could be shut down, its owner identified and possibly prosecuted.

Enter the dark web.

The dark web

The dark web provided a haven for the sorts of videos that would be illegal to host on the internet. Such videos could now be hosted without fear of the site being shut down, nor of the owners, uploaders or downloaders being identified.

The dark web allowed niche sites, such as animal snuff, to operate more openly. It is an odd quirk of human nature that people who are comfortable watching torture and murder of humans might balk at harm to an animal. The outrage directed at sites dedicated to animal harm far outweighed that directed to the ones that hosted violent human deaths. But such videos fared better on the dark web. One niche in particular, 'crush porn', which involved women in high heels crushing small animals to death, proved to be popular underground.

Despite this, the gore sites on the dark web were little different to those on the internet. No films hosted were worse than *3 Guys 1 Hammer* or *1 Lunatic 1 Icepick*.

However, such is the nature of people, new rumours circulated about deeper, darker sections of the dark web that housed new horrors. Not only snuff movies, but real-life gladiator fights to the death, and pay-per-view murder.

Such claims tended to be hazy on the details. Were the gladiator fights *Fight Club*-type events, where angry, muscled men willingly take the 50/50 chance that they will die in a sort of winner-takes-all scenario? Is there some sort of promoter who takes bets from punters, or who sells access to the live feeds?

Or were they perhaps *Django Unchained* situations, where unscrupulous millionaires force slaves to fight to the death in a 'kill or be killed' scenario, for their own private amusement and that of a select group of their similarly morally bereft millionaire friends?

While none of these potential situations seems likely, gladiator fights became one of the most pervasive myths on the dark web. Conspiracy website Words With Meaning ran a 'special investigative series' by someone claiming to be a cybersecurity expert who needed to remain anonymous because he was a former employee of the UK Centre for Cybercrime and Computer Security. This investigator was convinced that the underground fights to the death could be found on the dark web: 'There are literally gladiators who organise ways of fighting to death. I know how exaggerated this sounds—trust me, I'm the one trying to convince readers it is true—but there's no joke to this claim,' he wrote. The 'security researcher' was, unsurprisingly, unable to provide anything resembling proof for his claims.

That's not to say that there are never genuine forced fights to the death; they do occur, and are most notoriously engaged in by the drug cartels, in particular Los Zetas. 'The elderly are killed. Young women are raped. And able-bodied men are given hammers, machetes and sticks and forced to fight to the death,' reported the *Houston Chronicle* in 2011. The Zetas would force passengers off buses passing through San Fernando and stage gladiator fights to the death, with the survivor being forced to join their ranks. A cartel member told the *Houston Chronicle* it was a game they called 'Who's going to be the next hitman?' Nearly 200 bodies found in mass graves gave the man's story veracity.

Although videos of drug cartel atrocities have made their way to the gore sites, there is no evidence that these fights to the death were recorded. In particular, there were no livestreams with observers able to bet on the outcome, nor were tickets sold to the bloodthirsty rich.

Red rooms

A young man sits at his desk, door locked against any unexpected visitors. The screen in front of him shows a windowless room, dungeon-like, undecorated and sparsely furnished. Against one wall is an iron bedframe, topped by a bare mattress, indeterminate dark stains concealing any discernible pattern. The only other piece of furniture in the room is a wooden chair. A young woman strains against the ropes binding her to the chair, screaming.

As the clock clicks over to the allotted time, a huge, hooded figure enters the room, causing the young woman to scream more. On the screen, a chat box appears, with half a dozen usernames of those who are watching. The masked man looks up to the camera, awaiting his commands. The young man's fingers fly across the keyboard. 'Cut off her ear.' The hooded figure picks up a knife.

This is the scenario those who pay the requisite Bitcoin fee to a dark web red room expect to see. Red rooms are another staple story of the dark web. To describe them, you might think of the movie *Hostel*, with webcams.

In an interview with horror film site Dread Central, *Hostel*'s director, Eli Roth, said the idea came to him after a friend sent him a link to a site that allowed a person to travel to a place in Thailand and, for ten thousand dollars, walk into a room and shoot somebody in the head. 'The site claimed that the person you were killing had signed up for it and that part of the money would go to their family because they were so broke and were gonna die anyways,' he said. 'It was to give you the thrill of taking another human life.'

In *Hostel*, a shadowy Eastern European outfit lures foreign tourists to a hostel. The tourists soon find themselves bound to a chair in an isolated location. Rich Western businessmen bid for the right to torture and kill the victim, while others get to watch.

The dark web version provided the opportunity for people to take part without having to physically carry out the torture and murder. For a fee, punters would be provided with login credentials to a virtual 'room' at an allocated time. In that room, cameras would be concentrated on a person—invariably female—tied to a chair or bed, or chained to the wall by her ankle.

The entry fee provided the right to be a voyeur to the proceedings. Participants could pay extra to direct the action, typing commands into the chat section on the screen, which would then be carried out by a hooded man.

The sites became known as red rooms.

The enabling technologies of the dark web—Tor and Bitcoin—provided such scenarios with new plausibility. Tor technology meant that videos could be hosted without revealing the location of the film. Bitcoin allowed for instant, anonymous payment by the audience to watch or participate, directing the action.

A red room site will feature a creepy picture of a dungeon or room that looks straight out of a horror movie. It will typically have a countdown to the next 'show' and invite prospective participants to click to enter. Upon clicking, a welcome screen such as the one at the beginning of this section explains what you will get for your money and contains testimonials from previous viewers, which sometimes provide graphic detail of what was done to the unfortunate victim.

Potential participants will be directed to a Bitcoin address that will unlock a download of the special software required to access the show. Entry fees are typically significant, which deters journalists and the merely curious from signing up.

Such red rooms had all the hallmarks of a scam and certainly no evidence ever surfaced that any legitimate red room existed, or that anybody was ever harmed or killed for the entertainment of a live pay-per-view audience.

Then one day in August 2015, a different type of red room promised a very different type of dark web entertainment. And anyone could join in.

The ISIS red room

It started, as these things are wont to do, with posts on 4Chan and reddit, the discussion boards popular for dark web topics: *WHOA! Is this Real??* The posts provided no explanation, but just an onion (i.e. dark web) link. The curious, of course, clicked. If they had the Tor browser, they were greeted with a message:

Greetings!

Do you think you've seen the worst yet?

On 29 August 2015 at 00:00:00 UTC, right here, on this onion address, a new market will open. One that even the Feds will love. Do not miss the market opening. There will be a free event that you will not want to miss! Watch real life terrorists turn on each other!

The greeting went on to say the site owners had captured seven ISIS terrorists whom they would humiliate ('there will be bacon'), torture, set against each other in fights to the death, and ultimately murder live on webcam at the allotted time and date.

The site promised, it seemed, that the two most persistent dark web myths—gladiator fights to the death and the red rooms—were to become reality. As it was ISIS terrorists getting tortured and killed for participants' viewing pleasure, some of the guilt that potential voyeurs might have could be assuaged. After all, ISIS had regularly made videos of its atrocities available and the public was hyper-aware of the threat of terrorism.

Unlike other red rooms, this one was funded by 'wealthy interested parties' and would be streamed free to anybody who cared to join in. Those who joined would be able to type commands into a chat box, with suggestions of appropriate punishments for the captives. The prospect of a free show ignited the social forums of reddit, 4Chan, LiveLeak and YouTube.

'This is gonna be the best date night ever!' wrote one participant.

As the clock ticked down, the site updated periodically with its preparation and plans.

We are working around the clock.

We are around a warzone and got more urgent things to worry about. But we will deliver and we will hit the deadline.

Maybe not under optimal circumstances as hoped, but the circumstances also makes things even worse for our ISIS pigs.

Enclaves of mobs were forming on the various forums chatting about the event. Although some were sceptical, many expressed hope that this one was real. Few questioned how they could verify that the people being tortured and killed were, in fact, terrorists.

'I don't usually condone violence, but I can't wait to see these pigs suffer,' was a typical attitude.

A black and white photograph of a hooded man, seated on a bare hard floor, dog bowls at his side, greeted those who visited the site. He had the posture of defeat and his captors, calling themselves Enemies of Islamic State, delighted in updating their audience with preparations:

> The conditions are good here for the 'soldiers of god'. The dogfood (shit flavored) is free and we fill their water bowl with clean water and flavor it with piss.

> It's not our fault if they don't eat, they called for it. They are such heroes. Again, support us by watching. That's all we need.

The next update informed the potential voyeurs that the captors had already executed two prisoners, but not to worry, they still had another five who could be used for the entertainment.

> Expect fun games, mingle and torture as promised. All inter-active. Still fully free. We will make at least the first hour family friendly, and explicitly warn you before things get violent.

The soon-to-be-killers had also opened up the chat room, allowing what appeared to be an army of teenage boys to spout semi-literate racist slurs. When the event started, the chat room would be used to suggest punishments and tortures for the captured terrorists.

Once they opened up the chat room, the excitement built expo-nentially. People started exchanging ideas for commands they would type once the show got underway. They feverishly tried to outdo each other in imaginary punishments and humiliation to be perpetrated on the hooded figures.

Other than questioning the overall authenticity of the proposed show, nobody seemed interested in querying how any viewers could verify that the captives were who the webmasters said they were. How could we tell they were terrorists being punished for their sins and not innocent people being murdered for page views?

As the timer counted down, the suggestions became increasingly violent and cruel. Many had a sexual element to them, which the website promised to deliver.

We will sell their assholes a.k.a. human trafficking. We want to give ISIS-careers a promising future!

We will also upload materials for free. We call it the 'insta-gram' of happy ISIS whores or instagram of Jihad, what do you think? Having their asses sold is just too ironic to not document and eternalize and we promise exactly that.

We make Moviestars of Jihadists. It's part of the non-optional ISIS-employment with us.

By the time there were just a few hours left on the clock, the potential audience had gathered in the chat room. The few people who expressed reservations were howled down, and those who articulated concern at the bloodthirsty nature of the mob were branded terrorist sympathisers.

For some it was nervous anticipation: 'I'm nervous. I feel like it's wrong for us to be "excited" for this, but I've had the tab open for hours now, so who am I to bring up morality?' wrote one voyeur.

'Not gonna watch this since ive never been on the deepweb before and dont wanna get fucked—but pretty excited to see it [if] this shit is real or not,' wrote another. He was assured somebody would record it and upload videos to YouTube for those who were afraid of logging on themselves and watching via the dark web.

Some anti-vigilante vigilantes spammed the chat room with nonsense, trying to ensure the torture orders would not get through, and soon 4Chan took over, linking to child pornography sites. Between them, they succeeded in making the chat room all but unreadable.

Nevertheless, some torture requests made it through, and these involved everything from force-feeding bacon (which they considered to be the height of humiliation for people of the Muslim faith) through to anal rape, acid in the captives' eyes, removal of teeth, forcing them to drink bleach, dismemberment and, of course, eventual murder.

The voyeurs fed off each other's sadism. They discussed how they could drag the torture out for days and techniques for making sure the captives did not pass out.

The clock continued to tick down.

One participant summed up the atmosphere: 'OMG OMG OMG!'

A couple of minutes short of the start time, a refresh of the page resulted in the ubiquitous *404: Page Not Found* error.

The mob frantically refreshed in the hope that the site would come back up. Rumours began circulating almost immediately: the FBI had put it under attack; maybe ISIS had found out and stopped it; hopefully it simply buckled under the weight of all those people refreshing?

A little under an hour later, the site reappeared. 'Thank you for participating and directing the action! Stream over, will be uploading in parts.'

Shortly after, links to footage of one of the ISIS captives being tortured appeared. The video lasted a little over 21 minutes, during which almost nothing happened. Every time the 'torturer' carried out a punishment on the suspiciously pale-skinned jihadist, the video froze or jumped. There was, indeed, bacon involved.

While a few people desperately clung on to the hope that the video was genuine, the majority accepted that it was an elaborate hoax, which wound up being poorly executed. The disappointment was palpable.

'Wasn't real, it was just a hoax. And a bad one. Which is a shame because I was looking forwards to this shit for a couple of weeks!'

It was chilling to witness the mounting hysteria, the reactions of people who believed or hoped that this particular red room was real, and their anger and disappointment when the ISIS red room turned out to be a badly acted hoax.

Black Death and Facebook Live

In 2015 another dark-web site which purported to allow customers to browse photographs and sign up to bid in an auction garnered some attention. On the site Black Death, punters bid on young women whom they could purchase for any purpose they chose, including for the goal of creating a snuff movie. The site listed details of where the women had been kidnapped, their race, age, weight, height and breast size. Bids started in the high five figures, but ran well into six figures for blonde Western women. It was dismissed as yet another hoax (indeed, Motherboard readers soon uncovered BDSM porn movies from which it was apparent screenshots had been used to advertise the so-called victims) until a bizarre revival in 2017.

On 11 July 2017, British Page 3 glamour model Chloe Ayling was allegedly kidnapped in Milan, having been lured there by a fake modelling shoot. The model claimed to have been drugged with ketamine and bundled into the trunk of a car by two men. She was then held, bound to a chest of drawers, in a remote farmhouse a couple of hours out of Milan. Her kidnappers told her they planned to auction her with a starting bid of $300,000 on the dark web. She had, they said, been put up for sale on Black Death, where there had already been offers made to buy her.

In an implausible twist, the kidnappers decided to release Ayling six days later, after she told them she had a two-year-old child. It was against Black Death's rules, they claimed, to kidnap and sell mothers. The man who dropped her off, Polish-born (but UK resident) Lukasz Herba, was promptly arrested. His alleged accomplice, his brother, was arrested not long after.

Ayling's story came under scrutiny when it was revealed that she and Herba (whom acquaintances described as a deluded, narcissistic loner) had been spotted shopping for groceries and shoes together during the time of the ordeal. Witnesses claimed they thought the two were a couple. Upon her return to the UK, Ayling employed the services of a celebrity agent to navigate the talk show circuit. Nevertheless, she stuck to her story, claiming she did not try to escape during the shopping outing because she feared for her life. At the time of writing, the two brothers remain in custody, and Herba has reportedly confessed to the elaborate kidnapping. However, the mystery remains as to whether Black Death exists as a real or hoax website, and what, if any, role the brothers had in the site.

Hoax or not, how far are we from the real thing? If a red room ever comes to fruition, it is more likely to appear on the clear web than the dark web, perhaps even through our most familiar websites. Facebook Live, the application that allows anybody to broadcast live to their friends or the public at large, has already provided a platform on which people have livestreamed their crimes, including a number of suicides and at least one murder.

One of the most disturbing aspects during the suicides was that viewers responded much like the mob in the ISIS red room. They cajoled, insulted and encouraged the victims to complete the task.

In April 2017, Steve Stephens filmed himself on Facebook Live as he killed a homeless man. He said the killing could be blamed on his ex-girlfriend. 'She's the reason I'm doing this,' he told his victim.

And on the dark web, it remains a tediously common question: 'How can I go deeper in the deep web? Where's the *really* dark stuff?'

The really dark stuff exists. Truly horrific things take place on the dark web. Those who ask, however, are rarely prepared to face the truth of just how dark the dark web can go.

The darkest corners

We're building digital tools to fight human trafficking. Basically, the purchase and commerce for human trafficking is happening online, just like everything else now, and so we're building digital tools to fight back against it.

—THORN: Digital Defenders of Children

Innocent Screams is only for discussing and sharing the rape, torture and death of people (and animals). Yes, that does mean you can post pictures of children being violently raped and killed (there are even sections just for that) but it is not your place to post random CP [child pornography]. All posts must deal with real abuse of some sort or it will be deleted. Furthermore, if you are easily offended you should NOT join. You have been warned. If you're not a pansy ass bitch and still want to join, then welcome to Innocent Screams!

—Welcome page to a dark web hurtcore site

'Father accused of raping daughter, 2, in livestream on the dark web'. The headline is sickening, but it is not isolated. The dark web is a breeding ground for child predators, declares one tabloid newspaper after another, and the market continues to grow.

It's the stuff of nightmares. One of the most common fears of those venturing into the dark web for the first time is that they will stumble across child pornography. The fears are not without foundation; child pornography is rife on the dark web and anybody who goes searching for it will find it in no time. However, the chances of stumbling upon it accidentally are slim. The sites usually require registration and they leave the visitor in no doubt of what lies beyond the login screen.

When the first darknet markets started trading on the dark web, the idea was that they would allow and encourage completely free trade. But even the most hardcore libertarians found the belief in free trade tested when vendors began to offer child pornography and abuse materials for sale on the websites. The markets all had an XXX section and, in between codes for cheap access to premium porn sites on the clear web, that section would soon be flooded with questionable material.

No matter what people were browsing the darknet markets for, most balked at the idea of child exploitation material. This was something that was beyond the moral compass of decent people, and even the vast majority of otherwise indecent people. Any market that allowed the sale of such materials came under fire from its current and potential customers. Excuses of being unable to police what people bought and sold on an open market held no water. Some market owners argued that freedom meant freedom to sell *anything*, including those things that the majority thought to be abhorrent. After all, the typical users were themselves on the fringe of respectable society, buying drugs or weapons; surely it was hypocritical to try and ban the people who were even further to the fringes.

Freenet.org, a smaller anonymity provider than Tor, but one that was known for its population of child abuse sites, claimed, 'the true test of someone who claims to believe in Freedom of Speech is whether they tolerate speech which they disagree with or even find disgusting'. But such arguments fell on deaf ears, and black-market customers were quick to threaten a boycott of any business that allowed the sale or dissemination of child exploitation materials. Even if market owners wanted to allow such items for sale, it became commercially unviable to do so.

Not being able to promote their wares on the large and well-known markets did not stop child exploitation from proliferating. Pedophiles and predators simply created their own corner of the dark web, where their sites were grouped together—forums, chat, images, videos and worse—under different headings to cater to different tastes. These sites provided the opportunity to download all manner of porn that could not be found on the regular internet. This included child porn (pre-pubescent children), jailbait (young teens), zoophilia or bestiality and hurtcore, which involves children, adults and animals genuinely being subjected to pain and, in some cases, torture.

The sites had names like Playpen, Toybox, Child's Play, Kinder Surprise, Lolita City, Giftbox, The Love Zone; the pedophiles took all that was innocent and turned it into something sick and disturbing. It was not difficult for predators and pedophiles to find each other on the dark web. The most well-known gateway to the dark web, the Hidden Wiki, blatantly separated its porn section into adult and underage, the latter grouped in a section called Hard Candy.

The child pornography and exploitation market is the most disturbing aspect of the dark web. It's not just the images and videos that are uploaded by the terabyte, but social forums where child abusers share tips on how to sedate young children while keeping them awake, psychological tricks and ways of covering up their crimes. Seeing chat rooms in which offenders graphically describe sex acts with prepubescent children in the same terms you might expect to hear used for adult porn stars is beyond disturbing.

In October 2011, Anonymous launched Operation Darknet, with a goal of exposing those who accessed child pornography over Tor. Anonymous is the name given to the vigilante hacktivist (hacker-activist) collective spawned from 4Chan, a discussion forum and image board where most contributors post under the username 'anonymous'. Anonymous is not an organisation with central membership that one can join. It is at best a loosely associated collective.

Those who identify as Anonymous enjoy trolling people and organisations (the Church of Scientology is a favourite target) and they are quick to claim responsibility for distributed denial of service (DDoS) attacks on corporations they perceive as evil. They have often been accused of internet bullying. However, they have also become known for tackling social justice issues, some of which caught the attention of the world. One such initiative was Operation Darknet.

Operation Darknet was one of the early examples of a combination of technical know-how and social engineering as weapons to expose those hiding behind Tor's hidden services. Anonymous posted a pastebin dump of what they claimed were names and IP addresses of people who had accessed child pornography through the dark web's Lolita City, the largest site under the Hidden Wiki's Hard Candy banner.

Media coverage and a groundswell of support followed Anonymous' actions for the next few days. As usual with such events, the coverage started with online technical and gossip news services like PC World and Gawker, but within a few days spread to reports in *The Wall Street Journal* and on the BBC. Most of the services repeated the official line Anonymous had taken: 'We vowed to fight for the defenseless, there is none more defenseless than innocent children being exploited.'

Hard Candy continued to be restored from backups, and after the 20 October restoration the owner of the site sent Anonymous a message: 'To the vandals, you vandalize the page 1,000,000 times, we will correct it 1,000,001. It will just go back and forth. We are here to stay. People want to run DDoS attacks over tor and think it hurts us, it does. It is our GOD given right that we can choose to have our sexual preferences for youth. It is the same for any other porn community.

It is not what we choose to become, it is who we are. You Anonymous aka #OpDarknet do not have the right to censor us.'

Anonymous responded with the launch of Operation Paw Printing. In a clever form of social engineering designed to unmask some of the users of child porn sites and frighten the others, they tricked visitors to Hard Candy and Lolita City into clicking on a button, which had actually been placed there by Anonymous and would then log the user's information.

Disguising the button—which was only available on the Hard Candy gateway to child porn—as a 'Tor security update', Anonymous harvested the IP addresses of 190 unique individuals from around the world over a 24-hour period.

On 2 November, in another pastebin message, Anonymous described in detail how they had unmasked the IP addresses and provided their rationale for these actions:

> Operation Darknet was never intended to bring down Tor or the 'darknets'. The only purpose of Operation Darknet was to reveal that a service like the 'Tor Project' has been ruined by the 1% using it for Child Pornography. The rest, 99% consists of Chinese/Iran journalists, Government intelligence fighting a secret war with Al-Qaeda, and us Anons who believe in the right to Free Speech.

> However, Child Pornography is NOT FREE SPEECH. We proved beyond doubt, that 70% of users to The Hidden Wiki access the HARD CANDY section, 'a secret directory' used by the pedophiles to access sites like Lolita City and The Hurt Site, a site dedicated to trade of child rape.

Anonymous' efforts were in vain. Law enforcement was unable to use the IP addresses, illegally obtained, to track down users of child pornography. Their one small win was their regained popularity among many internet users who had become tired of apparently ad hoc attacks on businesses, organisations and websites under the Anonymous name. They earned their right to be classed as hacktivists, rather than garden variety hackers. In the following years, they hit the limelight again for forcing the authorities to investigate rape allegations that had been covered up, most notably the Steubenville High School rape incident. Two popular footballers had carried an unconscious teenager from place to place, sexually assaulting her and filming their crimes. The young girl did not know she had been raped until the pictures started circulating on social media. Most of the town rallied behind the boys until the intervention of Anonymous, which resulted in the conviction of the rapists. Three other people were indicted for obstructing the investigation into the rape. Anonymous also became known for unmasking and shaming trolls who stalked and bullied their victims, sometimes to death, from behind the safety of their keyboards.

They vowed to continue the fight against child abuse sites: 'We will continue to not only crash Freedom Hosting's server, but any other server we find to contain, promote, or support child pornography.'

But there was one consequence of Operation Darknet that the members of Anonymous could never have foreseen. When one particular person checked the sites to see what all of the fuss was about, instead of revulsion, he felt excitement; instead of turning away, he sensed he had found his people.

The making of a predator

There were many who watched the Anonymous takedown of Lolita City with interest. One of these was someone who was a regular on 4Chan, where much of Anonymous' work either originated from or was discussed in depth. He had given himself the name 'Lux', after a brand of soap. Lux desperately wanted to earn respect and cachet in the dark web. He fancied himself as quite the security expert, and had studied the darknet markets, hoping to be able to offer his services there. He found, however, that the markets' security was tight and clearly administered by professionals. They had no need for the comparatively rudimentary skills of Lux. So he turned his attention to other, deeper, darker, parts of the dark web.

'It was kind of a morbid curiosity that drew me towards it,' he would later say, claiming that at first he wanted to help Anonymous in their fight to take down the pedophiles. He would insist that he had no predilection towards children when he started logging in to the sites. But as he delved further into the murky depths of child pornography, his attitude began to change. 'It was quite a supportive community. And this was at a time where I was really struggling with depression and the aspergers was at its worst,' he said. 'I kind of found, I dunno, like a home in there. Like a support network.'

The child abuse sites, which did not have the millions of dollars of profits available to them that the darknet markets enjoyed, were significantly less secure, and those who accessed them far less technically proficient and security conscious than their drug-buying brethren. Lux was keen to offer security advice and the sites were keen to accept it.

Lux created the persona of an American pediatrician. He claimed to have had numerous sexual encounters with children, as well as maintaining an ongoing sexual relationship with a specific six-year-old. He said all the things he thought would give him a role and status among pedophiles. 'I guess as time went by I kind of gained the trust and respect of that small community,' he said.

Lux craved acceptance, approval, adulation; all things he could not get in his real life, or elsewhere online. He was not special or talented. Nothing he did made people interested in getting to know him, or even talking to him. When he entered this world, he felt at home. All the people within the virtual walls of the gated community

were reviled and hated, but also, they felt, misunderstood and perse-
cuted. Some wore the revulsion of others towards them like a badge
of honour.

'It wasn't until I came across the Tor pedo community that I was
able to truly feel comfortable with [my] attractions,' he told journalist
Patrick O'Neill in his one extensive interview.

Lux set about providing security tips and advice to keep pedophiles
safe from the long arm of the law. He knew how to strip metadata from
photographs and videos, and secure computers against prying eyes.
The people he helped were grateful; they thanked him and praised his
efforts to keep them safe. He was getting the acknowledgement and
appreciation he craved so badly.

One person became particularly close. Lux struck up a friendship
with a man who called himself Wolfman Jack. Together they created
Lux's first website in Tor, which purported to allow darker and more
extreme material than was permitted on most of the sites. It was
the first of many sites, and their development gave Lux a purpose.
'Most nights when I get home from work, instead of sitting back and
watching TV, I bust out my laptop and get working on the PedoEmpire
hopefully creating something which makes the community at least a
smidgen better,' he told O'Neill.

Another in his circle was Skee, who operated The Love Zone and
shared child abuse content with Lux's sites, including acts he had committed himself. Skee did not share the craving Lux and some others
had for publicity. 'WHY the hell would you give this information
out, why would you be stupid enough to risk ruining peoples lives by
destroying the secrecy we have spent years building?' he asked those
who were willing to cooperate with journalists. 'Information is power
and your just giving out information about a group of people doing
a highly illegal activity, its not a fucking joke, 250 years in jail is not
a fucking joke. You dont give out any information regardless of how
knowledgable you think you are.'

Lux, however, revelled in his growing notoriety. The ever-growing network of sex offenders on the dark web turned to him as the oracle of child exploitation, something that gave him great satisfaction and self-worth. He provided exceptional customer service and went to great lengths to ensure the users of his websites remained anonymous.

Abusers began to approach him for other advice. Pleased and proud to be called upon, Lux offered direction on how to groom and sexually abuse young children, how to ensure there were no signs of sexual penetration, how to drug children so they would be awake during the abuse but would have no memory of it afterwards, and how to kidnap, kill and dispose of a child's body.

Over the next couple of years, Lux created more sites to satisfy the tastes of different niches of the online pedophile population, providing what he believed 'the community' needed and wanted. As his sites grew in number and popularity, he created an umbrella group that housed a variety of sites dedicated to child porn and abuse material. He called it PedoEmpire, and Lux was the emperor.

PedoEmpire

Lux's PedoEmpire was designed to be a one-stop shop for all things pedophilia; anything from pictures of barely-clothed children—torn from underwear catalogues or downloaded from friends' Facebook updates of a day at the beach—to materials designed to satisfy the darkest and most depraved tastes of the sickest individuals. Grouped under five tabs—'News', 'Pedophilia & CP' ('verified selection of websites I personally use or recommend'), 'Empire', 'Utilities and Safety' and 'Uploads'—were links to everything imaginable.

There were forums for users to chat with like-minded individuals, with messages grouped under themes and subjects, like any other internet message board. There were video streaming (PedoTube) and image upload services. 'I would also like to find a way where I can have

PedoTube completely open to the public and not require an invite, but it's proven to be much more difficult than I originally thought it would be,' he told O'Neill, 'but it's definitely something that's on my to-do list!'

An entry point and one of the most visited of the sites was the PedoWiki. Just like its innocent wiki cousins, this was a receptacle for all types of education, history and knowledge-sharing which could be added to, corrected and updated by members of the PedoEmpire. It grew to nearly 600 articles over 1200 pages, under headings like:

- Child Porn Stars
- Debate Guide (a guide for arguments to use against anti-child-porn crusaders)
- Research
- History of Child Porn

The PedoWiki proved popular, with over a thousand active contributors. The pages within garnered over 3 million hits.

Elsewhere in the empire, while some sites required an invite from a trusted member to get access, most would allow basic viewing privileges, but members would have to prove themselves to gain access to 'premium' areas. 'Leeches'—those who consume without sharing— were frowned upon and would soon find themselves excluded from anywhere but the entry page to the site. New members were required to share images or film, with preference going to fresh footage that had not been shared elsewhere.

Lux required different levels of intensity of participation depending on the site and area within the site. The merely curious were free to browse photographs of naked or partly clothed children, but to gain access to more pornographic images, members had to upload pornographic images of their own. To earn entry to the exclusive Producers' Lounges, members had to prove they were personally active with a child, by providing never-before-seen footage that included the child holding a sign with a unique identifier, such as the name of the site or a phrase dictated by Lux. Some members scrawled their username onto the child's skin with a marker.

Such measures not only kept leeches at bay, but also assisted in keeping law enforcement out of the sites. It was one thing for law enforcement agents to purchase drugs from the darknet markets, but producing and uploading child pornography was a different matter altogether. As there is no way of producing the material without harming a child, certain areas remained off limits until somebody was arrested and handed over their login credentials. Even then, access might be short-lived, because the most exclusive areas required ongoing uploads of new materials.

Lux's PedoEmpire grew in membership, content and popularity as use of the dark web became more widespread. He never charged for any materials, nor, he told O'Neill, did he ever intend to. As far as Lux was concerned, he was providing a service to a marginalised section of the community, not a commercial enterprise.

Some pedophiles were content with the material provided, but others sought increasingly depraved and violent photos and videos. On 28 February 2013, Lux created a new site to satisfy the cravings of those who wanted the most extreme thrill. It gained thousands of followers and members in no time at all. Lux's new endeavour was universally agreed to be the worst child abuse website that ever existed.

Hurt2theCore

Hurt2theCore is a forum that's dedicated to open discussion and allowing people to express their uncensored thoughts and ideas about pedophilia and child sex. This means that we welcome <u>both</u> the Child Love and Hurtcore aspects of it.

If you do not feel comfortable in discussing or viewing material that deals with <u>both</u> these topics, then this is not the place for you. Otherwise, welcome to Hurt2theCore!

– welcome page of Hurt2theCore (2013)

'My name is Lux,' the man quickly becoming the most reviled person on the dark web wrote in a note to law enforcement officers. 'Not only do I maintain the largest suite of child pornography on Tor, I also have complete control over the largest number of proven producers in the world.' He had the right to make these claims thanks to the phenomenal and continued growth of his PedoEmpire.

The dark web was full of anonymous and pseudonymous characters who held various levels of fame or infamy within the net's dark underbelly. Some, like Dread Pirate Roberts and Bitcoin creator Satoshi Nakamoto, were lauded as libertarian heroes and visionaries. Many of the most prolific drug vendors were admired despite their outlaw status.

Then there was Lux. His name became known as it seeped out of the murkiest corners of the dark web, whispered with revulsion and disgust by some, while the majority tried to pretend he did not exist at all. Even the pedophiles who dwelled in the cesspools of the dark web had a hierarchy of the 'acceptable' level of abuse they could tolerate. The type of materials available through the Hidden Wiki's Hard Candy gateway varied widely, from otherwise innocent photographs of children through to increasingly extreme and exploitative materials.

'The issue I can't shake in my mind is that in the general population equates everyone like us with slime like Lux and his cohorts. It reinforces the sick shit they make TV and movie detectives uncover. It is so disheartening,' wrote someone in a 'pedo support community', whose forum profile stated he liked both boys and girls, aged four to fourteen.

The efforts of hacktivists like Anonymous did little, if anything, to stem the availability of child abuse material on the dark web. Following the brief and ultimately unsuccessful DDoSing of Lolita City, if anything, the type of material being shared got even more extreme. The most horrifying trend was towards filming not just sexual abuse of children, but the deliberate infliction of pain on them for the entertainment of viewers. Lux was the king of hurtcore and he gained a reputation of such cruelty, most pedophiles shunned him. However, to a small (but still disturbingly large) subset he was a hero and he revelled in that status.

Others tired of Lux's incessant self-aggrandising as he boasted of his empire being the biggest and best, the most extreme and shocking. Some were even suspicious that he was not one of them, procuring hurtcore materials not because it was something he was into himself, but because the attention it got him fed his ego.

It is difficult to determine the first use of the term 'hurtcore' but its etymology is clear—it is hardcore infliction of pain in a pornographic context. It describes a subset of pornography that involves rape, harm and even torture—not simulated, but real. There has always been a market for this sort of material, but the internet allowed like-minded people to congregate, discuss and share images, stories and film that would give most of us nightmares for life. Lux's new site delivered images that specifically dealt with pain and torture—it could apply to animals, adults (provided it was non-consensual) or children; given Lux's fan base, it almost universally applied to the latter.

Hurt2theCore was accessible by anyone, but there were sections that were cut off to those who did not provide new material. The base level was for Active Members—those who posted frequently and included child exploitation materials in their posts. But the pinnacle was to get entry to the Producer's Lounge, where the most senior members of the site shared their ongoing, real-life experiences with children in their lives.

H2TC was split into different forums, sub-forums and threads, just like millions of other forums on the web. By July 2013 it had 7728 members, with 22,236 posts on 2192 topics. Forums included Hurtcore: Discuss how you like to make them scream; Bestiality; Practical Child Education: Advice and guides on how to get what you want from kiddies; Sex Tourism and Prostitution: Where to find them sexy little kids. The videos and image forums were broken down into sub-forums of male and female, babies and toddlers, jailbait and adult.

Members were ranked according to how many posts they had, with the more prolific posters accorded a higher level of respect in the community:

0 Posts	Rape Victim
10 Posts	Kiddy Fiddler
50 Posts	Child Molester
100 Posts	Child Fucker
250 Posts	Certified Rapist
500 Posts	Hurtcore Master
1000 Posts	Your own custom title

Beneath their avatars, members would list their age and gender preferences. Once a member had 100 posts and had been a member for at least a month, Lux or one of his volunteer moderators would review the member's posting history and if they liked what they saw, they would grant access to the Active Members section. Members were warned that if they tried to game the system by posting short, undetailed posts, they would not be provided access to the more exclusive areas.

Lux was active in the community and nothing was off limits to him. One member wanted advice about filming the abduction, rape and killing of a five-year-old girl in Russia. Lux first had to be satisfied that the member was serious and not simply fantasising. 'OK good.

So you do have a plan and this is not just fantasy for you,' Lux said upon receiving the requisite proof. 'I have many contacts willing to purchase such a video.' He provided significant and detailed advice to the murderous Russian.

Lux would provide practical advice for those who were submitting videos, including how to clean them of metadata and, if the videos were shot by the members themselves, how to ensure there was nothing in the background to give them away. He deemed too dangerous for distribution the abuse of a seven-year-old girl who suffered from MS and was mute, as she was too recognisable. However, he told the member he should make videos for his own gratification. 'At least you know she can't cry for help.'

The members of his site came from all over the world, with many working in a field where they had access to children. One member, Jabber, worked in a home for mentally impaired children in the UK.

Such was Lux's craving for admiration and acceptance, he gladly took on the role of the most evil creature of the dark web. There was always a small group of sick, twisted predators who looked up to him.

With that reputation came pressure to keep producing and providing ever more extreme subject matter. Lux was always on the lookout for new material to satisfy his growing membership. He had already heard of the film that was reputed to be the most extreme depiction of hurtcore available. Lux was determined that Hurt2theCore would host *Daisy's Destruction*.

Daisy's Destruction

The dark web is home to all manner of rumours and creepy stories, most of which are exaggerations, lies or hoaxes. There were always stories of websites and videos that were gruesome beyond anything anyone had ever seen. Many people believed there was a further, deeper, darker section of the dark web, called Mariana's Web or the

Shadow Web, where the select few discovered the key to unlock the greatest horrors. Snuff movies, of course, and worse. There were sites that detailed cruel Nazi-style experiments on homeless people, who would die in the process. Gladiator fights to the death. A collection of psychopaths who played demented games of conkers, swinging babies by their ankles to try to crush the skull of their opponent's child. A man who created human sex dolls by severing the limbs of girls and women and removing their vocal cord, while keeping them alive.

Such things were no more than the imaginings of perverse and demented minds and could be relegated to pure fiction. The stories often had their genesis in the Random board of 4Chan or the nosleep subreddit, and were designed to be as shocking as possible.

In early 2013, rumours began circulating the dark web of a film called *Daisy's Destruction*. Details would vary in the telling and passing around of the content of the film, but one thing was for sure—it involved torture of a young girl. Many claimed it was torture and murder. As happens with such things, soon everyone had heard of the film, everyone knew somebody who had watched it, but there were few first-hand accounts, and those who claimed to have watched it seemed to recall different details of what was contained therein.

As the rumours swirled, the inconsistency of the stories caused most people to write the film off as being yet another dark web urban legend. The ratio of fiction to fact in the stories that made their way around reddit and other clear-web forums was skewed heavily to the former. On the other hand, there were enough coinciding stories that substantiated the fact that it did exist in some form. One site's name cropped up repeatedly as the source for much of the detail about the film. If anywhere would host it, Hurt2theCore would.

Lux wanted to maintain his reputation as the source for the most extreme materials on the dark web. He set out to find and host *Daisy's Destruction*.

His sources were able to point him to an organisation called No Limits Fun, a production company—complete with logo—that produced hurtcore videos of young Asian girls, tied in dog chains, being abused. Lux opened up negotiations with the producer, who went by the name Exciteagirl, to purchase the full video of *Daisy's Destruction*. He offered NLF $900 in Bitcoin, which was swiftly rejected. The producer wanted significantly more, claiming No Limits Fun videos could sell for up to $10,000 through private networks. Exciteagirl said that No Limits Fun could create more custom videos for Hurt2theCore if they were to enter into a business relationship. However, as Lux was not inclined to charge members to access any productions on his site, he could not afford the asking price.

Relations soon broke down between the two for the film that No Limits Fun dubbed 'a pedo-delicacy in 1920 × 780 resolution; more than 45 mins to enjoy!' However, Lux was able to procure four short extracts—a total of twelve minutes of footage—from other sources, which he released one at a time, free to his members in revenge for the deal falling through. Once it was available on Lux's sites, it would lose its value as a privately circulated film. As he released each part, he encouraged his viewers to post in the comments which part of the film—which tortures—they would like to see next.

Lux wanted to be sure everyone knew that *Daisy's Destruction* could be found for free exclusively on Hurt2theCore. 'Those NLF guys deserved me leaking DD. They were whiny bitches,' he told one forum, where he went for support and accolades. Lux loved the power and cachet he got from being the one who had the mythical film and the ability to grant access to others.

The footage was as horrifying as any rumours, short of the actual murder of a child on a screen. The words 'Introducing Daisy's Destruction' above the NLF logo in the opener were followed by a twisted pastiche of text and stills from the film: 'Come see a child's mental ruin . . . her innocence lost . . . Used as a tool . . . she will learn how to please her mistress . . . her body will be ravaged . . . her dignity stolen . . . Helpless, she will hang for your entertainment.' In the ensuing video, the eighteen-month-old girl was subjected to rape and excruciating torture—kicked, slapped, pinched, punched, penetrated with large pieces of ice and other objects, her genitals burned with a lighter, sex acts performed on her by a masked female, and hung upside down while being urinated on. The child screamed in agony throughout in a soundtrack that haunted the dreams of those who had to watch it in an attempt to bring the producer to justice.

Lux posted links pointing to Hurt2theCore, but in almost every case, it was considered too extreme and was soon removed. But there were those who sought it out. Download after download, the snippets of film spread throughout the network of pedophiles and then out into the clear web to those whose curiosity could only be sated by watching it for themselves. Lux had delivered what nobody else could. He was the emperor.

In pursuit of monsters

'What would happen if Lux is caught?' mused a member in a post on Hurt2theCore. He was assured in the responses that Lux was too careful to ever get caught. Lux himself joked that if it ever happened, everyone would know because he would go down in a blaze of glory.

International law enforcement agencies were well aware of Lux and his PedoEmpire. The dark web served to gather the worst producers of violent child exploitation materials in one place, but the technology meant it was more difficult than ever to trace them to their physical locations. The monsters were scattered across the globe, but able to communicate with each other with a few mouse clicks.

In 2013, Operation Downfall, a joint Europol/FBI Violent Crimes Against Children initiative, had seized the servers of Freedom

Hosting, the same service that had been the target of Anonymous' Operation Darknet in 2011. The service's willingness to host any site without question or censorship meant that it was the most popular choice for child exploitation sites.

What the authorities found was a collection of the largest and most egregious child sexual abuse sites in the world. Not just repositories of child exploitation materials, the sites encouraged members to actively and frequently produce child pornography and child exploitation matter. The sites depicted child abuse including sexual penetration, bondage and torture involving toddlers and infants.

FBI and Europol intelligence had determined that a user known as Lux was infamous as one of the top child sexual abuse facilitators around the world. He was known as the most powerful and prestigious of child abuse offenders, having strong supporters, but also abusers who did not like him because of his cruelty.

Operation Downfall put Lux squarely in the sights of law enforcement around the world. Although it was the nature of the dark web that authorities could not determine the locations of those who used it, when people post online often enough, they start to leave hints and clues that experienced detectives could use to narrow in and, hopefully, pinpoint them.

The closure of Freedom Hosting did not deter the child exploitation sites for long. Lux moved his empire to its own personal hosting where he built anonymous image-sharing services, video streaming, chat rooms, forums and a hosting service—his PedoEmpire. He took great delight in what he saw as a win over law enforcement:

> Well, it looks like this Empire hasn't fallen yet! To any LEA [law enforcement agency] whom may be reading this Fuck you. You can not keep us down, and every time you try we will just get bigger and bigger, so thanks for the publicity and leading more pedophiles to where you cant catch them.

To my fellow pedos: it won't be long now until all of the major CP sites are back up and running. In the mean time, I suggest you spend your newfound free time by going out and fucking some kiddies!

Lux believed himself to be invincible, administering his sites and sourcing the most depraved material while seemingly impervious to any law enforcement efforts to track him down. He continued to be a polarising figure on the dark web and in the child exploitation community. To appease those who were highly engaged in the pedophile world but disapproved of hurtcore, he opened Love2theCore, which was devoted only to the twisted version of 'love' in that world—what he called 'the softer side of kiddy porn'—while Hurt2theCore would continue to cater to hardcore and hurtcore. As with other sites, accessing discussion forums was free to anybody, but to view any media, users had to upload at least 25mb of their own media first. Lux even created two-tier access—apply with non-nude material and be granted access just to non-nude boards, or apply with preteen hardcore to be granted access to all content.

The majority still wanted nothing to do with Lux, or any of the sites he administered. 'The operator of that site is known to be a dishonorable man,' a 'regular' pedophile warned somebody who had posted in a forum asking about membership to Love2theCore. 'I'd stay away from it. It ain't worth being associated with someone personally responsible for the distribution of *Daisy's Destruction*.'

In early 2014, Lux became spooked. He felt law enforcement closing in and made a bizarre decision. He sent an email to the FBI's cybertip line offering up details of his customers: 'My name is Lux and not only do I run the largest online suite of child pornography websites on Tor, but I also have a knowledge about its users (and their identities) unrivalled by anyone out there.' Lux said he was willing to hand over control of his empire, including administration details for all sites under the PedoEmpire and server details, as well as access to his emails. Law enforcement would have full control of his Lux persona. 'On top of that I also have complete control over the large group of proven producers on any site,' he told them. 'I am sure that access to this, let alone everything else I am offering you is merit for the conditions I will outline below.'

The conditions included $50,000 in Bitcoin and immunity across all jurisdictions. Not surprisingly, the task force was not interested in acquiescing to either demand.

'It is clear you are not taking my offer seriously,' a frustrated Lux wrote when it was obvious no money or immunity would be coming his way. 'It is NOT a game, these are real lives you are bargaining on. It's now clear that if I want to fix this problem I need to do it myself. I will get rid of these people because no one else will. As you do not want to be part of the solution, I bid you farewell.'

Lux announced to his inner circle that he would be closing down the sites under the PedoEmpire umbrella. Some reacted by posting child abuse in his honour. One fan sent him a number of images of his nine-year-old niece, naked and forced into a sexualised pose, with a note scrawled on a piece of paper balanced on her legs: 'Lux, you'll be missed' followed by a crude reference to her uncle's activities. The two men had built up something of a friendship after Lux tutored him in removing identifying features, such as his tattoos and his victim's face, from the videos he supplied.

On 24 June 2014, true to his word, Lux closed down his sites, saying: 'today is the day that I walk away. There are personal issues which my close friends have been made aware of that have forced me to make this decision.'

It did not take long before hubris and his desperate desire to be emperor in his own sick, twisted world resurfaced. Early in August 2014, he boasted in a private chat to someone he trusted that he had killed off 'Lux' and had been reborn as 'Buddha'. Buddha was working on a new site, Innocent Screams.

Lux captured

When detectives swooped on a house in a suburb around 20 kilometres out of Melbourne on 26 August 2014, they were confident they had their man. Countless hours of infiltrating the world of child exploitation and hurtcore had led them to this nondescript house in a quiet street in a country not usually associated with such extreme subject matter. What would Lux, the worst of the worst, the most reviled pedophile in the dark web, be like?

Lux had presented himself as an American pediatrician with considerable life experience. Detectives knew that in the house was a white, working class man in his fifties who worked as a mechanic, his wife, son and daughter. 'We thought for sure we knew who it was,' a police officer involved in the case said.

As they tore apart the house, they soon realised it was not the mechanic they were seeking, but his son: a young man barely out of his teens, who rarely left his bedroom where he sat day and night hunched over a computer. He was eerily calm as they read him his rights.

Matthew Graham, born 21 September 1992, was, like many young men his age, shy and insecure around people. Unable to develop friendships at school and unsuccessful with the opposite sex, he had no social life and increasingly turned to his computer for comfort. Online multi-player game World of Warcraft was his only form of social interaction, and he spent many hours in his room gaming and forming his only relationships outside his immediate family.

Soon the discussions in the gaming room led him to explore forums populated by other young socially awkward boys and men, in particular the discussion board favoured by gamers, outcasts and deviants: 4Chan. There a whole new world opened up to him, a world of anonymity, where he could be anyone or anything he wanted. He was fascinated by 4Chan's most famous accomplishment, the spawning of the hacktivist collective Anonymous.

Matthew considered himself asexual. He had a single unsatisfactory sexual experience as an adolescent, and a neutral response to pornography. As the teenager had become more and more isolated, crippled by social anxiety, and threatened by his peers, he withdrew from his family and spent all of his time in his bedroom. His desperately worried parents sought help from a psychologist, who tried to treat him for his extreme social phobia, but Matthew was uncooperative.

Towards the end of high school, Matthew watched with fascination as Anonymous announced on 4Chan that it would be attacking Lolita City, the underage porn section of The Hidden Wiki, a gateway site to the dark web. Matthew thought it would be fun to help, and for the first time he went and looked at what could be found in this new, dark version of the internet he had not visited before.

Anonymous did indeed take down Lolita City for a short time, but were ultimately unsuccessful in making any lasting dent in the dark web's child pornography websites. Anonymous was not interested in Matthew Graham's help. The pimply teen had once again been rejected and deemed useless by those whose acceptance he craved. But now he had been exposed to new communities of even greater misfits than those he found in online games and on 4Chan.

Things did not get any easier when Matthew started at La Trobe University, where he was a nanotechnology student. Although he was intellectually quite bright, he was socially immature, more comfortable around children than people his own age, although not sexually attracted to them. He was a babysitter for his neighbour's young children, but there was no evidence that he ever touched them inappropriately. University did not last long. 'I just started at uni and it was kind of not really a good time and all that,' he told police later. 'Even though I don't then and still don't consider myself a pedophile . . . and then yeah.'

Once he dropped out, he stopped interacting with his parents, and spent all his time in his bedroom. Over the next three years he rarely emerged. He had developed an anxiety condition that meant he could not eat in front of other people, so he did not join his family for meals.

In between playing online games, he became increasingly intrigued by the dark web and what could be found there. He desperately wanted to become somebody, and thought there would be people there who would appreciate his computer skills. He started looking at drug and weapons sites, and eventually wound up at child porn sites and entered a world that both repulsed and fascinated him. Inside the chat rooms he found people whose warped views distorted lines of reality and fantasy; he could never tell what were true tales of depravity and what were fevered imaginings. He was most drawn to the forums where like-minded people tried to top each other with how outrageous and disgusting they could be.

From text-based forums it was not a huge step to move on to image boards. The infamous Random forum (known simply as /b/) on 4Chan was a repository of twisted images that sometimes included death and mayhem, and occasionally child pornography. Graham started needing more than /b/ could provide. He moved into the depths of the dark web, seeking out more and more depraved images, and became titillated by what he saw. He never had a normal emotional response to abhorrent images, and now he started compulsively masturbating to them. Previously asexual, he could eventually only masturbate to images of children being harmed.

When he discovered a requirement for his technical proficiency in some of these sites, Matthew Graham moved into a world that gave him the respect that he craved and a sense of satisfaction. The unemployed teenager who lived with his parents finally felt as if he was someone special. He was Lux, and Lux was emperor.

The police tore apart the Graham household, seizing all of Matthew's electronic equipment, including USB sticks which they soon discovered held the most depraved collection of pornography they had ever encountered. They heard about his multiple psychiatric diagnoses of schizoid personality disorder, anxiety and depression. They spoke to his bewildered parents, who had no idea how to help when, like so many troubled teens, he refused their comfort and aid. As the teen grew into a young man, it had become increasingly difficult to draw him out of his room. They thought he was gaming; they could never have dreamed he was building his wicked empire right under their noses.

Within the dark web, the child abuse communities were abuzz with news of the arrest, as well as others that seemed to be related. Also in Australia, 33-year-old former childcare worker Shannon McCoole, known as Skee on the dark web—he who had implored Lux and others to eschew any form of publicity—was jailed for 35 years for the sexual abuse of seven children, six of whom were in his care. Authorities also caught the uncle of the young girl who had been forced to hold a farewell sign when Lux retired. He too received a hefty jail sentence.

There was nothing high-tech about the way these dark web predators were identified and captured. They were caught thanks to methodical, unrelenting police work combined with clever, targeted social engineering, carried out by law enforcement agencies working together across the globe. Task Force Argos was responsible for the Australian arrests. Skee, for example, had been caught after a high-ranking member of his site The Love Zone had been busted and had handed over login details for his VIP membership. Those credentials provided access to exclusive sections where members were less reserved with each other and shared materials more freely.

Among those materials were images by Skee that had not yet been stripped of metadata, including information about the camera used.

Skee's home country was an open secret among those who knew him, and from there police set about narrowing down his interests and studying the grammar, spelling and form of his writing. One officer noticed that he began a post more often than not with the greeting 'hiyas'. This was unusual enough that, after scouring millions of websites and forums, they were able to narrow their target down to about 5000 suspects. Continuing to pare down the list, they matched men who had similar interests to Skee through normal clear-web social networks. Of those, only one worked with children according to his Facebook, which also had a picture of his vehicle, registration number visible. They raided his house when they determined from his history that he was most likely to be online, and caught him with his laptop open. Once they had him, they were able to match the camera found in his home to the metadata on the pictures, as well as identifying a freckle on his finger.

After catching Skee, police were able to impersonate him online and continue the chain of unmasking child abusers around the world.

The child abuse communities applied their own twisted version of morality to make sense of the arrest of Lux. A user called Chairman on Pedo Support Community wrote:

> Lux was a pathetic little boy. Endearing in his own way, but providing passages for the monstrous to occur. A secret community none of us would admit to knowing the name of would never have existed without Lux giving them an initial platform. A certain girl has had her life ruined—despite having what we could argue was a healthy sexual relationship—because of Lux's arrogance. He rolled over exactly as expected—for love and attention, as I'm sure law enforcement agents promised him. Lux was incredibly insecure and that

made him incredibly dangerous—nothing mattered as much as his ego. Thus H2TC, then L2TC, and on and on . . .

We should pity him to some extent.

We should pity the lives he impacted much more.

The girl whom Chairman considered had been in a 'healthy sexual relationship' was the nine-year-old girl who had been abused by her uncle for three years. Chairman proudly declared his own preference for sexual partners to be girls aged six to eleven.

Others were shocked that the sophisticated American pediatrician was not what he seemed. 'What!? This kid is Lux!? Guy is younger than me! And weirder! How's that possible!?' wrote Unleashed Loser, predator of six-to-twelve-year-old girls. 'He was supposed to be Darth Vader! But he's a 4channer!'

When a reporter from Melbourne's *Age* newspaper, Chris Johnston, visited Matthew Graham's South Morang house a while after his arrest, he found that it had been sold to unsuspecting new owners. The house had been vacated quickly, it seemed; a mess was left behind and the new owners discovered graffiti scrawled inside a bedroom wardrobe: 'Parents should be afraid of raising children like us.'

They painted over it.

Peter Gerard Scully

Once *Daisy's Destruction* gained notoriety, an international manhunt set out to track down those responsible for the vile video. Cross-border task forces studied every detail of the No Limits Fun footage to narrow down the geographic region of the abuse. On 20 February 2015, Peter Scully, an Australian man living in the Philippines, was arrested, literally with his pants around his ankles, and charged with an array of offences. Later it emerged that not only was he behind *Daisy's Destruction* and various other films produced by NLF depicting the rape and torture of children, but the remains of an eleven-year-old girl were found buried in a shallow grave at a house Scully previously rented.

Scully, a father of two, had fled Australia some years before to avoid fraud charges. He had orchestrated property and computer scams that allowed him to fleece millions of dollars from duped investors. He told *60 Minutes* that he was not a pedophile while in Australia, nor when he first arrived in the Philippines. He claimed he could not pinpoint when or why he became such a monstrous abuser of children.

Scully and his girlfriend, Liezyl Margallo, ran NLF from Mindanao in the Philippines, producing videos of themselves carrying out heinous crimes on children from as young as eighteen months. Scully would force children to perform sex acts on each other and his girl-friends, as well as himself, as he filmed them for distribution. He also forced the children to dig their own graves in his backyard, telling them they would eventually be buried there.

In some cases, the parents of the children willingly handed them over to him, believing him to be a benefactor who would provide them a better life than they, in their desperate poverty, were able to. Other times Scully's 'girlfriends'—former child prostitutes in their late teens—were tasked with finding street kids for him to 'adopt'. Scully would send his girlfriends out with instructions to find specific-aged girls—never older than twelve—and lure them back to his home with the promise of food.

Despite allegedly absconding with millions of dollars in ill-gotten gains from Australia, and earning up to $10,000 for a single video, Scully did not seem to live an extravagant lifestyle. The house in which he was captured was modest and unrenovated, as was the house where the body of eleven-year-old Cindy was found.

Wearing a grotesque Mardi Gras mask, Liezyl Margallo carried out the physical torture of Daisy, as well as children in other films. She and Scully were charged with kidnap, rape, torture and murder. Heinous though his crimes were, they were not crimes that carry the death penalty in the Philippines. There were reports that authorities considered reinstating the death penalty to execute Scully, an initiative that had considerable support from the public, but that never eventuated.

Daisy was found alive and taken into care, but she sustained permanent physical injuries from her treatment by Scully and Margallo, and will never be able to bear children. Margallo claimed Scully had filmed Cindy being strangled to death, but police did not discover any such footage. There were many hours of documented sexual abuse and torture of children, but it stopped short of film of any murder.

There is little doubt that Peter Scully harmed many more than the three children whose abuse he has been charged with. However, much of the prosecution's evidence against Scully, including computer hardware, memory card, camera, computer monitor, video recorder and chains, were destroyed in a fire that gutted the Hall of Justice in the Philippines earlier that year.

Scully's accomplices—his 'girlfriends' who carried out much of the abuse on the children, while wearing masks under Scully's direction—could be considered more victims of his depravity. Liezyl Margallo, the young woman who featured in *Daisy's Destruction*, however, showed little remorse and went on the run soon after Scully's arrest. NLF released more videos and it emerged that Margallo remained in touch with Scully, who many believed continued to carry on his business from prison.

Lux in court

'It was my clear duty to watch it,' the judge said. 'I wish it hadn't been. It is the worst thing I have ever seen.'

The County Court justice who had been allocated the sentencing hearing of Matthew Graham was reluctant to view *Daisy's Destruction* and was now letting Matthew Graham—and the rest of the court-room—know what he thought of it. 'To you it was just footage for your stock,' the judge said. 'It was pure evil.'

The prosecutor had insisted that the judge view *Daisy's Destruction* to understand the true nature of the materials Lux sought out for his site. Some allowance for the judge's sensibilities had been made by way of removing the sound. (One police officer involved in the case mentioned that the sound—the continual screams of a toddler being brutalised—was the most gruesome part of the video.) The judge was not at all keen. 'Do I really need to see it to form a view that this material is depraved?' he asked.

Graham's own barrister had not seen the clips, nor did he have any desire for the judge to see them. Graham was silently sobbing in the back of the courtroom as the learned people had their debate.

'There was prestige in being able to deliver *Daisy's Destruction*. It was highly sought after?' asked the judge.

'Yes,' agreed both prosecution and defence.

'And it was for a reason, right?'

'Mr Graham does not dispute the description of the material,' the defence barrister said, acknowledging that it was the 'worst of the worst'.

The prosecutor read out precedents supporting her request. 'Seeing it brings it home,' she said, 'in a real and tangible way rather than just reading a description of it.'

Although the judge agreed he was legally obliged to view the video, he was in no hurry to do so. The discussion was held in the morning, and it was agreed that His Honour would watch the film at lunch-time. After lunch, however, he reported he had not been able to bring himself to watch it. At 4:00 pm the prosecutor suggested he might like to watch it then. 'I don't think I'm quite up to it right now,' he said.

The judge eventually excused himself for half an hour the next day to view the footage. When he returned to the courtroom he was pale and quiet.

'How any human can view that impassively . . .' he said. 'The infant was being tortured, actual physical torture . . . an extremely trusting, vulnerable child who begins smiling wearing a nappy and ends a wailing physical wreck.'

In a quiet, high-pitched voice, the young man with no prior criminal record answered 'Guilty' to each count read out to him. Life had not been easy for Matthew Graham since his arrest. Although housed with other sex offenders, he had been assaulted and abused by both prisoners and guards. Just as it had been online, in prison he was looked upon as lowest of low for his crimes. He had been in protective custody, where he would remain for the foreseeable future. Members of his family, including his sister and his father, the man police had originally thought was Lux, sat through the hearings in a show of support.

When a scene-by-scene description of *Daisy's Destruction* isn't the most depraved thing you hear before noon, you know you are in for a really tough day. Among the charges, Lux was accused of aiding and abetting the abduction, rape and murder of a five-year-old child in Russia. But it was the detailed description of the abuse of a seven-year-old profoundly disabled girl—in a wheelchair with MS—that forced several people to leave the courtroom and caused the eyes of the father of the defendant to well up. Graham's father wept openly as the court heard a transcript of the conversation between Lux and the abuser, where Lux advised him that the film would be too dangerous to sell, but he should make it for his own gratification. Even more vile was the cavalier way in which they spoke about their victims. Joking that as the seven-year-old was mute, 'at least you don't have to worry about her accent giving her away'.

As more horrors were read out in court, spectators, including some members of Graham's own family, stumbled from the room, traumatised by what they were hearing. Those who stayed heard of three-year-old Sarah, with a plastic bag over her head and rope around her neck and the word 'rape' scrawled across her stomach. There were descriptions of images of children engaged in bestiality and photographs that purported to show children decapitated or raped to death. A fifteen-year-old girl had been blackmailed into penetrating and torturing herself on video while holding up signs as a sick advertisement for Hurt2theCore.

Matthew Graham spent the two-day hearing alternating between looking around the courtroom defiantly and sitting hunched over in apparent distress, occasionally sobbing quietly. His defence team made a valiant effort in introducing mitigating circumstances that should reduce his sentence. No contact offending had been alleged against Matthew Graham. He never profited from his crimes in any way. He was a sad, friendless little boy who was desperate for attention and accolades from his peers.

Meanwhile the people who had given him healthy and positive attention—his family—stood by him in court, even while their hearts broke. Graham's family had the most difficult situation of 'hate the sin, love the sinner' there could possibly be. No doubt there are those who would judge and revile them for standing by their son, nephew and brother. But nobody looked more bewildered than Graham's father about how the monster came to be. Certainly, there was nothing to suggest that he in any way created the fiend. No abuse, no neglect; there was no suggestion of anything but love and helpless support as he and his wife struggled to help their son cope with the world.

'They would never in their wildest dreams have imagined you were living the twisted, evil life you were in the dark shadows of the cyber world,' the judge told Matthew, who bowed his head.

On 17 March 2016, the County Court sentenced Matthew Graham to fifteen years in prison. With good behaviour and concessions, he could be released in as little as ten years.

'I have seen some shocking things over the journey of my career and I have never seen anything like that,' said the judge. 'I can find no like cases—your case is without parallel.'

Many were outraged by the apparent leniency of the sentence. Some compared his sentence to that of serial pedophile Geoffrey Robert Dobbs, who had molested at least 63 girls aged between a month and fifteen years old over 28 years. He was given two consecutive terms of indefinite imprisonment with a nominal sentence of 30 years.

Is setting up websites and encouraging others to perform vile sexual acts and commit vicious violence as evil as carrying out child molestation personally? It is a question the courts must wrestle with.

As this was a high-profile dark web case, comparisons were naturally drawn between the sentence handed down to Lux, who ran a website dedicated to the torture of children, and Dread Pirate Roberts, who ran a website to sell drugs. Most would agree the former is a far greater crime than the latter (and it is hard to compare sentences from different jurisdictions), but Matthew Graham will still be a relatively young man upon his release, whereas Ross Ulbricht was sentenced to never be released, and is expected to die in prison.

It is safe to say Lux will spend his next ten to fifteen years in similar conditions to those he had in the time already served—in protection and solitary confinement. Just as on the dark web he was reviled; in prison even the most hardened criminals have no sympathy for the likes of Lux. He may not survive the process at all.

Online, the news was met with ambivalence from much of the pedophile community. 'For me Lux always stood for NLF and hurtcore and as such I despised him,' wrote BabyBoyLove, whose preference was boys and girls aged three-plus. 'He is now paying the price for his deeds and he is now another name in the past of darknet. I figure it is best to let him be in the past and fade away.'

'Not only was this asshat responsible for torture and likely death of children, he has made life so much more difficult for the remainder of this community,' said foolsareus, who likes nine-to-thirteen-year-old girls.

But one user appeared quite happy at the sentence that seemed lenient for the crimes. 'Cannot wait to see him in 15 years. He'll be still quite young to admin a site, really,' said Chairman.

Fighting high-tech predators

While law enforcement around the world continues to do what it can to close down these sites, and identify and prosecute those behind them, the technology can be tricky to navigate. Most children sold as sex slaves online are advertised on the clear web—most notably Craigslist—but the anonymising technologies of the dark web provide a safe haven for predators to meet, discuss, share and develop methods to evade detection.

Despite Lux's PedoEmpire falling, replacement sites began operating to fill the void immediately. Law enforcement agencies find it can be more difficult to intercept the child abuse circles than the commercial enterprises, because often, like Lux's empire, they are run not for profit but purely for the purpose of sharing with like-minded individuals. The numbers quoted for Scully's No Limits Fun productions seem to be unverified and, given his living arrangements in the Philippines, can be treated with some scepticism.

One member of the online community said, 'nobody is making any money whatsoever. Mainstream media has fostered the impression that children are being rampantly abused to fuel a multi-million-dollar industry, but that is just not the case. I've been "consuming" on[-]topic material for over a decade and I have never even provided a real email address to any website, much less any form of money. The only thing we spend is time. There have been only a handful of fleeting companies that tried to turn a profit peddling child nudity. They always get shut down, people who paid get busted and all the content becomes freely available and even ubiquitous. Exclusivity is all someone has to offer when selling child porn and it doesn't take long for that to go away the way stuff is traded and shared. That's why it has never been and never will be a sustainable business as long as child pornography remains illegal.'

On the other hand, many pedophiles are desperate to befriend like-minded people, which leads to them providing personal information that can eventually be used to identify and locate them. The police officers who go undercover to elicit this information have one of the toughest jobs around.

International law enforcement agencies, including Task Force Argos, continue to infiltrate the realms of child abusers operating within what the predators believe to be the anonymity of the dark web. Sometimes their methods raise troubling questions. The FBI took over and ran one of the internet's largest child porn sites, Playpen, for a couple of months in 2015. The FBI infected the site with software designed to identify users. One of the pedophiles charged from that sting subsequently sued the government on the grounds that the agency enabled him to access the site.

Then Task Force Argos, in conjunction with US Homeland Security and Canadian and European authorities, was revealed to have run another major site, Child's Play, for over a year. Child's Play had over a million users, around a hundred of whom were regular producers. When agents infiltrated and took over the sites, they purposefully rose as high within the networks as possible to enable them to gain the trust of more users, and hopefully save more lives. But sometimes to keep up the charade, the infiltrators had to post child exploitation images themselves.

Meanwhile, a man who sought 'ideas for a blackmailed 15yo' from Hurt2theCore's customers and then posted videos of the results was revealed in October 2017 to be a Cambridge-educated doctor. The depravity of 28-year-old Dr Matthew Falder rivalled that of Scully and Graham as it was revealed he had similarly blackmailed over 50 people of all ages, forcing them to carry out degrading acts which he uploaded to the dark web. He was an active member of H2TC and encouraged another member to rape a four-year-old boy and post the video.

In February 2017, the masked woman in *Daisy's Destruction*, Scully's live-in partner Liezyl Margallo, was arrested. She had been living a life of luxury, Instagramming herself in exotic locations, and had exchanged telephone calls and text messages with Scully, leading Philippine authorities to suspect he continued to mastermind a dark web pornography and child torture operation from his jail cell. Peter Scully seems to have certain comforts and luxuries not afforded all prisoners in the Philippine system. He escaped the looming threat of capital punishment and pleaded not guilty to all charges, forcing a protracted court battle within a sometimes corrupt system. Much of the evidence against him was—some would say conveniently— destroyed in a suspicious fire.

We can hope that Margallo's arrest is the end for No Limits Fun. Sadly, children, especially those in impoverished countries, continue to be exploited and abused to satisfy the twisted desires of a demented few. Technology continues to develop to provide protection for those who want to carry out their heinous crimes.

And for those who want to know just how far the dark web goes, they have an answer. This is the darkest web.

AFTERWORD

I struggled with whether to include certain events and people in this book and decisions to do so were not taken lightly.

Dark

I was unabashedly a fan of Silk Road prior to its demise. As an active drug law reform advocate who is firmly against the war on drugs, I knew Silk Road offered drug users a safer alternative for procuring their drugs. I believed in the philosophy of the Dread Pirate Roberts which allowed people to purchase drugs for their own use in a violence-free environment. I loved that the site took the high moral ground and refused to allow the sale of anything the purpose of which was to harm or defraud another person.

I was devastated when the peace-seeking libertarian I thought I had come to know was accused of blithely ordering the murders of six people, three of whom had never done him any harm. When the accusations failed to materialise into charges in court, I held onto the possibility that the conversations were never held at all; perhaps they were even planted to turn DPR's followers against him.

However, not only was there a mountain of evidence to support their existence, once I personally spoke to people on the other sides of the discussions with Dread Pirate Roberts, I could not deny those conversations took place. DPR and Variety Jones were prepared to kill people to protect their business.

Whilst I find the cavalier attitude to murder abhorrent and DPR lost my support, I still believe that Ross Ulbricht was not granted due process and that his sentence is manifestly excessive. I also believe that Silk Road was a safer place to purchase drugs than the 'real life' alternatives and operated on a more ethical model than any of its successors. To me, the Silk Road I knew provided an insight into what a post-prohibition world might look like and it was overwhelmingly positive.

Darker

My opinion of Yura did an about-turn in the process of writing this book. When I started, which was before Amy Allwine's murder, Yura was threatening me and carrying out his scam with little regard for potential consequences. It was purely a money-making exercise for him and I did not feel I owed him any obligation of confidentiality.

By the time I submitted the manuscript we'd had many hours of conversation. The murder shook him and he subsequently claimed to actively inform law enforcement organisations around the world of the details of people prepared to pay large sums of money to harm or kill other people. I can't help but hope that writing this book does not put him in danger of arrest so that he can continue his twisted version of being a dark web Robin Hood.

In the interests of full disclosure, some minor parts of ThcJohn's chapters have used creative licence to imagine thoughts in his head and conversations with friends, having built up a picture of him from his many emails to Besa Mafia and to Chris. I do not think they affect the integrity of the story.

Darkest

Part III of the book was incredibly difficult to write and I often considered abandoning it. I never downloaded or viewed any illegal pornography and did not personally view Daisy's Destruction, instead relying on a scene-by-scene description by the officers who had to document it.

Nevertheless, it is safe to say I never want to return to that part of the dark web again. I wish I could say I exaggerated the horrors, but if anything, I sanitised them.

ACKNOWLEDGEMENTS

As with any work of non-fiction, *The Darkest Web* could never have happened without the assistance of many people.

I thank Chris Monteiro aka deku Shub aka Pirate London for sharing his experiences, for doing the tedious work of creating an accessible database out of the thousands of pages of the Besa Mafia files and for providing me with the transcripts of his police interviews following his arrest.

As with my last book, I again have to acknowledge the incredible work of the much-underrated LaMoustache. His research skills when it comes to the dark web are unsurpassed. On that note, contrary to popular belief, most journalists bend over backwards to help each other out. For their willingness to share information and provide insights, I want to thank Chris Johnston, Andrew McMillan, Patrick O'Neill, Tom Lyden, Chris DeRose, Joseph Cox, Jamie Bartlett (and I know I've left some out, for which I'm truly sorry).

The wonderful people at Allen & Unwin worked hard to make this a better book, fix my errors and bent over backwards to accommodate me when I was cutting it so very, very fine on the deadlines.

I especially thank Tom Gilliatt for championing it in the first place, my publisher Kelly Fagan, Rebecca Kaiser for whipping it into shape and Maggie and Klara for pimping it out.

My travel hacking community has saved me thousands of dollars in airfares over the years and I have to give a special shout-out to Mahir Hodzic, who turned what was going to be a very expensive world trip in economy class into an affordable trip in business class with his know-how and points-fu.

To the people of Cottage Grove, in particular the friends of Amy and the Cottage Grove police department, with a special shoutout to Randy McAlister and Jared Landkamer for their time and insights.

To my amazing family and friends who support me, cheer me on and worry for me, I love you all. To my stepkids, James and Steph, that goes for you too, but I don't want you reading this book for a few more years, okay?

Finally, to my incredible partner Cam, who takes death threats from hitmen in his stride, spends his holidays being my chauffeur and bodyguard, who never complains as I drag him to prisons or to meet people who either don't have real names or have too many names, who has been my biggest fan and my greatest support and who gives better advice than anyone, I love you and could never have done this without you.